A TEXAS TRAGEDY:
Orphaned By Bootleggers

© 2002 Elva Edwards
All rights reserved.

For information about this book,
write to
Elva Edwards
13318 West Exposition Drive
Lakewood Colorado 80228

A TEXAS TRAGEDY / Elva Edwards
ISBN 0-925854-24-7

Published by Elva Edwards
Lakewood, Colorado

Printed in the United States of America

CONTENTS

PREFACE 4
DEDICATION 7
ACKNOWLEDGEMENTS 9
INTRODUCTION 11

CHAPTER ONE 13	CHAPTER TWENTY-NINE 137
CHAPTER TWO 16	CHAPTER THIRTY 141
CHAPTER THREE 19	CHAPTER THIRTY-ONE 143
CHAPTER FOUR 24	CHAPTER THIRTY-TWO 146
CHAPTER FIVE 27	CHAPTER THIRTY-THREE 148
CHAPTER SIX 30	CHAPTER THIRTY-FOUR 150
CHAPTER SEVEN 34	CHAPTER THIRTY-FIVE 153
CHAPTER EIGHT 37	CHAPTER THIRTY-SIX 155
CHAPTER NINE 39	CHAPTER THIRTY-SEVEN 159
CHAPTER TEN 40	CHAPTER THIRTY-EIGHT 161
CHAPTER ELEVEN 43	CHAPTER THIRTY-NINE 164
CHAPTER TWELVE 46	CHAPTER FORTY 168
CHAPTER THIRTEEN 48	CHAPTER FORTY-ONE 171
CHAPTER FOURTEEN 53	CHAPTER FORTY-TWO 174
CHAPTER FIFTEEN 66	CHAPTER FORTY-THREE 177
CHAPTER SIXTEEN 71	CHAPTER FORTY-FOUR 180
CHAPTER SEVENTEEN 83	CHAPTER FORTY-FIVE 184
CHAPTER EIGHTEEN 91	CHAPTER FORTY-SIX 186
CHAPTER NINETEEN 97	CHAPTER FORTY-SEVEN 188
CHAPTER TWENTY 103	CHAPTER FORTY-EIGHT 191
CHAPTER TWENTY-ONE 110	CHAPTER FORTY-NINE 193
CHAPTER TWENTY-TWO 119	CHAPTER FIFTY 200
CHAPTER TWENTY-THREE 121	CHAPTER FIFTY-ONE 203
CHAPTER TWENTY-FOUR 124	CHAPTER FIFTY-TWO 224
CHAPTER TWENTY-FIVE 128	CHAPTER FIFTY-THREE 228
CHAPTER TWENTY-SIX 130	CHAPTER FIFTY-FOUR 230
CHAPTER TWENTY-SEVEN 133	CHAPTER FIFTY-FIVE 236
CHAPTER TWENTY-EIGHT 135	CHAPTER FIFTY-SIX 238
	CHAPTER FIFTY-SEVEN 240

APPENDIX 249
CAST OF CHARACTERS 251
ENDNOTES 252

PREFACE

I needed to write this book for five reasons:

1. To be my parents' voice.
2. To heal my wounded heart.
3. To touch the hearts of others who have suffered the loss of a parent as a child.
4. To challenge our society to re-examine our feelings about the pain and suffering of children, and to consider how we can best help them through loss.
5. To show how our lives play out the imprints made in our earliest years.

To be my parents' voice:

My parents have been buried for many, many years. How would their story possibly be told unless I wrote it? I didn't want Mike Cochran's Associated Press series of articles on Pinkie to be the final word. When I discovered the truth about our accident, I felt it was my story to tell, for the sake of my parents' and grandparents' memories and for the sake of my heart.

To heal my wounded heart:

Everything in my life was different after our car accident, at least everything that was important to a nineteen-month-old baby. The traumatic feelings and sensations that I experienced from the physical injury, the vanishing of my parents, and the lack of stability due to the health challenges of my grandmother after our accident were frozen in my body and psyche. They remained there, frozen for more than thirty-nine years. Crystalline structures full of intense feelings were hidden far beneath the surface, much like a glacier.

Clues to the hidden structures were strewn along the path of my life, but the events in my life reinforced the rigid necessity of not noticing. Then one day I read a series of articles written by Mike Cochran. His stories ignited a flame in the center of my being that started melting the frozen structures, the residue from my past. It was the part of my past that stayed with me, and ran my life, though it was hidden, even from me.

The ice began to thaw. Feelings surfaced and tears began to flow as I followed the flame, melting all in its path, allowing me to identify and deal with the feelings I had not known were hidden far below the surface. One change catalyzed another.

As the ice melted and became water it developed its own flow, like a river, flowing in its own course and creating its own path. I was like a log in the river, going where the flow of the water took me.

To touch the heart of others who have suffered the loss of a parent as a child:

A poignant moment in my life was at the death bed of my best friend's father. He was an interesting man with a history similar to mine. His mother had died when he was one-and-a-half years old. His father dropped him and his older brother on the steps of the boy's aunt and uncle. The father was off to enjoy his life as a musician leaving the children in better hands, but with broken hearts. The father visited only once. The boys grew up in a loving home. But this man could never dull his pain from being abandoned enough that it did not consistently show up in dynamic ways. I witnessed the way his life was affected by never dealing with his abandonment issues. It shook me to the core knowing that if I did nothing, I too might end my life feeling bitter and angry about events I had no control over. I decided at that moment that I wanted to do whatever it took to heal my heart, but I didn't know what to do. It wasn't long after that when Mike Cochran's articles appeared. When the student was ready, the teacher appeared.

To challenge us as a society to examine our feelings about the pain and suffering of children and how we can best help them through loss:

This book will show that even though I had few, if any, behavioral problems, my family and I needed professional help to lessen my burden as a child. Children, by their very nature, tend to blame themselves for the many things that go wrong in their lives, just as I did. We as adults need to help the children to see their true qualities regardless of the circumstances in their lives. We need to help them understand what has happened in their lives, to reassure them that it isn't their fault, and to encourage them to recognize and deal with their feelings.

To show how our lives play out the imprints made in our earliest years:

One of the most difficult things for me to understand about my life has been the number of negative events I have endured. Only after learning not to take things so personally did I begin to relax about how many car accidents I've been in, how many acts of crime I've had against me, and so forth. None of my friends or family have had such a life. I've come to understand that our lives are like a piece of fabric that is made up of threads of different colors and textures, woven together to create a pattern that is repeated over and over. The patterns in our lives are created by our earliest experiences and our reactions to those experiences, which make deep impressions on the body and the personality, causing us to repeat them over and over. Therefore our issues tend to be the same throughout our lives, at least until we have worked through them. Understanding that it is life living through me—in the same patterns that were created in my earliest years, has allowed me to relax and do the best I can with what life places before me. One pattern created in my earliest years was trauma. As I have understood my early life and my reactions to it, I have learned to take care of myself in ways I was previously unable to do. Things continue to happen in my life, but now I work with myself in such a way as to see that what happens in my life is not who I am.

Cover Credits:
Design: gretadesign. L.L.C.
   303-733-5490
Photography: Stephen Ramsey
   303-777-9411
Family Portrait: Author's Collection

DEDICATION

Written
For My Parents,
Who Lost Their Voices
and
In Loving Memory
of My Grandparents,
Whom I Adored
and
With Compassion For All
Who Suffered
the Loss of a Parent as a Child

ACKNOWLEDGEMENTS

Bill Vidal, my spiritual teacher, for helping me understand my life and for showing me the way home.

My sister, Calva Ledbetter, for being the one who understands.

My aunts, uncles, cousins, niece and her family for my sense of family.

Mike and Shirley Nosler for their years of friendship.

Bill and Nancy White and my group for their compassion.

Hameed Ali and the Ridhwan school for their teachings.

Mary Ann Edwards for her willingness to approach me in the face of my pain.

Dr. Scott Walker for his committment to the chiropractic community and the world of hurting people.

My Neuro-Emotional Technique™ buddies, especially Dr. David Ackerman, Dr. Wayne Braddock, Dr. Theo Gruska, and Dr. Barry Faecher, for helping me with the "issues in my tissues."

Polly and Wilson Edwards for their openness about my parents.

Glenda Mathers, Leonard Coffman, and *Bill Pendleton* for their contributions to my healing.

Attorney *Mitchell Williams* and the late Judge *Truett Smith* for their kindness in responding to my letters.

Jon Hunt for opening my eyes.

Mike Cochran for inciting me to action.

Carol Lehr for support to publish the book.

Trey Spangenberg, my computer angel, for his computer expertise.

Elaine Long, for editing.

INTRODUCTION

This is not a big story. It did not merit national headlines or attract hordes of media to the small town where it happened. But it is a true story and an important story. It is important to the more than twenty people who were victimized by the members of a large illegal organization. It is also important to every thinking person who cares about the effects of illegal actions upon our society as a whole. When politicians praise criminals and give them community awards, it is the business of the members of the community to ask why.

My investigation of this accident took me back to the lawyers who represented the state as well as my sister and me. Their responses to my letters led me to the Lynn County Courthouse to retrieve copies of the court cases and the depositions involved with the law suit filed for wrongful death of the parent of a minor, the law suit against Roy Maxey for the death of my mother, and the courts decision finding Maxey guilty of bootlegging. The Texas Court of Criminal Appeals sent me the documentation regarding the appeals Maxey filed all the way to the Supreme Court of Texas. My sister and/or I had conversations with my parents' friends, my family, Melvin Burks, Glenda Mathers and others who added bits and pieces of information.

After Mike Cochran's article about our accident appeared in many papers throughout Texas, Leonard Coffman and Bill Pendleton called me and further enlightened me as to the events that occurred in 1951. The book has gone through many revisions and now I consider it an honor to inform you of what happened on May 21, 1951 and how that moment in time has influenced my life.

CHAPTER ONE

*"'Pinkie never considered bootlegging a crime...
He considered it a public service.'"*[1]

May 21, 1951

Across the street from Pinkie's Farm Store, a liquor store located twenty-one miles outside Odessa, Texas, a state "liquor agent huddled in a West Texas corn field, his eyes fixed on the rear entrance of a modest frame building."[2]

The Farm Store had a high fence around it allowing cars to drive into the back area to be loaded with bootleg liquor without being seen from the street. Roy Maxey, a runner for Pinkie Roden, pulled into the back area and gave the warehouse boys his written order for whiskey and beer. The order had been prepared by D.C. Turner, the manager of Pinkie's bootlegging business in and around Lubbock, about one hundred miles to the north. Roy sauntered to the front of the store to get a Coke and say hello to the store manager while he waited for his car to be loaded. As he pushed open the swinging doors to the front of the store, Roy saw Pinkie, his boss, jawing with another runner. Pinkie turned around and grinned, "Hello there Roy."

"Hidee Pinkie," Roy replied.

Pinkie leaned against a case of beer, "How's your car running?"

Roy quickened, "Just fine. Ain't noticed no trouble."

"That's good! How is the heat up in Lubbock?" Pinkie asked lazily. Roy knew that Pinkie meant how were the Liquor Control boys treating him.

"They haven't been too bad," Roy muttered chewing on a wad of tobacco. Roy took his time getting a Coke, jawing with Pinkie and the other runners who were also waiting for their car to be loaded. They let time pass by shooting the breeze.[3]

"I best be gettin' going," Roy said, heading toward his car before spitting remnants of tobacco along with its juice. Satisfied with the way the boys loaded his car, he checked the other two cars. Convinced everyone was ready to roll, he signaled to the good-old-boy manning the door to open it for the three waiting cars.

"Suddenly, the garage door opened and out lunged a late model red Cadillac, its engine growling and its tires squealing. The driver spun the steering wheel sharply to the left and sped off in a flurry of dust.

Within seconds, the liquor agent who was waiting in the cornfield and a colleague raced away in pursuit. As those two cars disappeared from sight, the two vehicles that were waiting in the garage quietly emerged from the building and headed in the opposite direction."[4]

These two cars were the ones filled with bootleg whiskey. The first car was for the purpose of diverting the attention of the liquor control boys and tricking them into following the car without any liquor inside.

"A short time later, the investigators overtook the red Cadillac on a lonely country road. They searched the vehicle and found nothing.

'A damn decoy,' the agent grumbled."[5]

Meanwhile, the other two cars broke formation, with Maxey turning northwest toward Lubbock, and the second car turning southeast toward Abilene.[6] Both were crammed with half pints of bootleg whiskey and beer. "Unchallenged and unhurried by the liquor control boys, both cars were bound for a thirsty clientele in different 'dry' West Texas counties."[7]

"Vast stretches of West Texas were dry, and would remain so for years to come. Across thousands of square miles, Prohibition was not dead or even gravely wounded. Those wanting to purchase legal whiskey often had to travel a hundred miles or more . . . Large sections of the region remain dry except for scattered tiny and remote crossroads still selling beer and liquor."[8]

Roy headed toward Lubbock in a 1951 Lincoln. He was a married man in his mid-thirties with two teenage children and was employed by Pinkie as a runner. That meant he was behind the wheel, running from the law, with a load of bootleg beer and whiskey that was owned by Pinkie.[9]

Pinkie Roden, the largest and most powerful bootlegger in the state of Texas, was a man with an actualized vision of satisfying the always thirsty West Texans who had a lusty affection for cold beer or whiskey. If Pinkie couldn't do it legally, he was just as comfortable bootlegging.[10] "The Big Spring store provided a facade of legitimacy and an early base for what would become a multimillion dollar enterprise, both legal and otherwise."[11]

Heading toward Lubbock, Maxey drove on highways as well as back roads, known in Texas as farm-to-market roads, mostly composed of dirt, gravel, and sand. Always dodging the law, the runners usually drove late in the day or at night and often with their lights off. As Maxey turned off the paved Lamesa highway and drove miles down a dirt farm-to-market road, he approached the small town of Sands, one of the tiny communities located on the back roads Maxey frequented. He pulled into the graveled driveway of the house in which his cousin lived and moseyed up to the porch since he had a little time to spare.

"Hi Sam." Roy greeted Samuel Riley with a smile as he walked into his farmhouse.

"Come in and take a load off, Roy." Samuel welcomed their guest while his youngest child, two years old, held his arms up for Samuel to pick him up.

"What kind of car is that? It sure is perty." Samuel commented, lifting the child into his arms and then lighting a cigarette. Samuel had recently lost his job, and since the couple had ten children, Roy hoped to offer them an opportunity to get back on their feet financially.

"It's a Lincoln. Can you believe ol' Roy's driving a Lincoln?" Roy asked.

"Not really," Samuel said with a laugh. "I never have rode in one of them hydraulic cars, but sure would like to. How's the job going?"

"It's good," Roy said placing his palms on the arms of the rocker he lowered himself into. "Hey, the guy who gives me my orders—his name is D.C. Turner. He has to go to jail for eighteen months on some kind of bootlegging charge.[12] I could bring you up to talk to him about working, 'cause he'll need extra help while he's in the pen.'"[13]

Mrs. Riley hurried into the room, joining the men, and having heard Roy's comment, she jumped at the chance to get a job. "Would he want to work the both of us?" she asked.

"That's a good question, but I wouldn't doubt it," Roy answered taking the cold glass of beer she offered. "Business is real good."

"I might work awhile just to catch up on bills if the older kids could watch the little ones. That is if Samuel don't care," she announced handing her husband a cold one.

Samuel said, "We sure could use the money. The sooner we start working, the sooner we'll bring home some money."

"Ride up to Lubbock with me now and I'll bring ya back tomorrow. I make this trip six days a week. But I can't wait too long because they are expecting my load up there pretty quick," Roy said.[14]

It was little more than a look and nod at each other before Samuel and his wife quickly moved into action. They waved goodbye to their children as the Lincoln pulled out of the driveway with Roy at the wheel.

CHAPTER TWO

*"Across thousands of square miles,
Prohibition was not dead
or even gravely wounded."*[1]

Tahoka, Texas, May 21, 1951

At lunch the same day, seventy miles north of Odessa, on a cotton farm outside of the small town of Tahoka, Calvin Edwards climbed off his tractor. Tired and hungry, he walked to his house. Opening the door, he bent down, offering each daughter an arm to jump into. His girls giggled with joy at his arrival. Calva An was two months shy of four-years-old and Elva Jo was just nineteen-months-old. The children didn't care that his clothes were full of dirt and dust from the field, but were interested in the hugs and kisses he'd give them. He walked into the dining room, put Calva An down and instructed her, "Go wash your hands."

He lifted Elva Jo into her wooden high chair at the dining room table. Walking over to his wife Pearle, he held her at the waist, kissing her gently on the cheek. "How are you feeling?" he asked.

"I'm past the morning sickness," she reported smiling. "I feel really well."

"I'm already in love with that baby. I think we should have a half-dozen—maybe more," he grinned, but Pearle ignored him.

Next to Pearle, Calvin's five-foot-eleven inch frame gave him the appearance of being a large man. Calvin had a muscular body and compared to Pearle, who stood five-foot-two inches tall and had weighed only one-hundred-four pounds when she became pregnant, he appeared large. Her fifth month of pregnancy was barely noticeable.

Changing the subject, Pearle said, "Your Dad called. Your mother is sick and in bed again. I'm afraid she needs that surgery."

With a voice full of concern he asked, "What's bothering her this time?"

"Colon problems I think, Calvin. She is looking to you to help her decide what to do. Perhaps if she had that surgery, she would feel better." Nellie, Calvin's mother, had discussed colon surgery for some time. Pearle continued, "Honey, will you help Mother get Granddad in here for lunch?"

Granddad was Pearle's eighty-six-year-old grandfather who lived ten miles north of Tahoka on his farm. He was visiting for a few days which he would do from time to time. He wasn't exactly sick, but more fitting to say he was old, feeble, and sometimes simply lonely. His two great-granddaughers were full of life and energy and would chase his blues away. When they became too much for him, he retreated to his farmhouse.

Calvin, Pearle, and their two children lived with Pearle's mother, Granny Rogers, in the very house where Granny and her husband, D.T. Rogers, had raised Pearle, their only child. This family was Grandad's only family. Pearle and her family had become the center of both her mother and her granddad's life, especially after Pearle's father died.

At lunch they planned their quick trip to check on Nellie, Calvin's mother. "I'll quit planting a little early today. Let's plan to spend the night, so if I need to take Mother to the doctor in the morning, I can," Calvin said as he delivered a big spoonful of black-eyed peas to his plate. "I'll tell the boys what to do tomorrow so they can continue planting if I'm not back."

That evening, Pearle asked her mom, "Do you think Granddad can stay here by himself tonight?"

"Yes, he'll be fine. He should be in bed before we leave, and I'll prepare everything he'll need while we're gone," Granny Rogers said.

Calvin's mother's fears of death weren't unwarranted. Nellie Edwards had many times become sick suddenly, flirted with death, and recovered. Each sickness took a bit more of her vitality, and since she was fifty-six years old, the family wondered if "this time" would be her last. Calvin felt he could determine her physical condition better by looking at her with his own eyes, instead of hearing about her condition over the telephone. Even though he was tired from planting cotton all day, he was never too tired, and it was never too late for Calvin to travel the thirty miles necessary to be with his mother if she needed him.

That evening when it was time to leave for Brownfield, Calva An, Calvin's namesake, crawled into the back seat of the car with Granny Rogers, and within minutes laid her blond curls on Granny Rogers lap. Elva Jo was named after both of her Grandmothers. Granny Rogers' name was Elva Pearle while Granny Edwards' name was Nellie Josephine. Calvin picked Elva Jo up and passed her across the front seat to her mother, after rubbing her dark head of hair and tickling her under the chin. Her green eyes danced as she giggled. Calvin closed the back door of the car, turned to Pearle, and flashed her his crooked grin as he slid into the front seat.

Pearle smiled and said, "I love watching you play with the girls."

"I'm crazy about them," Calvin said. "You know that."

Pearle patted her barely noticeable tummy and said, "I know it doesn't matter, but I hope the little one in here is a boy."

Calvin and Pearle felt fine about obvious displays of affection for their girls. After all, they had waited a long time for children. At a time when most people had children within a year or two after marriage, Calvin and Pearle had been married ten years before Calva An was born. They had tried to have children, but after several miscarriages Pearle discovered she needed surgery to carry a child to term. Of course, the war had carved out four years while Calvin was in the service and Pearle lived with her parents. They were a couple who definitely were ready for the job of parenting.

Calvin drove down the dirt road bordered on each side by freshly planted cotton. He turned left onto state Highway 380 which would lead them directly into Brownfield. After a few minutes of silence Calvin asked Pearle, "Are you happy with the house plans?"

"There are a few things I'd like to change," Pearle said, "but I'll sure be glad to have the additional room. We are so crowded, especially when Granddad comes to spend a few days."

Calvin replied, "Don't worry, it won't be long and we will be in our new house."

Calvin loved his new Chevrolet. It was comfortable for his family, ran smoothly, and went fast. The sun had descended below the horizon and darkness had arrived. Three miles outside of town they passed by the road leading to the T-Bar Ranch, where one of Calvin's farms was located. As they passed the road, Calvin smirked and asked, "Remember when we lived out here?"

Pearle joined Calvin in a laugh at their personal joke. Once Calvin had gotten upset with his mother-in-law and decided he and Pearle would move to T-Bar. They stayed in the God forsaken house one night before returning to their familiar surroundings where Calvin settled his problems with his mother-in-law. She was a fine woman, and he was a fine man, but with a healthy temper. Able to laugh about the night they "moved" to T-Bar, they recalled lying in bed and seeing the stars through the cracks in the wooden roof. The house was still standing years later, but was never inhabited again.[2]

Silence descended into the car as Calvin and Pearle encouraged Elva Jo to fall asleep. She lay between them with her head in her mother's lap as Pearle gently patted her on the back.

CHAPTER THREE

"Pinkie Roden's boys had struck again."[1]

West Point, 9:00 p.m.

Nine miles further down the road, half way between Tahoka and Brownfield, was a farm-to-market road which intersected the highway. With a cotton gin located on the northeast corner, it was well-known to the farmers in the area. In cotton country, a gin made the intersection a landmark, and it was known as West Point.

Roy Maxey was traveling north on the farm-to-market road. A stop sign marked the approach to the highway, but Maxey didn't stop. As Calvin reached the West Point intersection, his headlights flashed on Maxey's Lincoln roaring into the intersection, and in the twinkling of an eye, the lives of twelve children were changed forevermore. Calvin hit the brake pedal, but ramming the bootlegger's car was unavoidable. Calvin's Chevrolet broadsided the Lincoln. Screeching brakes and banging metal created a chaos of sound as the cars crashed into each other. The smell of alcohol filled the air. As the cars came to a halt, all sounds ceased, and then the children began to wail.

As Calvin's overwhelmed senses returned to near normal, he heard the cries of fear and pain coming from his children. He wanted to jump to the aid of his babies, but his body simply would not cooperate. He was trapped behind the steering wheel wedged in every possible way to prevent movement. With broken bones and injuries to nerves, the body simply would not do what the mind directed it to do. Sharp objects had pierced his flesh, and blood ran down his face and into his eyes. Calvin couldn't even move to wipe the blood off his face. He listened to the cries of his children, the belabored breathing of his mother-in-law, and then the silence from his wife. Calvin was the only conscious adult in the accident and could only muster a beseeching "God, please help me."

Behind the gin and close to the intersection was a house where Kevil Coffman, the gin manager, lived with his wife and son. "What was that?" Marie, Kevil's wife, yelled after the deafening crash of vehicles.

Kevil jumped up from his easy chair and ran out the screen door with Marie close behind.

He quickly surveyed the scene and turned, yelling at Marie, "Go call for the ambulance."

Marie ran back to the house as Kevil ran through the rubble and tremendous debris toward the cars. Kevil found Calvin's car north of the Brownfield highway and east of Maxey's Lincoln. Calvin's car was standing right side up, facing west. The Lincoln had landed upside down in the ditch on the north side of the road after apparently rolling over several times.

Kevil heard a voice cry out, "Can you help us?"

Running to the car Kevil found Calvin wedged between the steering wheel and the front seat. Kevil, not recognizing Calvin, asked, "Can you move?"

"No, not really," Calvin moaned, "but please see about my two little girls. I hear them crying."

Kevil sent a quick glance across the front seat toward Pearle and noticed she wasn't moving. He hurried but had to be careful as it was dark and the area was full of broken beer and whiskey bottles and shards of glass from the windshields.

Kevil found Calva An, the oldest little girl, standing up in the back seat screaming. Kevil said, "Come here little girl." She limped toward him. There seemed to be something wrong with her hip. Having no medical training, Kevil did not know the first thing about how to determine her injuries. Though no blood was evident, she was crying as if she were hurting.

Kevil picked her up and held her close while moving her to a location away from the broken glass and out of harm's way. His heart was racing and he blinked back tears as the child winced in pain crying, "Mama, Mama."

Marie returned in a run from calling for help and yelled, "What can I do, Kevil?"

"Come sit with this little girl," he said as he rushed Calva An to his wife. Passing her from his arms to hers, he said, "There's another little girl I'm trying to find. And, be sure to watch for oncoming traffic." Kevil scurried back to the car.

Kevil asked Calvin, "How old is the other little girl?"

"She's just a baby. She's one," Calvin answered haltingly.

"It's so dark out here," Kevil said as he looked for the child. No headlights were visible from either car.

"Where was she in the car?" Kevil asked Calvin because he wasn't finding a child. Perhaps she was thrown from the car, he thought.

"She was riding between my wife and me," Calvin's breath came labored.

Kevil searched the seat of the car, tearing at the floorboard between Calvin and his wife. He found no child, but he could hear her crying. Perhaps the child had flown through the window. Kevil tracked the sounds from the baby which intermingled with the cries from the older child, confusing his investigation. If the child were outside the car, she could be cut to bits on all the broken beer and whiskey bottles. Just breathing the fumes from the wreckage was intoxicating. "Where are you little girl?" Kevil looked around the scene and called to the baby.

Kevil rummaged around the car in the dark attempting to locate the child. He backtracked the likely path of the car and ended up in front of the car. Suddenly, Kevil yelled to his wife, "It sounds like she's under the hood!"

"Oh, dear God," Marie said biting her lip. She called, "Leonard, come over here." Kevil and Marie's ten-year-old son had been in the bathroom when he heard the crash. He scrambled to the accident scene to discover the cause of all the commotion. Marie didn't like his young eyes witnessing the sight, but right now she knew she had to help these little children.

Calvin's car had hit the side of the Lincoln and crumpled, so there was no way Kevil could open the mangled hood to look for the child. The dashboard was curved down upon itself from the impact of the car. Kevil contorted himself inside the backseat of the car, reaching over the front seat between Calvin and Pearle. Miraculously, underneath the pummeled dashboard, his hand suddenly touched squirming wet flesh.

"I've got her," he screamed to his wife. His large hands clutched her trapped body dislodging her out of the coiled dashboard. The child was screaming hysterically and blood dripped everywhere. He cradled the crying baby girl to his chest and tried to comfort her. He hurried over to his wife and placed the child in her arms and exclaimed, "I don't know what's wrong, but she sure is bleeding."

Kevil rushed back to Calvin and said, "I've got the children over by my wife. I can't tell how badly they're hurt, but help is on the way."

"Please get my little girls to a hospital," Calvin begged.

"I promise," Kevil said laying a comforting arm on Calvin's shoulder, "I will as soon as someone gets here."

"Is my wife hurt?" Calvin asked suddenly. Kevil hadn't even thought to check Pearle. Her eyes were closed and she sat unmoving and silent.

"Don't worry. We are going to take care of everything," Kevil said. He couldn't tell this man the mother of his children might be dead. The wail of sirens chased all thoughts from his head, and he looked up to see the red lights of the ambulance coming toward him. "Here comes our help." Kevil had no time to attend to anyone in the other car.[2]

The wailing ambulance came to a halt and two men lunged from the pink-and-white unit with one attendant rushing to each car. Within a minute the blaring of another siren announced the arrival of Deputy Sheriff Roan. He first noticed the children crying and the smell of alcohol in the air. He kicked the broken whiskey bottles out of his way with his cowboy boots to walk to Calvin's side of the car. He overheard Calvin asking again, "Is my wife hurt?"

Sheriff Roan was shocked at the sight before him. He listened intently to the conversation between Calvin and the ambulance attendant.

"Calvin, where were you going?" the ambulance attendant knelt by his side.

"Brownfield," he managed to reply.

"What happened?" the attendant asked, attempting to make conversation with Calvin while determining how best to get him out of the car.

"I don't know," Calvin said wincing. "I didn't see any lights from the other car. And, he surely didn't stop."[3]

The ambulance attendant informed Kevil that a second ambulance was on its way, but it was apparent that the adults would take all the space in the ambulances. This was 1951 and before the time of emergency medical technicians. Lynn County had only one ambulance and one hearse, which doubled as an ambulance when necessary. With a crowd of new arrivals gathering to help, Kevil went to get his car to fulfill his promise to Calvin. He backed it up close to the accident site where he and his wife picked up the girls and placed both of them in the front seat. They were particularly concerned at the baby's emotional response. They had understood her earlier crying, but now she did not cry at all. She was completely quiet with her eyes darting from side to side. It was clear she could not comprehend what was happening to her. It appeared she was too scared to cry. Calva An's crying was less unnerving than Elva Jo's silence. In 1951, the symptoms of shock were not widely known or understood by the average person.

With the children loaded in the car, Kevil informed Calvin he was taking the children to the hospital. Kevil's wife and son watched his departure from the accident scene where he left gravel flying and tires squealing. Kevil and his family were shaken by this first hand view of the fragility of life.

Kevil spoke to the children in his most comforting voice. "It's going to be OK, little girls." Even as he said the words, he knew in his heart the previous moments had changed these girls lives forever. Kevil knew how much children need their mother, and the mother of these children appeared to be dead. Witnessing the horror of this accident left a wound for him and each member of his family. Not a bloodletting wound needing stitches, but a wound that created a scar nonetheless. The scar was buried in their psyches.[4]

Kevil's car screeched to a halt in the emergency driveway of the hospital in Tahoka. He opened the passenger door, put Calva An in one arm and Elva Jo in the other, and carried them into the emergency room. The children's cries quickly got the attention of the nurse who took the baby out of his arms. Kevil blurted, "These are Calvin Edwards' little girls. There's been a terrible accident at West

Point with at least four adults hurt."

All the emergency systems that were available in a small West Texas farming community in 1951 were thrown into motion. Calls for additional personnel to attend to the accident victims were made. In Tahoka, located thirty miles south of Lubbock on the Texas Panhandle, the Edwards' family was well-known and well-liked. The adults were considered community leaders. News traveled fast in a small town and soon people started arriving at the hospital to support the Edwards' family. With Kevil's assistance to the children complete, it was time he return to his family.

CHAPTER FOUR

*"For Pinkie, life was a game.
Like politics, he played it to the hilt,
but by his own unique rules."[1]*

Same night, 9:40 p.m.

A second ambulance arrived at the accident scene. The ambulance drivers worked quickly and carefully extricating Calvin from the car. "Calvin, I'm going to open this door and see if I can get you out of the car from this angle." The attendant wanted to keep Calvin talking.

Calvin knew he was hurt badly because he was in a great deal of pain if he attempted to move any part of his body. "It seems like I'm trapped." The metal car was twisted around him in such a way that he was not able to move at all. The attendants carefully lifted Calvin's body from the car by opening a door and, with minimal jarring, placed him on a gurney.

"Calvin, we are putting you in the ambulance with a man who was in the other car. Roy Maxey is his name. We are leaving for the hospital as soon as I get this door closed," the attendant said. Although he spared Calvin the information, Roy Maxey was the man they had pulled from behind the steering wheel of the Lincoln, the car that had sped onto the highway from the farm-to-market road. While the ambulance was in transit to the Lynn County Hospital in Tahoka, a second ambulance was being loaded with Granny Rogers, who was unconscious, and Mrs. Riley, who had been taken from the Lincoln.

Upon arrival at the Lynn County Hospital in Tahoka, Calvin found the needed support of his friends. While being x-rayed he could hear people talking outside the room. As the doctor entered the room Calvin said, "I want to talk to W.T. I can hear him outside the door."

Dr. Thomas said, "Let's take care of you first. There will be plenty of time for you to talk to your friends later."

Calvin voiced concerns, "How are my girls?" Calvin refrained from asking about Pearle.

Dr. Thomas assured Calvin, "We took some x-rays and it looks like they will be just fine Calvin." As he talked, Dr. Thomas stood in front of the x-ray light reading the radiographs just taken of Calvin.

"Calvin, the x-rays show you have a badly broken right leg, a broken right arm, and a broken left hip. And I'm sure you can feel the severe lacerations on your head, face, and body. We need to send you to Lubbock because these kind of injuries need an orthopedic surgeon, and Lubbock has the connections for those services. We just aren't equipped here to treat problems this extensive, and we want you to have the best care possible." In 1951, even Lubbock was not large enough to enjoy the talents of all medical specialists. Calvin's injuries would require the knowledge and expertise of a skillful orthopedic surgeon, who flew into Lubbock from Dallas when needed. Such a large and tragic car accident was a first for the small West Texas town of Tahoka.

"I'm fine with going to Lubbock, but I want my girls to go, too. I want them to be with me," Calvin's voice trailed off.

"That's fine, Calvin. We will transfer all of you to the West Texas Hospital in Lubbock for treatment," Dr. Thomas said. "Is there anyone in particular that you would like to take your girls? It would probably be best if they ride in separate cars."

Ruby Harvick was the nurse in the room attending him. Calvin looked at her and asked, "Ruby, could you and Lawrence take Calva An? I know she will be in good hands with you."

"Of course we can, Calvin. We will help you any way we can." She left the room to tell her husband to get the car ready. As she walked into the lobby area, everyone gathered around her asking about the injured parties.

Ruby said in her professional voice, "It's really too early to tell yet. Please be patient with us as we have our hands full. Lawrence, I need to talk to you." She led him into an area where only staff were allowed. "It looks pretty bad. Calvin's injuries are bad, and he has to be transferred to Lubbock and wants the girls to go with him. We are going to take Calva An to the hospital in Lubbock for him. I think she will be all right, but she has a broken leg. Will you get the car, make sure we have enough gas, and bring it around to the emergency room door so we can transfer her to the car?"

Ruby went back into the room with Calvin and said, "Lawrence is getting the car. Is there someone in particular you want to take Elva Jo to Lubbock Calvin?"

"Isn't W.T. out there?" Calvin asked.

"Yes, he and Esta Mae are both here," Ruby said.

"Will you ask them to take Elva Jo to Lubbock for me? She knows them and maybe she won't be so scared," Calvin said.

"Ruby, I'll ask him, if you will stay here with Calvin. I'll be back in a minute," Dr. Thomas said.

W.T. Kidwell was around Calvin's age and had two children of his own just older than Calva An and Elva Jo. W.T. and Calvin were both farmers and W.T. also owned and managed the local grocery store in Tahoka. He and his wife, Esta Mae, had learned of Calvin's accident when one of W.T.'s farm workers came by his house with the news. They had come to the hospital to discover the extent of the injuries and to see if they could be of assistance.[2] The doctor approached W.T. and asked him to step into his office.

"W.T., Calvin is hurt badly enough that he needs to be taken to Lubbock, and he wants the girls to go with him. We can't take the girls in the ambulance with him, and he requested that I ask you and Esta Mae to carry Elva Jo to the West Texas Hospital for him."

"Sure, anything we can do to help. How is Pearle?" asked W.T. as he had heard rumors.

"Pearle hasn't been brought in yet, so I can't really say. It was a bad accident. I'm sure Calvin thanks you for taking Elva Jo. Drive up to the emergency door, and we will put her in your car," Dr. Thomas said as he left the room.

Rumors were flying. It didn't take long for the Tahoka grapevine to spread word about the liquor involved in the accident as Lynn County and most other counties in West Texas were dry. Being dry did not mean liquor was not available, as West Texas was a haven for the bootlegging industry.[3]

CHAPTER FIVE

*"A multi-million dollar syndicate,
controlled by one Tom (Pinkie) Roden of Odessa,
sold most of the liquor which ended up
in Lubbock and other dry West Texas cities."*[1]

Same night, 10 p.m.

At the site of the accident, the ambulance attendant, Jeno Jones, found Pearle's body in the front seat of the Chevrolet. He placed his finger on the carotid artery and confirmed what he had feared to be true: that Pearle was dead. She had gashes on her forehead, lip, and chin, a large laceration on her cheek as well as a broken right forearm and a crushed and bruised chest.[2]

Ten minutes after the arrival of the ambulance at the Lynn County Hospital, Mrs. Samuel Riley was pronounced dead. Only five minutes later Granny Rogers, Elva Jo and Calva An's grandmother, was also pronounced dead. In less than an hour, four adults were dead, two adults were critically injured, and two children were injured and desperate for their mother, who would never return.

The Edwards' maroon Chevrolet had crashed into the passenger side of the 1951 Lincoln. The cars were reduced to little more than twisted metal. As the rescuers continued to clear the accident scene, they moved the Lincoln. An ambulance attendant yelled, "Someone's under the car!"

They found the body of Samuel Riley, forty-nine-years old, whose head had been crushed by the car after he was thrown from the passenger's side.

Maxey, the driver of the Lincoln, had massive injuries. In fact, he was at first thought to be dead. The authorities called his wife and informed her of his death. She was told that his body would be at the funeral home in Tahoka, but after she and her two teenage children arrived at the funeral home, they were informed there had been a mistake. He was alive, but seriously injured and was at the Tahoka hospital. His injuries were critical, and he was transferred to a hospital in Lubbock. He had a broken jaw, severe lacerations, a fractured left arm, broken ribs, and bruises.[4]

Calvin's parents, Carroll and Nellie Edwards, were expecting their son and his family to arrive the evening of May 21, 1951, to help with Nellie's illness. Instead, they found a friend, Benny Moore, from Tahoka at their door. Benny asked to speak to Carroll outside the house. "Carroll, Calvin and Pearle were on their way over here with the kids, and, er, well, they had an accident. It was right there at the West Point gin."

"Is everyone ok?" Carroll asked.

"Well, I know they got some ambulances out there and they took them to the hospital in Tahoka, but that is about all I know."[5]

Carroll and Nellie had absolutely no idea how vastly their lives were about to change. Nellie was already ill and became immediately worse upon hearing of the accident. She was in no condition to go to Tahoka. She stayed home while Carroll and his twenty-five year old son, Robert, and seventeen year old daughter, Freda, drove to Tahoka to see Calvin. En route to the hospital they had to drive through West Point and they stopped to survey the accident site. The sheriff, still on the scene, was writing down necessary information and directing traffic. The awesome destruction was still visible. The two cars were totally demolished, and the debris and smell from alcohol left Carroll feeling very apprehensive about the condition of his son and his son's family. Carroll could only pray incessantly, "God, please help Calvin."

Because the ambulance attendants directed their attention to those accident victims who could benefit from emergency care, Pearle was still sitting upright in the passenger side of the Chevrolet. She would be the last person to be taken from the scene to the mortuary. The people in charge were unable to shield Carroll from the sight of Pearle. Tears welled up in his eyes.

"Oh, Daddy, let's go," Freda said.

Carroll left the scene knowing his son would need him in ways he had never needed him before. Carroll, a godly man of strong character and integrity, knew that he would be available for whatever kind of assistance Calvin would need.

Arriving at the Lynn County Hospital in Tahoka, Carroll, Robert, and Freda were briskly escorted in to see Calvin. There were gentle hugs and kisses given, but no mention of Pearle or the scene of the accident. Calvin had lacerations on many areas of his body and bones broken, but he seemed to be mentally sound. Hurting on the inside, physically and mentally, he was not one to show it on the outside as he had a whole family for whom he felt he needed to be strong. Calvin was like his father. Men didn't show their true feelings. He made a few poor attempts at joking because being the jokester and prankster in the family, he felt if he acted carefree, everyone would know he was all right. His concern for his children and wife created internal turmoil, but outwardly he spoke about his mother. Calvin wanted them to go home and care for his mother as he was being cared for by doctors and nurses. He knew his mother's condition was fragile, and he was not emotionally ready to speak of his concern for Pearle and the girls.

Calvin rushed to tell them, "The hospital in Lubbock is having an orthopedist fly in tomorrow to do my surgery. I think he's flying in from Dallas." The family was unaware that his accelerated speech was a sign of being in shock.

Dr. Thomas assured Mr. Edwards his son would be kept comfortable while awaiting surgery the next day.

Before Carroll, Robert, and Freda left, Calvin said, "Hey, Robert, keep my wallet for me until I get out of here. OK? And, sister, be sure and tell Mother I love her."

"Just take care of yourself, Calvin. We'll take care of mother," Robert said unable to keep the sadness out of his voice. "Don't worry. I'll keep your wallet for you."[6]

Returning to Brownfield to update Calvin's mother on his condition, they again passed by the intersection at West Point, but this time they did not stop. The police were still on the scene measuring Calvin's skid marks at fifty-four feet and making notes about the specifics of the accident. The Lincoln was an obvious bootlegging vehicle, with the back seat removed and filled with bottles of gin, whiskey, and beer. In fact, there was so much alcohol at the scene of the accident, two cars and a pickup truck were needed to carry the bottles of intact liquor and beer back to Tahoka.[7]

Meanwhile, rumors continued to fly through Tahoka among the young couple's friends that Calvin had hit one of Pinkie's runners who was driving the back roads with his lights off, running from the liquor control boys.[8] Carroll's nephew, Wayland Edwards, was the pastor at the Southcrest Baptist Church in Lubbock. He was asked to meet Calvin as he arrived at the West Texas Hospital. It was sad enough for the Edwards' family to lose a family member in a car accident, but for *alcohol* to be the reason for the death made it harder on them all. The Edwards' family had strong Southern Baptist roots and Carroll had always frowned upon alcohol in any fashion, although Calvin had been known to have a beer. It was a prime example of how, although you may never touch alcohol yourself and you teach your children to shy away from it, the drug can still have a massive, catastrophic effect on your life. Wayland drove to the hospital and waited for Calvin to arrive.[9]

The Riley couple, Roy Maxey's cousins, were both dead. They were not known in Tahoka, but tragedy is tragedy, even when it strikes strangers. The townspeople were aghast when they discovered that the couple had ten children, with the oldest being about twenty years old.

CHAPTER SIX

"For one-year old, Elva Jo Edwards and her sister, Calva An who is three and a half, the tragedy itself happened unbelievably fast."[1]

Same night, midnight

Calvin arrived at the West Texas Hospital in Lubbock about midnight. He was swiftly moved into the emergency room area. He called Ruby Harvick, the nurse from Tahoka, over to him and asked, "How are my girls?" "They will both be fine. Calva An has a broken leg which will be set tomorrow, and Elva Jo has cuts on her shoulder and elbow that need stitching. Both girls are in shock. But, Calvin, I promise you they will get good care because I will see to it." Ruby decided not to mention Elva Jo's internal injuries as the doctors were uncertain as to the diagnosis. There would be time to inform Calvin of her condition after his surgery. He needed to reserve some of his internal strength for himself.

"Thanks Ruby. I know you will," Calvin said in a soft, strained voice.

In the emergency room, his vital signs were taken. He was talking rapidly as a reaction to the shock ravaging his system. The doctors were aware of the severity of his fractures, but there was little to do until the orthopedist arrived. The doctors were also concerned about Calvin's mental health. He had not asked about his wife or mother-in-law. But, the doctors said nothing. They felt it best to defer his grief until after his surgery as it appeared he was not ready to face the truth.

The doctor said, "Calvin, the orthopedist from Dallas will fly in tomorrow morning. We have a few tests we'll have to perform on you tonight so you'll be ready for the surgery tomorrow. Be patient with us, Calvin. And, I want to assure you that your little girls will receive the best care we have."

"Thanks, Doc, I appreciate it. I think I hear a friend of mine out in the hall. If Wilson Edwards is out there, will you tell him I need to talk to him?"

The doctor left Calvin's room and asked, "Is there a Wilson Edwards here?"

It isn't often that two married couples are as compatible as Wilson, Polly, Calvin, and Pearle. But they were two very well-matched couples whose love for each other extended beyond friendship into family. They enjoyed each other's company and could depend upon each other for needed support. Even though Wilson and Polly lived forty-five miles away from Lubbock, they had come immediately after hearing of the accident and dropping their young son off at his grandmother's home in Tahoka. It was after one o'clock in the morning when they arrived at the hospital in Lubbock.

"I'm Wilson Edwards," said a handsome looking, thin man, about Calvin's age.

"Calvin Edwards is asking to speak with you," said the doctor, "but I would like to talk to you for a moment first, so if you don't mind, please step over here with me." The doctor, Wilson, and Wilson's wife, Polly, stepped into a semi-private area where the doctor asked, "Are you related to Mr. Edwards?"

"Yes, we are cousins and best friends," answered Wilson with his hat in his hand.

The doctor put his arm on Wilson's shoulder and said, "I am concerned about your mentioning anything about his wife. Did you know she was killed in the accident?"

"We heard that, but tonight I'm hearing a lot of things, and I don't know what is true."

"I was told by Dr. Thomas in Tahoka that Calvin's wife was pronouced dead at the scene," the doctor said.

Polly's tears rolled down her cheeks. Wilson put his arm around Polly and asked, "Does Calvin know about Pearle?"

"He hasn't been told," the doctor answered. "But, he hasn't asked either. You know, he has such a difficult surgery to get through tomorrow. I feel it would be better if you didn't tell him about her death," the doctor said.

Wilson hugged Polly a little tighter around her shoulders, "I won't mention it, but, you know," Wilson paused, "we are best friends, and if he asks me, I can't lie to him. Not at a time like this."

"I understand," the doctor said nodding his head. "If you need us, we'll be available. He asked for you. Go in and close the door behind you and don't stay too long."

Wilson turned to Polly as tears continued streaming down her cheeks. She could not turn the tears off. "I just can't go in, Wilson," Polly said.

Wilson understood. "It's OK Polly. You don't have to. Just stay in the waiting room because I've got to talk to Calvin. I won't be in there long."

"Wilson, tell Calvin I love him." The state of shock caused by this horrific evening was descending on the friends and family of Calvin and Pearle. Polly kept repeating to herself, "I just can't go in," as she walked toward the waiting area. She wanted to see Calvin and tell him how much she loved him, but she knew she couldn't contain her emotions. There would be time to assure Calvin of her love and concern after his surgery, when her pain from the evening was not so fresh, not so raw. She sat down and began pulling herself together by considering how she could help the little girls, while Wilson entered the emergency room where Calvin was lying on a gurney.

Signs of the accident were starkly visible in his torn, ragged and blood-soaked clothing. He had dark, dried blood in streaks and clots on his skin, and matted in his dark brown hair. Wilson said, "Hi, Calvin. I came as soon as I could."

"I knew you would. You just wouldn't believe what we've been through. I guess you know Pearle didn't make it," said Calvin.

"Well, I heard that and our hearts are broken," responded Wilson. He had known Calvin wouldn't be fooled by the doctors. Calvin was just the kind of man that wouldn't speak of "it" until he was ready. It would be his decision when and with whom he confided. "What can we do to help you Calvin? Polly is in the hall and they told me I couldn't stay in here very long. We are here to help you however we can."

Haltingly Calvin said, "I'd like Polly to stay with Calva An and Elva Jo tonight. The doctors tell me that they'll be ok, but I know they must be scared." Calvin started crying. "I'd feel a lot better knowing she's with them."

"You bet she will. I'm sure Polly will want to stay with the girls," Wilson replied, choking up. "How are you feeling?"

"It hurts, but as long as I don't move, it isn't too bad," Calvin said.

"Why haven't they cleaned you up?" asked Wilson. "I'm going to get you out of these clothes." Wilson walked over to a medical tray and picked up a pair of scissors and began cutting Calvin's blood-soaked clothing off of his body. He asked about the accident, "What happened?"

Calvin responded with each word in rapid succession. "We were on our way to Mother's when it happened so fast. This car came out of nowhere. I was going fast, and they didn't have any lights on and it was dark. There was no way I could see he was there. All of a sudden, my lights hit this car cutting across the highway in front of me. I slammed on my brakes, but it didn't do any good. There was nothing I could do to stop it. I didn't have any time to warn Pearle or her mother. I saw the car, and the next moment we hit. I'll never forget the sounds of that crash. It all happened so fast........" Calvin's voice softened as if his consciousness was back at the accident. After a long pause, he continued speaking. "We hit the car, and the next thing I knew we were stopped. From that moment I knew it was really bad. I couldn't even move. But the worst part was I could hear the girls crying and calling for us, but I couldn't move to help them. It tore my heart up to hear them crying like that. The gin manager came over after he heard the crash and took the girls to the hospital. I just pray to God they'll be all right. I wish I'd had one last good-bye with Pearle," Calvin's tears cleaned a path of blood off his cheeks.

Wilson got a tissue off the medical tray and wiped Calvin's cheeks since Calvin's own arms were broken. Calvin said, "Would you go to the funeral home for me? I'm almost sure Pearle's mother is dead, but they haven't told me. She is isn't she?"

"Yes, Calvin, I heard she didn't make it." Wilson knew he must soon leave as the longer he was in the room, Calvin inched closer and closer toward hysteria. But he was unwilling to leave him alone.

"You and Polly went to the funeral home with Pearle and me when we made arrangements for her dad's funeral, so I figure you would know what Pearle would want for herself and her mother. Would you handle all of the arrangements for me? Mother is sick, and I want my family to take care of her. I don't know how long I'll be in the hospital." Calvin's voice turned into sobs again as his crying took over.

"Yes, Calvin. I'll go tonight. I'll leave Polly here with the girls, and I'll go to the funeral home and be back tomorrow for your surgery."

A nurse walked in and advised Wilson to leave. She calmly told Calvin she needed to wash his wounds and take him to X-ray. She seemed very kind so Wilson bid Calvin good-bye. "Calvin, you know you don't have to worry about anything because I'll handle everything for you. I'll see you tomorrow."

Wilson left the room and returned to Polly. While with Calvin, Wilson had been fine, but after he left, his voice and hands were shaking while he reported the conversation to his wife. They sat for a few minutes consoling and comforting each other. Then together they found their way to the front desk and asked the nurse for the room number of the children.

The two girls were sharing one hospital room. Polly and Wilson walked into the room and hugged the children they knew so well. The girls appeared glad to see them and made simple conversation. Polly and Wilson felt a natural desire to pick them up and rock them, but Calva An's leg was broken and Elva Jo had cuts that continued to ooze blood. Polly and Wilson certainly didn't want to cause the children more pain.[2]

CHAPTER SEVEN

*"Attention was first given the little girls.
Calva An was found to have a fractured left leg,
just above the knee, and bruises.
Elva Jo had lacerations and
bruises all over her little body."*[1]

May 22, 1951 3:00 a.m.

Polly settled in for the night with the children, while Wilson left the hospital and headed for the funeral home in Tahoka. With the events of the night, he knew the people at the funeral home would be available. He told Polly he would return in the morning with a fresh change of clothing for her so they could wait through Calvin's surgery together. They bid each other goodnight with a kiss and a heartfelt hug, but tried to avoid tears for the sake of the children.[2]

Calvin was wheeled from the emergency room and was headed toward the x-ray room when Ruby Harvick, the nurse from Tahoka, walked up beside his gurney, "Calvin, if you need anything, you let me know and I'll see that you get it."

Calvin didn't answer and in fact was becoming more and more distraught. Ruby said, "I am going to stay by your side until they put you to bed for the night. So I'm here, no matter what. Don't worry about anything. I'll take care of you."

Calvin's gurney was rolled into the x-ray room parallel to the x-ray machine. Ruby watched from the doorway. She knew it would be painful for Calvin to be transferred to the x-ray table with so many broken bones. A group of nurses, working as a team to lift Calvin onto the table, were preparing to count to three to lift him up and over to the table. Because of his condition, Calvin was unable to be any help in shifting his weight. As the team captain said "one, two, and three," they lifted him up and across the gurney toward the x-ray table. Calvin gasped for a breath. His head fell backward as silence momentarily filled the room.

"Doctor," yelled the nurse. The doctor was in an adjoining room and quickly responded, but there was nothing to be done.

"He's gone," the doctor said after putting his finger to Calvin's neck to check for a pulse. The doctor looked up at Ruby and said, "I'm sorry."

For a moment time stood still. Then Ruby went to Lawrence and cried, "Calvin just died."³

Wilson had been gone from the hospital for about twenty minutes when a nurse arrived at the door of the girl's hospital room. Looking at Polly, the nurse inquired, "Are you a friend of the family?"

"Yes." Polly replied.

"I'm sorry to tell you, but Mr. Edwards just died," the nurse said.

"Oh, my God!" Polly whispered. She left the room so the children would be spared her conversation "What happened?" she asked.

"It is hard to tell, but either he had some bleeding in the brain or his heart was punctured by a rib as they moved him. We aren't quite sure. He started crying and became somewhat disoriented which made us think he had some bleeding in the brain. But on the other hand, when we were moving him from the gurney to the x-ray table, the way he gasped with his head falling backward made it seem like maybe his heart was punctured by a rib. Immediately there was no pulse. The only way to really tell is have an autopsy, and I don't know if it matters enough that the family would choose to do that. I'm so sorry to have to give you this news," the nurse said.

"How could he have died?" Polly asked, "My husband went in to see him and said he was messy and bloody, but didn't mention his being close to death. He was talking, and my husband didn't think he seemed to be in too much pain for what he had gone through. It's hard for me to comprehend. Could you stay with the children a moment?" she asked, and the nurse nodded yes. Polly walked down the hall to get a cup of coffee and compose herself before returning to the children. In the course of a couple of hours both of her best friends were simply gone. And the children they wanted so badly were orphaned at such a young and tender age. Her sadness turned into pure anguish, and she felt she must call Wilson. She went to the pay phone down the hall and called the funeral home in Tahoka.

As Wilson drove back to Lubbock, he flashed on memories of the four of them together: the many laughs and good times they had shared over the years. He remembered the many trying experiences that had bonded them. Once when Calva An was in the hospital in Tahoka with pneumonia, there was an incredible ice storm. Calvin was not pleased at Calva An's improvement in the Tahoka Hospital so he had picked her up and started out of the hospital, but was stopped by a nurse who informed him he couldn't take the child out of the hospital. Calvin said, "Watch me," and out the door he went, driving her to a hospital in Lubbock. The weather was brutal and, of course, it would have been wise to stay home. After Wilson arrived at the hospital in Tahoka and found Calvin gone,

Wilson had a gut feeling Calvin had taken his daughter to Lubbock and nothing could have kept Wilson from following. When he arrived at the hospital in Lubbock, Calvin looked at him and said, "I knew you would come."

Once Calvin called on Polly's birthday and said, "I'm going to take you out tonight for your birthday, so be ready when we come by to get you." Calvin forgot to mention they were taking them to Fort Worth. They returned three days later.

Wilson knew that the girls would be his and Polly's to raise, as he knew in his heart that was what Pearle and Calvin would want. He knew Polly would feel the same way. Approaching the family would be necessary, but he was certain they would know Calvin and Pearle would want them to raise the girls.[4]

CHAPTER EIGHT

*"It didn't take long—it never does
when two automobiles smash together at high speeds
—for two little girls, now lying pale and listless
in large white hospital beds, to become orphans."[1]*

May 22, 1951, 3:30 a.m.

Calvin's father, Carroll Edwards, was from a large family and had eight brothers, one sister, and countless nieces and nephews, most of whom lived in the Lubbock vicinity. Wayland Edwards, Carroll's nephew and approximately Calvin's age, was the preacher at Southcrest Baptist Church in Lubbock. He had registered as Calvin's pastor while waiting for Calvin's arrival at the hospital in Lubbock. Wayland had met the ambulance and after speaking to Calvin and sitting with him for about thirty minutes, he was informed of the surgeries that would take place the next morning. He had bid Calvin good night so he could return for the surgery and minister to Calvin's family. Arriving home very late, he'd been asleep only a short time when he received a call from the hospital, about three-thirty in the morning, informing him of Calvin's death. The hospital granted his request to allow him to inform his Uncle Carroll and Aunt Nellie of their son's death. He drove to their house in Brownfield. For Carroll and Nellie Edwards, the night was filled with the kind of life changes that would make this event the center of the rest of their lives.[2]

Back in Odessa at Pinkie's favorite hangout, the bar tender said, "Telephone's for you. It's D.C."

Pinkie, back slapping patrons all the way to the telephone answered, "Yeah, this is Pinkie."

"Pinkie, this is D.C." D.C. Turner, was the manager of Pinkie's bootlegging activities in the Lubbock area. "I jest got word Roy had a wreck."

"Oh, really," Pinkie questioned. "How bad is it?"

"Don't know fer sure," D.C. answered.

"Where did it happen?" questioned Pinkie.

"Somewhere around West Point," D.C. muttered.

"Don't worry about it.," Pinkie said. "I'll take care of everything."

Pinkie took care of it by finishing his drink at the bar and going home and getting a good night's sleep. For Pinkie, life was good. He would have preferred that Roy had not had the accident. After all, Roy was driving an expensive car and had a load of Pinkie's alcohol in the car. And besides, Pinkie liked Roy. But the accident was really only a small inconvenience for Pinkie. His runner might be out of commission, but there was always someone who wanted a good paying job. He had lost a bootlegging car, but Pinkie had money to buy as many cars as he needed. He wasn't happy about it. He hadn't become a rich man by things not going his way, but these things happen, and Pinkie considered it all part of the expense of doing business.[3]

While Carroll and Nellie were awakened in the night with bad news, ten-year-old Leonard Coffman woke up from a bad dream. He had seen too much that night for his tender years. The events of that night were indelibly imprinted on his psyche and would remain in his subconscious, for the rest of his life. He tossed and turned that night. Finally, the early morning hour arrived for him to "rise and shine" as his mom would say. But this particular day his mom came into his room, sat on his his bed, and tenderly nudged him awake. Leonard readied himself for school, ate breakfast, and joined the other children who normally waited at the intersection to catch the school bus. This morning the students were drawn to the accident site where Leonard joined them. He relived some of the events of the previous night in conversation with his friends.

The accident site was riveting to Leonard. The police cars and ambulances were gone. Even the cars involved in the accident had been towed away. But for Leonard, it was still a horrific sight. What was left, the blood-drenched highway flanked by more broken glass than he had ever seen, captured the essence of the tragedy from the night before. It was an eerie sight for such a small boy. He wondered, "if that blood right there belonged to the little girl who was bleeding so much?" He hoped the little girls were feeling better. He knew they must be very sad, and he was sad for them.

As a neighbor girl appeared at the site Leonard said, "There were two little girls in the wreck. One was just standing in the back seat crying, but my dad had to dig the little one out. She was crunched inside the dashboard."

"Really," she said staring at the blood and glass. Leonard was glad when the bus picked them up and carried them far away from the gruesome site.

Leonard's dad, Kevil, knew the children were orphans. News of Calvin's death spread rapidly in Lynn County. Kevil's heart was heavy as he knew that the children's cries for Mama and Daddy would never be answered again. Yes, he had heard there were grandparents, and probably aunts and uncles, thank God, but isn't there something about the comfort of one's mama and daddy that allows a child to relax and feel that all is right with the world?[4]

CHAPTER NINE

*"The days of the wild West may be over,
but the legacy left by the bootlegging
'Wizard of the West' may never die."[1]*

May 22, 1951

Upon arising the following morning, Pinkie left his house early, stopped at the Farm Store, the package store where Roy had loaded his car the previous day, and grabbed a Lubbock newspaper. At the counter he positioned the paper to read the opening sentence about the accident, "One of the worst automobile accidents in South Plains history Monday night at West Point snuffed out the lives of five people, made orphans of two little Tahoka girls, left ten Sand children parentless, several of whom are dependent minors, and seriously injured the driver of a liquor-loaded car."[2]

Pinkie skimmed the newspaper article until he found information about Roy which read, "Maxey was also given emergency treatment, and was later carried to a Lubbock Hospital. He had a fractured left arm, broken right ribs, possible fractured jaw, and severe lacerations and bruises."

Pinkie tossed the newspaper aside and dialed the telephone number for D.C. Turner.

"Hi, Pinkie. What's going on?" asked D.C.

"Just read in the newspaper about Roy's wreck," Pinkie informed D.C..

"Yeah, I read that a bit ago myself. Too bad, huh?" D.C. remarked.

"Have you talked to Wells?" S.F. Wells, Jr. owned the car Maxey had been driving when he had the accident.

"No, can't say that I have. Do you want me to call him?" D.C. asked.

"No, I'll take care of everything." Concluding his conversation with D.C., Pinkie bit into a donut he had brought to the store. While eating his donut, he poured himself a cup of coffee and picked up the latest book that had caught his fascination. He was an avid reader even though his formal education had been abbreviated.

Pinkie was not known for sitting still, so after an hour of reading, he was ready to hit the road. He drove to the local Lincoln dealership and looked at a couple of new Lincolns he was considering buying. A powerful bootlegger like Pinkie needed the fastest cars money could buy, because after all, business depended on it.[3]

CHAPTER TEN

"As both a legal and illegal whiskey merchant, he (Pinkie Roden) cast a long shadow over the lives of many Texans."[1]

May 22, 1951, 9:00 a.m.

The morning after the accident, Wilson Edwards got out of bed with a burdened heart. He planned how to approach the families of both Calvin and Pearle about raising the children, although he didn't really expect any obstacles.

Pearle's side of the family was quite small: she was an only child and her only close relative was her granddad, J.A. Pierce, whom Wilson had met several times with Calvin. The night of the accident, a nephew took him to the hospital in Slaton where he spent the night.[2] The morning after the accident, Mr. Pierce was told of the death of his daughter, grand-daughter, and her husband. He was told the only survivors were the children. Though shaken, he went to his farm ten miles north of Tahoka to grieve privately.

Wilson drove to the farm to see Granddad Pierce, who answered the door. Wilson said, "Mr. Pierce, I don't know if you remember me, but I'm Wilson Edwards. I've been here to visit you with Calvin and Pearle several times. I want to tell you how sorry my wife and I are about Calvin and Pearle and Mrs. Rogers. We will all miss them terribly."

The old man held back his tears and said shakily, "Thank you." He invited Wilson into the house and they both sat down.

"Mr. Pierce," Wilson continued, "Pearle and Calvin's deaths leave two little girls without parents. My wife Polly and I have been around Elva Jo and Calva An ever since they were born. Our own boy, Craig, is two years older than Calva An and we aren't going to have any more children. I know Calvin and Pearle never dreamed of such a horrible thing happening to them and neither did we." His voice cracked. Regaining his composure, he continued, "Calvin and Pearle would want Polly and me to take the girls and raise them. We'd like to do this for them just as they would have done the same for us in opposite circumstances. I'm here today to ask for your blessing. I know you love the girls, and we'll bring them to see you often." After a pregnant pause, Wilson asked, "What do you think, sir?"

"I do love the girls, and they are my closest living relatives now," Mr. Pierce said as he reached for a tissue to wipe his eyes, "but I've been giving Calva An and Elva Jo's lives some serious thought. I'll provide for them financially, but I never want them to have to go through losing their parents again." He paused, wiping his eyes, and then said heavily, "I think it would be best for them to go to the Baptist orphanage. That way, they will never lose their parents again."

Wilson wondered if he was dealing with a man who was mentally competent! Squatting down beside Mr. Pierce's chair, Wilson said, "Mr. Pierce, don't you think having a home where they will be loved would be better than living among strangers? I mean, they are such little girls." Wilson stood up, and continued, "And besides, when you think about it, what do you think Pearle would want? Polly and I were best friends with Calvin and Pearle." Feeling overwhelmed with emotion, Wilson said, "Putting the girls in an orphanage would be second best. They don't know anyone there. Pearle would want her babies to be with people who love them and that the children know. Just think about it," Wilson concluded.

There was a long silence.

"Well, what is your name again?"

"Wilson Edwards. Calvin and I are cousins." Wilson forgot to refer to Calvin in the past tense.

Mr. Pierce cleared his throat, then said, "I can't take the girls because I'm too old. If you and your wife want the girls, I suppose I won't stop you."

Relieved, Wilson said, "Thank you Mr. Pierce. I assure you I will stay in contact. I'm going to go talk to Calvin's family now. Take care of yourself and thank you for seeing me." Wilson walked out of the small house with his mind awhirl. That old man wanted those two poor little girls to go to an orphanage!

Wilson found Robert, Calvin's brother, in Tahoka. "Hello, Robert," Wilson said.

"Hello, Wilson," Robert said as they shook hands.

"Robert, you know how Polly and I loved Calvin and Pearle." Overcome with emotion, Wilson gulped a couple of times and averted his eyes momentarily before he could continue. "How are Uncle Carroll and Aunt Nellie doing?"

Robert looked down at the ground first and then at Wilson. "They're devastated. I'm trying to help them out a little by doing some of the footwork. And, Mother isn't well."

Robert took his handkerchief out of his pocket and wiped his nose as Wilson began, "Robert, I want to talk to you about the girls."

Assuming Wilson wanted to know about their medical condition, Robert said, "They're in the hospital in Lubbock. Wilma went up there today to stay with them."

Putting his hands in his pockets, Wilson started with, "Well, Robert, you know Calvin and Pearle and Polly and I were best friends. I know Calvin and Pearle would want us to raise the girls for them. If it had been Polly and me that had been killed, they would raise Craig for us. Polly and I want to do this. I just know Calvin and Pearle would want it that way." Wilson put his hand on Robert's shoulder and continued, "The girls know us, and they'll fit right into our family. Three kids would be great. I know your parents love them, but your mother isn't well and your parents aren't getting any younger." Removing his hand from Robert's shoulder, he gestured, as he said, "Elva Jo and Calva An are going to need parents for almost twenty years. I talked to Pearle's grandfather this morning about Polly and me raising the girls, and he gave me his blessing."

"Well, Wilson, I don't know," Robert said as he moved a pebble around with his foot. He looked Wilson in the eye and said, "I don't know how Daddy will feel about it, but I will tell him what you said."

"What do you think, Robert?" Wilson asked.

Robert leaned against his car. "I don't know, Wilson. I'm in no position to take the girls myself." Pausing momentarily he continued, "If you and Polly are in agreement and if it works out for your family, I have no objections. But, you know, Daddy will have the final word."

Nodding, Wilson said, "I'd appreciate it if you'd talk to Uncle Carroll for me and tell him I'll wait for him to call me." Carroll and Wilson were cousins, but out of respect, Wilson always referred to Carroll as Uncle Carroll. Wilson knew Uncle Carroll well enough to know that it would be best to let Robert speak with him first. Wilson felt Uncle Carroll and Aunt Nellie were not healthy enough to take the children and they would be glad Wilson and Polly wanted to raise Elva Jo and Calva An.[3]

CHAPTER ELEVEN

*"Triple funeral services, one of the saddest
in the history of this town, were held
for Mr. and Mrs. Edwards and Mrs. Rogers."*[1]

May 23, 1951

For some people in the community, the days passed quickly. But for the two little girls whose only desire and greatest need was for their mommy and daddy to hold them and comfort them, each day was an eternity. With friends and family taking turns staying with them, Calva An and Elva Jo were not alone, except in their hearts where the hole got bigger and deeper with each passing hour. Even though they didn't understand why or how, their hearts understood that the loving voices and warm arms of mommy and daddy had been taken away.

Brother George Dale, the pastor at the First Baptist Church in Tahoka, was to officiate at the triple funeral and burial of Pearle, Calvin, and Granny Rogers. The church was overflowing with people. Sadness and despair filled the auditorium where the large extended Edwards and Rogers families were in attendance. Flowers filled the church sanctuary with mixed fragrances. The grief was a mix between the loss of the lives that were being remembered and the sadness for the lives that remained, especially the two orphaned girls.

Several of the young cousins on Pearle's side of the families were left with a baby-sitter while their parents attended the funeral. The children were too small to grasp the gravity of the situation, but they could sense the grief of their parents. They acted out their parents' sadness by having a pretend funeral which began with a procession, included singing and preaching, and culminated with the burial of their dolls. Later in the day one of the girls returned to the burial site, dug up the dolls, and life went on.[2]

Before the funeral, Brother Dale approached Calvin's parents privately. In Southern Baptist tradition, the preacher was addressed as brother. The minister spoke freely to Calvin's parents as he sat down with them saying, "Thank you for giving me a few minutes privately. Mr. and Mrs. Edwards, I know you would like to have the time to mourn your losses without having to deal with a lot of problems right now." He crossed his legs and clasped his hands over his knee, and continued speaking. "However, your situation is not so simple with two little girls who have to be considered. I know that you and your family have been attending to them in the hospital, but they will soon be ready to go home and several families in the community have approached me about the possibility of adopting the little girls." Uncrossing his legs, he leaned forward putting his hands on his knees. "They want to be sensitive to your sorrow, but time is of the essence for the two children. The families have asked me to speak with you on their behalf. No decision needs to be made right now, but I'm wondering if you've considered options for the girls?"

Without hesitation, Carroll replied, "We're going to raise the girls ourselves."

"Is that a final decision, Carroll?" the pastor asked.

"Yes." Carroll was a man of few words who felt no need to explain himself.

Brother Dale continued, "People in the community care about Calva An and Elva Jo and are asking me questions. I would like to be able to respond to them. Are you moving the girls to Brownfield with you?"

Carroll removed a package of Camel cigarettes from his shirt pocket and said, "We're moving into Pearle and Calvin's house, and Robert and I are going to farm his land." Carroll's manner of speech was matter-of-fact. "I just ask God to let me live long enough to raise the girls."

Brother Dale responded, "I will pray for that too, Carroll, and I certainly understand your desire to provide a home for them. I know it won't be easy as you and Nellie aren't young people. You have a supportive family, and people of this community will help you." Brother Dale stood up, shook Carroll's hand, offered his hand to Nellie and said, "And Mrs. Edwards, I will be praying for your health, too."[3]

Before the gravesite service was over, word was flying through the grapevine in Tahoka, "Calvin's parents are going to raise the girls." People were in disbelief. The Edwards' were too old! Mrs. Edwards had been near death for years! Her health made the possibility of her living until the girls were grown remote at best. Conversations like the one at the Milliken's house took place throughout the community during the next few days.

Polly and Wilson Edwards were at her parents, the Millikens, and several of Polly's sisters were sitting around the Milliken dining table drinking coffee and visiting with her parents. Polly said, " I just can't believe Uncle Carroll and Aunt Nellie are going to do this. It's crazy. She's in such poor health." Polly pulled her hair behind her right ear and continued, "Pearle always told me Calvin's mother had one foot in the grave when she and Calvin got married, and that was thirteen years ago!"

Wilson, nodded in agreement and said, "I can't stand it because I know Calvin and Pearle wouldn't want his parents to take the girls." Wilson took a drink from his coffee cup, but barely paused before saying, "We know they'd prefer that Polly and I take them. They've been our best friends for years, and we know what they'd want."

Polly continued, "Yes, I know Pearle would want me to take her girls. You know Pearle once said she...."

"STOP. NOT ANOTHER WORD!" Mr. Milliken interrupted Polly, his daughter, in mid-sentence in a loud, commanding voice. Into the silence Milliken continued speaking in a booming voice, "You may not agree with Mr. and Mrs. Edwards' decision, but they love those girls, and I know they're doing what they think is best for them." After a short pause, Milliken continued, "Their hearts are broken and they don't need people questioning their decision. They'll do the best they can by those girls." Milliken began emphasizing every word, "Each one of you will get out to that house and help Mr. and Mrs. Edwards. Now, I don't want to hear another word about it." The room was silent. Polly and Wilson knew Calvin's folks loved the girls. Besides, it was out of their hands. Polly and Wilson accepted the idea that the care of the girls was best left to Carroll and Nellie and God.[4]

CHAPTER TWELVE

"He (Pinkie) was a gambler and a bootlegger and as crafty and cunning as a West Texas coyote."[1]

May 25, 1951

Living on the farm at West Point was sometimes lonely for an only child so Leonard Coffman always enjoyed Bill Pendleton's visits. Bill was one year older than Leonard, and was welcome company when Bill visited his grandparents. Bill's grandparents owned and managed the West Point Grocery Store that was located beside the gin at the intersection. It was only a few days after the accident, so Leonard was full of all kinds of information for Bill. And Bill was all ears. Because the parents did not talk to the boys about the accident, they only had each other to help them put into perspective what Leonard had witnessed and what Bill had only heard about.

"Feel this dent in the pole," Leonard said to Bill as they stood in front of the telephone pool that had been hit by the Edwards' car. They rubbed their fingers back and forth over the indention as Leonard described in great detail the gore of the scene etched in his memory. "The car that had the little girls in it hit here," he continued filling his friend in on the details.

Bill was mesmerized. Even though the accident was gory and sad and horrifying, there was an attraction toward knowing every detail.

"The car with all the beer and whiskey in it ended up over there," Leonard pointed toward the site.

The broken glass that lined the highway was tinged with different colors. Bill said, "I'll bet this piece of glass came from a whiskey bottle." He sat on his knees playing with pieces of colored glass, holding them between his eye and the sun, guessing the previous contents of the bottles. Bill tried to see how many different colors of glass he could find. "Here's a yellow, here's a brown, here's a clear." All of a sudden he stopped noticing the colors of glass when a coin caught his eye. He excitedly blurted out, "Look what I found. I found a penny!" Instantly Bill imagined, in the way only little boys can convince themselves, that this penny had been in the Edwards' vehicle.

"Leonard, I'll bet this penny was on the dashboard of that car that had the little baby all crumpled up inside it."

"Maybe it was. Or, it might have been in the other car," Leonard countered.

Bill dismissed the thought. He wanted to believe it came out of the car the little kids were riding in, because he felt so bad that they didn't have parents anymore. He put the penny in his pocket and kept it.

In a certain way the boys were spellbound by the accident scene. They were drawn to talking about it with each other, because they both had an inward sense that they weren't to speak of it to their parents.[2]

As the boys were walking around the accident site, the little girls were in the hospital lying on big white beds missing their parents. Numerous people, aunts, uncles, and friends stayed in the hospital with the children and everyone did their best to give them comfort.

A male doctor walked into the doorway of the room, and Elva Jo cried desperately, "Daddy, Daddy." With her needs unmet, she cried, throwing her head onto the mattress. These emotional scenes were difficult for the caregivers, but they could at least understand what had happened. The emotional impact of the abandonment and the abrupt break in the primary relationships of the girls would best be understood in their adult life, if ever. The children couldn't possibly comprehend that an accident had occurred that had taken their parents away. The children could only sense the tragedy as loss, abandonment, betrayal, and rejection. The girls vacillated between periods of crying and more lighthearted moments of playing with their caregivers.[3]

Calva An and Elva Jo were playing with a toy, when they looked up to see a newspaper reporter and a photographer appear at the door. They were writing articles for the newspaper and wanted to take photographs of the children lying in their beds. About that time, Carroll walked through the door of the children's hospital room. Carroll's grandchildren would _not_ be used for sensationalism to sell newspapers. He felt the girls had been through enough and demanded that the photographers leave. Absolutely no photographs would be taken.[4]

CHAPTER THIRTEEN

*"Calva An and Elva Jo are young.
They do not realize what has happened."*[1]

May 28, 1951

Carroll arrived at the West Texas Hospital on May 28, 1951, at 10:15 in the morning to take the children home. His demeanor made him appear larger than his size. He was five-foot-nine inches tall with the beginning of a pot belly. It was evident that in his younger days he had been quite a handsome man. Though he normally smoked cigarettes, Carroll could occasionally be seen smoking a cigar and wearing a Stetson hat.

Carroll parked his car and walked toward the hospital entrance. The drive from Tahoka had given him time to consider the one thing no one had attended to this week: the fact that the girls needed to be told that their parents were dead. The week had been full of so many things to do like burying the dead and moving from one town to another that it was easy to postpone the most undesirable job. Carroll was a man who took responsibility seriously, and he had decided he would finish the job of parenting that his son started. He was unwilling to look at the facts that the townspeople felt were so important. His wife had been ill off and on for at least twenty years and was ill now. He was fifty-eight years old and his wife was fifty-six years old. His youngest daughter had graduated from high school the same week as the fatal accident. He had been considering a life of retirement where his young grandchildren would visit for short periods of time and go home with their parents. And yet, his life and that of his family were altered irrevocably. He could have chosen to let the girls be adopted by other people who would, most likely, be good parents to them. He could have let them go to the Buckner Baptist Girls' Home. But for Carroll, a stubborn man who was very unlikely to ever change his mind about anything, the girls were left for him and Nellie to raise. For him, it was his only option. And since Calvin and Pearle had been young and healthy and had never suspected life would turn on them in such an unkind way, they had not made arrangements for the care of their dependent children in case of their deaths. Carroll would not give up his grandchildren.

But Carroll was uncomfortable taking Calva An and Elva Jo home without their knowing about Calvin and Pearle's deaths. At some point, something needed to be said. How would he and Nellie answer the inevitable questions? He decided it was the hospital's job to tell the children about their parent's death. He knew it was not a job he had the capacity to do. He wasn't the kind of man who could hold a child and tell her that her parents would not be coming back. That might require him to be soft. In 1951, men didn't do that sort of thing, certainly not the kind of man Carroll was. For him, anything would be better than facing the pain he and the children shared.

After riding the elevator to the appropriate floor, he stopped at the nurse's station closest to the girls' hospital room. The nurse said, "Hello, Mr. Edwards. The children are doing real well today. Elva Jo's fever is normal, and they are ready to go home."

Calva An's broken right leg was put in a cast and Elva Jo's jagged lacerations were stitched and had quit bleeding. Elva Jo had been diagnosed with a lung infection and medication had been administered. Some of her bruises had faded, her fever had disappeared, and her lungs were clear.

"Well, I'll tell you," he said hesitantly, "I'm ready to take them home as soon as you tell them what happened to their parents."

The nurse was startled. "Mr. Edwards, that is not my job." She felt bad for the man, but she was not going to be put in that position.

"Well, it is someone's job," Carroll said with anger seeping into his voice, "and I am not taking these children home until someone tells them. Find someone to do it." Carroll's voice was a little too loud for a hospital. "Mr. Edwards, you can talk to the doctor if you'd like. You know nurses only follow the orders of the doctor."

Perturbed because the nurse was unwilling to be of assistance, Carroll walked to the doctor's office located in the front of the building and a nurse ushered him into a private room. The doctor entered and asked, "What can I do for you, Mr. Edwards?"

Carroll said, "Before I take the children home, I want you to tell them about their parents."

The doctor wrinkled his forehead and scratched his head, "Mr. Edwards, I know you and your family are in a great deal of pain. I took care of the physical needs of the children, but it's not my responsibility to tell Calva An and Elva Jo that their parents will never be coming back. I'm not sure how to do that, and it isn't my area of expertise. It would be better for them to hear about the deaths from people who love them."

"I am not taking the children out of this hospital until someone tells them," Carroll persisted.

"Well, Mr. Edwards, feel free to go in the room and talk to the girls yourself. You are their grandfather. I know you love them, and I know this has been a tragedy for you and your family, but we won't tell the children their parents are dead. You do really have all of my sympathy as you are in a difficult situation. Maybe it would be best for you to take the girls home, and then, perhaps their grandmother could talk to them."

Carroll muttered, "Lord Geminy" under his breath, but where it could be heard. Carroll was a religious man and did not cuss. However, he had his own vocabulary of expletives that he used when irritated or frustrated. He saw that these people had no intention of helping him and decided to take Calva An and Elva Jo home, still uncertain as to the particulars of telling the girls their parents were dead.

The nurses carried the children out the front door of the hospital and deposited them in Carroll's car. "Bye, bye," the nurses said. The children responded verbally and waved bye to the nurses and were on their way home. The drive was to the same farmhouse in which they had always lived. The only difference: it was occupied by different people. There would be no mama, no daddy, and no Grandmother Rogers to welcome them home. Instead there was Granny Edwards, Grandpa Edwards, aunts, uncles, and cousins. There were many people who loved them. But Carroll knew they would call for mama and daddy. What child wouldn't?

Carroll drove the thirty miles between Lubbock and Tahoka and turned left towards Post. The first farm road on the right led him to the farmhouse which was home to Calva An and Elva Jo. He put one girl in each arm and carried them in the house to their Granny. "Granny, Granny," the girls screamed as they were obviously pleased to be with her as she cradled them on her lap kissing and hugging them. Mona, Calvin's sister, was there to help her mother with the children, because Nellie's health was compromised to the point that she was physically unable to care for them. Emotionally she was spent. Nellie required bed rest and, in fact, had scheduled an appointment with the doctor in a few days.

Calva An and Elva Jo appeared to be glad to be back in familiar surroundings. The big, white hospital room had little warmth for small children. Calva An had a cast on her leg and, since a three-year-old is not coordinated enough to use crutches, she crawled around, pulling her leg behind her. Elva Jo was walking around inspecting her toys.

The girls were in the living room, a large room with wall-to-wall carpet and long, narrow windows covered with brown curtains. The front door, located on the east wall, opened to the living room and had a locked screen door to keep the children inside. Outside the front door, past a large cement porch, you could see flowers blooming in the flower beds located next to the porch. Past the porch was a grass-covered yard with two apple trees, one planted as a celebration for the birth of Calva An, and one celebrating the birth of Elva Jo. Beyond the yard was a road that created a semi-circle around the house, and beyond that, acres and acres of farmland. On the flatlands of West Texas, the cotton fields continued until they met the horizon. Someone drove Calvin's red 1949 pickup on the road that created a semi-circle around the house. Elva Jo saw the pickup and squealed, "Daddy, Daddy!" running toward the door in anticipation of her daddy.

Calva An stopped playing with her toy, turned to Elva Jo and said, "That's not our daddy. Our daddy is dead." Carroll was in the room with the girls and overheard the conversation. He sat speechless, looking at the girls. How did she know? He had no idea, but was relieved that the children knew their parents were dead. The dirty deed was done, thank God, and now nothing more would need to be said.[2]

Over forty years passed before I knew the information in the story I have just told. I was the baby, Elva Jo, who was thrown into the dashboard of the Chevrolet that dark night in May of 1951. The events of that evening provided a defining moment that has unconsciously run my life and patterned it with the threads of trauma.

My grandparents wanted to make a home for us. But due to the circumstances in their lives, it took several years for our household to settle down.

My grandparents were good, religious people who willingly took on the burden of more children. They did what they could for us and we grew into adulthood. However, there was one area that was unapproachable territory: we were unable to talk freely about our parents, the accident, and our feelings about not having parents, as well as their feelings about their loss of a son. There was no meaningful way to approach the chasm, filled with pain and sorrow, that our shared sadness over their deaths created. At this point in time, psychology had not been fully embraced, at least not on the small farms in West Texas.

I grew up knowing my parents had been killed in an accident because a bootlegger was driving without his lights on and didn't stop at a stop sign. That was basically all I knew until I was forty-one years old.

There were a few occasions where my parents' names or the accident would come up in conversation. I listened intently, but usually did not feel I could ask for further information. If any emotion was seen, a tear or a grimace, all talk ceased. My grandparents, good as gold as they were, did not have the capacity to help themselves or my sister and me through such tortuous emotional terrain. We all needed help.

CHAPTER FOURTEEN

*"It may take a long time
to explain why it had to happen this way. . .
A long time. . . Maybe forever."[1]*

It isn't as if the deaths of my parents were the only traumatic circumstances I endured in childhood. Before the accident, I had been hospitalized twice. Once I was given a blood transfusion in my head because I was anemic. They held me down and a nurse told my granny, "You had better leave the room because you aren't going to like what we are going to do." Big people were doing things to my body which hurt and were very scary. I had no way to fight back or understand what was being done to me.[2]

Granny was sick at the time of our accident. Not long after that it was necessary for her to go to Temple, Texas, about five hours away from our farmhouse, to have an operation. Granny was expecting to be in the hospital for two weeks, but the day she was supposed to return home to us, her stitches burst open. That required her to have additional surgery, and to stay in the hospital for two more weeks. During the month Granny was in the hospital, my sister and I were passed around to aunts, uncles or whoever in the community could keep us on any given day. Those were hard times for my family, and everyone did what they had to do to make it through each day. However, that didn't mean it gave my sister and me a sense of our place in our confusing world.

My earliest memory was looking out the window in our living room with my sister. Grandpa drove up and got out of the car. We ran out the front door to greet him. He had returned from being with Granny in the hospital and brought us each a red purse. I loved the purse, but more than that, I loved Grandpa!!

Upon Granny's return home, she required domestic help for about a year until she could care for us by herself. Having help in the home was not something she was particularly comfortable with, but it was necessary. Two small children can be a handful in the best of circumstances.

Our eighty-six-year-old great-grandfather, whom we called Granddad, had to be cared for, and my sister and I were his closest living relatives. The responsibility for him fell on the Edwards' side of the family, because with the death of my mother and grandmother, the Edwards' side of the family was all that was left. Uncle Robert and his family moved in with Granddad and cared for him until the following year when he died.

I remember being at the funeral home with Granny when my great-granddad Pierce died. I was wearing a red coat and hat that was trimmed with gray fake fur. I ran from a chair across the room to Granny, and threw my head into her lap as she talked with other adults. Of course, I did not understand the sober circumstances: the only relative I was close to on my mother's side of the family had died. Now the Edwards' side of the family was the only family my sister and I had.

Tahoka was just miles down the road from Pinkie's empire of legal and illegal alcohol. While my grandparents were adjusting to moving into their son's home and parenting his children, you wonder if, when Pinkie drove past Tahoka, he ever thought about the two little girls who were growing up without parents?

Calva An and Elva Jo Edwards

FAMILY

Calvin and Pearle Edwards; Pearle's mother, Elva Rogers, Calva An and Elva Jo

EDWARDS

Three generations of Edwards' - Calvin, Calva An and Carroll

Calvin and Pearle

Calvin and Pearle Edwards on the beach.

THE GENERATIONS

*Four generations of the Pierce Family taken in 1948
J. A. Pierce, called Granddad; Elva Rogers, his
daughter; Pearle Dee Rogers, his granddaughter; and
Calva An, his great-granddaughter*

*Granny and Grandpa with their two oldest
grandchildren, Milton and Calva An, in June 1949.*

*J.A. Pierce:
Great-Granddad
to Elva Jo and Calva An
Pearle,s grandfather.
He died the year after
the accident.*

A Texas Tragedy

A FEW MONTHS BEFORE THE ACCIDENT

Pearle Edwards

Calvin Edwards

Calva An Edwards

Elva Jo Edwards

SHOPPING

*On a shopping trip - Pearle Edwards holds Elva Jo, as Granny Rogers follows.
Calva An is on the left side of photo.*

THE HIGHWAY

The crash site — Photo above shows the highway the Edwards' car was traveling on. Below is the intersecting dirt road the Maxey car was traveling.

EDWARDS' CAR

The Edwards' wrecked car.

A Texas Tragedy

BOOTLEGGING CAR

The Maxey wrecked car was a Lincoln.
Photo below shows broken beer and whiskey bottles in the back seat.

12 Pages

"Oldest Business Institution In Lynn County"

The Lynn County News

PATRONIZE LOCAL MERCHANTS

"I wholly disapprove of what you say but will defend to the death your right to say it." —Voultaire.

Volume 47. | Tahoka, Lynn County, Texas, Friday May 25, 1951 | Number 34

Five Killed In Two-Car Crash Near West Point

More Showers Add Moisture In Lynn County

Heavy showers which fell over much of Lynn county Wednesday night covered a lot of country which did not receive sufficient rainfall last week. More rain is needed, especially in the east half, but that Wednesday will help.

The gauge kept by The News showed .28 of an inch in Tahoka. Draw reported a half inch, Grassland about .4, New Lynn about a quarter. Rainfall was heavier in some areas, with Midway reporting .8, Wells and Three Lakes a half inch, and West Point from a half to three-quarters.

Especially over the west half of Lynn county, farmers have been very busy this week planting cotton. More rain was recieved over this area last week, one and a half to two or more inches, than in the east.

Many farmers in the east half have been planting, but most of them feared there was not sufficient moisture. Most of the east half had received from one inch to an inch and a half last week. The ground was so dry that this was not enough.

The additional rainfall Wednesday night will help many farmers.

Sheriff's Posse Wins Honors

Lynn County Sheriff's Posse has contributed $50.00 to the Olney Tornado Relief Fund, according to Sheriff "Slick" Clem, president of the local riding organization.

Wednesday of last week, the local posse carried away first place honors in the Odessa Rodeo Parade in competition against posses from Pecos, Monahans, Brownfield, Big Spring, Midland, and Odessa. The prize was $25.00 in cash, which the Lynn County Posse will use to buy a trophy to add to its rapidly growing collection.

The Lynn County Posse rode in the Post Stampede parade late Wednesday evenig and won the second place trophy. Graham carried away top honors.

Tahoka Wins Softball Games

Tahoka has won two games the past week in the Square Deal Softball League, but Southland remains undefeated in four starts so far.

Last Friday night, White Auto of Tahoka nosed out Post 16 to 15 in a game played here. In an excellent game played at O'Donnell Tuesday night, Tahoka was the 4 to 2 winner. The Tahoka entry in the league had previously dropped a game to Southland 8 to 2, and one to Grassland 13 to 1.

Friday night, Southland defeated O'Donnell 9 to 2, and Tuesday night Grassland dropped a 10 to 9 decision to Story Motor Company of Post.

Tonight, Friday, Southland plays at Tahoka, and Grassland goes to O'Donnell.

Next Tuesday night, Grassland will be at Southland, Story Motor Company, Post, will play at O'Donnell, and Tahoka will be idle.

The standings, according to E. L. Short, secretary, of Grassland, are as follows.

	Won	Lost
Southland	4	0
Tahoka	2	2
Post	2	2
Grassland	1	3
O'Donnell	1	3

J. T. Rogers, formerly of Sunset, is now making his home here in Tahoka with his brother, Will R. Rogers.

Thompson Well Makes 37 Barrels

Terry Thompson reports that his recently completed shallow oil well in northwest Tom Green county has been granted an allowable of 37 barrels daily. It was completed at a depth of 1,008 feet.

He is now preparing to drill an offset to the discovery on the lease he holds on which the oil was discovered.

New City Court To Enforce Laws

Setting up of a Corporation Court in order that Tahoka City Ordinances may be more easily enforced was made possible Monday, when a special election was held to name a City Recorder.

Russell McGee, City auditor, was named to the new office, which he will fill along with his other duties.

The City Council, according to Mayor James Applewhite, is passing a number of city ordinances that will stand up in court, and the Council proposes to do something about many law violations within/the city limits.

Citizens are being given due warning City police are instructed to enforce City laws. Ordinances are being passed that will stand up in court, a Corporation Court is being properly set up that meets all legal specifications, and fines will be assessed for violations.

Police are being instructed to give special attention to traffic violations. Most citizens have become careless in observing rules of safe driving in the City limits, creating a threat to life and property.

Various local organizations and individuals have given their support and encouragement to the "city dads" along this line, and the move will meet the approval of most law-abiding and safety conscious citizens.

Church of Christ Vacation Bible School Opens May 28

The annual Vacation Bible School held by the Tahoka Church of Christ will begin next Monday, May 28. The school will close Friday night with a commencement program.

In addition to classes held from 9:00 to 11:00 o'clock each morning, the church has invited Brother Quentin Fanning of Tucson, Arizona to preach each evening at 8:00 o'clock during the school, closing out the week's special services on Lord's day, June 3.

Teachers for the school include: Miss Ina Ledbetter, Miss Myrtie Ledbetter, Mmes. Douglas Finley, Ernest West, O. C. Sikes, L. A. Forsythe, Welch Flippin, Reuben McIlroy, Howard Draper, Farris Stevens, and Leonard Pyburn. Class music instructor will be Mrs. Dick Mitchell. Assistant teachers are Mmes. Fred McGinty, Bob Connolly, and Regan Reed.

Brother Fanning, visiting evangelist, and Ernest West, local evangelist will instruct a ladies class in the auditorium of the church building. All mothers bringing children will be provided an opportunity for profitable study while their children will be in classes.

The public is cordially invited to attend both the school and the gospel meeting.

BOOK REVIEW WILL BE GIVEN WEDNESDAY

Due to the funeral services here Wednesday, the Phebe K. Warner Club book review scheduled this week has been postponed until next Wednesday afternoon at 3:30 p. m. at the Methodist Church, according to Mrs. Paul Pittman.

At that time, the public is invited to hear Mrs. Fred B. Hegi review the book, "Root Out of Dry Ground" by Archie Biggs.

THE TWO WRECKED CARS that were involved in the wreck Monday night which brought death to five people are shown above. At the top is the Lincoln, driven by R. M. Maxey of Ropesville, which was said to be loaded with illegal liquor. Below is the Calvin Edwards Chevrolet.

Tahoka Ladies Head District VFW Auxiliary

Three Tahoka women were elected to places of honor in the Veterans of Foreign Wars District Seven Auxiliary convention held in Lubbock last week end.

Mrs. J. B. (Thelma) Oliver was named district president of the Auxiliary for the ensuing year. Mrs. Preston (Avis) Buchanan is the new district conductress. Mrs. Bill (Eloise) Griffin is the new secretary. The officers were elected at a Saturday afternoon business session. Mrs. Oliver served last year as second vice president.

In addition, Mrs. R. L. Richardson will serve again this year as the district musician.

Local members of the VFW and Auxiliary, were elated over the recognition given Tahoka by election of all these officers from this post to district offices.

Among others attending the convention were Mr. and Mrs. Dan Curry, Mrs. Pauline Smith, and Miss Laquita Smith.

Chas. A. Guy of the Lubbock Avalanche-Journal was the principal speaker at the afternoon general session. About 600 delegates were present at the meeting of the two groups.

Mr. and Mrs. Richard Taylor returned Tuesday morning from Houston and Galveston, where they spent several days vacationing, fishing, and swimming.

Mr. and Mrs. C. C. Garvin of Amarillo have been here this week visiting her mother and her brother, George McCracken.

Two Fined In Tahoka Courts

A Meadow citizen was fined $25.00 and costs for disturbing the peace and $1.00 and costs for drunkenness, a total of $54.00, by Justice of the Peace P. D. Server Monday morning. The man was charged with attempting to enter a local home Sunday night.

Another man, who gave Eden as his home address, was hauled into County Court on drunken driving charges. Judge W. M. Mathis assessed his fine at $100.00 and costs.

New Residences Are Being Built

Five new residences have been started within the last few days, as the growth and improvement of Tahoka continues.

John Fulford, who recently completed a new brick home on North Second Street, has sold this residence to the Methodist Church for a parsonage.

This week, Mr. Fulford started construction of a similar new brick home across the street from this one and immediately west of the W. D. Nevels place.

Stanley Sigman, who recently moved here from Lubbock, is erecting a nice five room home on North Fourth, out in the Roberts addition.

W. L. Knight is erecting a four room residence on Petty Street, between North Second and Third.

David Renfro, having sold his home to Mr. Harvey, is erecting a new home on North Seventh.

Another new home going up on North Seventh is a nice home for Ray Adams.

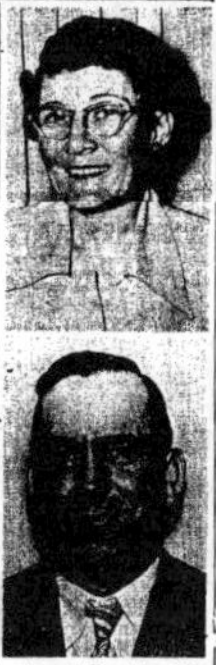

Mr. and Mrs. Calvin Edwards, commander and president, respectively, of the Tahoka American Legion Post and Auxiliary, who were killed in the automobile accident.

Go To Church Sunday.

46 Receive Diplomas In Final Tahoka High School Exercises

Diplomas of graduation were presented 46 Seniors at Commencement exercises of Tahoka High School last night in the school auditorium.

The program ended the 1950-51 school year in Tahoka. Report cards had been presented students of all grades Thursday morning.

James G. Allen, Dean of Student Life at Texas Tech, was the principal speaker at the closing exercises. A special vocal number was rendered by Mrs. W. H. Kenley. Mrs. Marcus Edwards was her accompanist and also played the processional and recessional. Rev. Lee Ramsour gave the invocation, and A. L. Smith the benediction. Supt. Vernon Brewer introduced the speaker. Calloway Huffaker, president of the school board, presented the diplomas.

Last Sunday night, the class sermon was given by Rev. C. A. Holcomb, Jr., pastor of the Tahoka Methodist Church. At this service, Mrs. E. W. Patterson sang "The Lord's Prayer," and Mrs. I. J. Hart presided at the piano.

Final examinations were completed Tuesday. Wednesday was a holiday for students, while the teachers graded papers, completed report cards and other records.

A list of this year's graduating Seniors follow:

Girls

Jane Adair, Joyce Andrews, Jo Anne Bennett, Jo Ann Benson, Elna Dunagan, Sue Findt, Katherin Hickman, Jo Hogan, Dovie Jenkins, Margilene Jester, Patsy Locke, Patsy McGinty, Wanda Marlin, Margaret Norwood, Betty June Paris, Billie Louise Patterson, Joyce Patterson, Wilma Payne, Margaret Roberts, Emily Slover, Minnie Lou Stanley, Martha Stevens, Geraldine Thormaehlen, Patsy Fox Waldrip.

Boys

Wayne Adair, Parker Blair, Charles Brookshire, Kenneth Calloway, Elwayne Crotwell, Jimmy Drager, Bland Draper, Glenn Evans, Jerry Ford, Ronny Gurley, Durwood Jones, Dean Laws, Danny Lockaby, Wendell Moore, J. W. Phillips, Jackie Slover, John Shepherd, Jerry Stevens, Bill Waldrip, Randall Waldrip, Dale Willhoit, L. F. Williams.

News Want Ads Get Results.

Three Tahoka People Are Among Victims

One of the worst automobile accidents in South Plains history Monday night at West Point snuffed out the lives of five people, made orphans of two little Tahoka girls, left 10 Sand children parentless, several of whom are dependent minors, and seriously injured the driver of a liquor-loaded car.

The dead are:

Mrs. Calvin Edwards, 30, of Tahoka, killed instantly.

Mrs. D. T. Rogers, 59, her mother, also of Tahoka, died in Tahoka Hospital at 10:15 p. m., less than an hour after the wreck.

Calvin H. Edwards, 33, of Tahoka, died in West Texas Hospital at 3:34 a. m. the next morning, Tuesday.

Samuel E. Riley, 49, of Lamesa, route 3, killed instantly.

Mrs. Samuel Riley, 44, of the same address, died in Tahoka Hospital at 10:10 p. m.

Serisouly injured is Roy Monroe Maxey, 37, of Ripesville, believed to have been driver of the liquor-laden car, which was also occupied by Mr. and Mrs. Riley.

Also injured were little Calva Ann Edwards, nearly four years of age, and Elva Jo Edwards, not yet two, daughters of Mr. and Mrs. Calvin Edwards.

Triple funeral services, one of the sadest in the history of this town, were held for Mr. and Mrs. Edwards and Mrs. Rogers in the First Baptist Church here at 3 p. m. Wednesday, with Rev. Lee Ramsour, pastor, and Rev. Geo. A. Dale of Lubbock, former pastor, officiating. Burial rites followed in Tahoka Cemetery under direction of Stanley Home.

No Charges Filed

Double funeral services were held at 3 p. m. Thursday for Mr. and Mrs. Riley in a Lamesa Funeral Home, Rev. Jesse Davis of Second Baptist Church offiriating, and burial followed in Lamesa Cemetery.

No charges had been filed in connection with the wreck Thursday, but local officials are expected to prefer charges against the driver of the Lincoln.

Mr. and Mrs. Edwards, their two little daughters, and Mrs. Edwards' mother, Mrs. D. T. Rogers, left Tahoka at about 9:00 p. m. Monday en route to Brownfield to visit Mr. Edwards' mother, Mrs. Carroll Edwards, who was ill. Calvin was driving his 1951 Chevrolet, his wife beside him in the front seat, and Mrs. Rogers and the two children were in the back seat.

Officers Investigating

Investigation by officers revealed that Roy Monroe Maxey,, driving a 1951 Lincoln, coming from "somewhere south" en route "somewhere north" stopped at Sand, on the Dawson-Gaines county line, between 7 and 8 p. m. and picked up Mr. and Mrs. Riley. It is said Mr. Maxey and Mr. Riley are cousins. The three are believed to have been riding in the front seat of the Lincoln.

As the Edwards neared the intersection of a farm road with U. S. Highway 380 at West Point, suddenly from the south the Lincoln drove out into the highway. Tire tracks showed that Edwards had applied his brakes, but the two cars crashed on the paving, veered to the right, and came to rest about thirty feet apart at the northwest corner of the intersection. The Edwards car, after the impact, crashed head-on into a telephone pole and the Lincoln rolled over on its top.

Kevil Coffman, operator of West Point gin, heard the crash, rushed from his near-by home to the scene. After surveying the scene of carnage momentarily, he grabbed up the two children, put them in his car and rushed to Tahoka Hospital with them.

Aid Rushed To Wreck

Stanley ambulances and local officers rushed to the scene. By aproximately 10 o'clock, only 40 minutes after the accident, they had the injured in Tahoka Hospital.

Mrs. Edwards was dead when ambulances arrived. Mr. Riley was also dead. The other three died later.

Maxey was pinned behind the steering wheel in the Lincoln. Mrs. Riley, still alive, was wedged against him. Mr. Riley had been thrown out of the machine, and the car had landed on top of him. His head was crushed.

Around the gory scene, covering a wide area, whiskey bottles and beer cans were strewn. Evi-

(Cont'd. On Back Page)

Rev. Holcomb Is At Conference

Rev. C. A. Holcomb, Jr., pastor of the Tahoka Methodist Church, along with all Methodist pastors of the Northwest Texas District, is in Abilene this week attending the Annual Conference in session Wednesday through Sunday at McMurry College.

The pastor was accompanied by his wife. Several members of the local congregation expect to attend some of the sessions.

No indication has been given as to whether or not Rev. Holcomb will be returned to the Tahoka charge, however it is presumed he will return.

Rev. J. W. Hawkins May Not Return To Draw Church

Rev. J. W. Hawkins, pastor of the Methodist Church at Draw, and wife are attending the annual Northwest Texas Methodist Conference, being held this week in Abilene.

Rev. Hawkins has been at Draw three years, and has plans to move to a pastorate in the Clyde area.

Since he lacks only four years reaching the age for retirement, he is desirious of moving to that section in order that he may supervise the improvement of some property he owns at Clyde. On being retired, he hopes to make his home in that little city.

Ross Smith's Father Dies At Aspermont

Ross Smith was called to Aspermont Tuesday by the death of his father, Willie Smith, age 85. Funeral services were held in the Methodist Church there Wednesday.

Mr. Smith had been in ill health about ten years, the end coming at noon Tuesday. He had been a stock farmer near Aspermont since 1900.

He is survived by his wife; one daughter, Mrs. Peg Finknay of Fort Sumner, N. M.; and three sons, Waymon and Lee of Aspermont and Ross of Tahoka.

Congratulations:

Mr. and Mrs. Charlie Lee on the birth of a daughter weighing 7 pounds and 7 ounces, Friday, May 18 at 5:58 p. m. in a Lubbock hospital. The father operates the Lee & Lee Service Station here.

Mr. and Mrs. Barron D. Cave of Route 5 on the birth of a son weighing 8 pounds 4 ounces in Tahoka Hospital at 2:46 a. m. Saturday, May 19th.

A Texas Tragedy 63

LITTLE GIRLS

In this photograph, Elva Jo is four years old. She was four when Grandpa had his major heart attack.

Ready for Grandpa to take them for a swim (about 4 and 7 years old).

Elva Jo and Calva An with Uncle Robert one year after the accident. Robert and Calvin were brothers.

GROWING UP

Elva Jo and Calva An pay Santa a visit.

Elva Jo in the first grade. This is the year she had to stand in the hall for talking too much.

CHAPTER FIFTEEN

"But it's not the end for the little girls."[1]

Growing Up

At three-years-old, I was asleep in my bed one night when I woke up with Granny crying over me. She was hugging and kissing me saying, "Oh, I'm so sorry I got mad at you today. I didn't mean it. I love you so much. Will you forgive me?" I didn't want Granny to be sad.

I told her, "It's OK, Granny. I forgive you." I hoped I didn't make Granny feel bad. I would try to be better so Granny wouldn't be so sad. I started taking care of Granny's feelings instead of my own.

In the evenings, Calva and I would sit on the floor as Granny and Grandpa would listen to the radio. We had an open stove we could edge up to when we wanted to get warm as we colored in our coloring books. Sometimes we dressed our dolls with the new clothes Granny made on the sewing machine.

One day Calva and I were on the front porch, which was raised off the ground about eighteen inches, when we heard a rattle that sounded like it came from beside the porch. "You look and see what it is," I said to Calva.

"No, you look," I said.

Since Calva was the oldest and could get me to do almost anything, I looked. I screamed, "It's a snake."

We both screamed and ran inside the house to Granny.

Granny wasn't scared of anything. She made us stay in the house where we looked through the screen door and watched as she got a hoe and battled with the snake. She raised the hoe several times with both arms and planted it firmly on the ground. The snake became wrapped around the hoe and as she raised it, this big, long, scary snake was hanging from the hoe, just above Granny's head. I was so scared that the snake would fall on Granny and kill her. Granny won. The snake was dead.

When I was four-years-old, my great-aunt and uncle came to visit. Our extended family came to our house to visit with them. Normally my sister and I were not allowed to jump on the bed. But when my cousin was visiting, the rules always changed. We did what she wanted to do, and if she wanted to jump on the bed, we did. It was thrilling for me to get to do something I ordinarily wouldn't be allowed to do. One evening during my great-aunt and great-uncle's visit, we were jumping on the bed when he said, "They will be dragging the bed in here any minute."

And, before long, we heard a thunderous noise. "Uh oh," we said in unison. We looked under the bed and saw a slat had fallen. We decided to take it to Granny so she could fix it.

As we pulled the slat into the dining room, my great-uncle said, "I told you they would be breaking the bed down." Granny was not a woman to get upset with child-like behaviors. She and my aunt said they would take care of it. Later that night my Granny's brother told her she was "crazy" for taking my sister and me. Granny was upset about his remarks. I didn't want to be too much trouble for Granny. I would try to be good.

Our house was often full of children, as my grandparents now had seven grandchildren with my sister being the oldest. When I was four-years-old, my granny and I went to Lubbock with my aunt and her children to shop. We were in a nice store and I was mesmerized by the escalator. I was watching it magically moving, when suddenly, I wondered, where is Granny? I looked for her and called for her. When I couldn't find her, I started crying. A nice man dressed in a white shirt and tie picked me up and talked to me. "I want Granny," I cried.

The man walked around with me looking for Granny, but I couldn't see her. We walked outside on the sidewalk and there she was.

"Granny, Granny," I cried.

"There you are," said Granny.

She took me out of his arms saying, "you need to stay with me." Granny was upset that I was lost. "Thank you so much for helping her find me."

Granny tried to comfort me, but I was so scared when I couldn't find her that it was hard for me to stop crying. I was scared I wouldn't be able to pay enough attention to stay with Granny, but I would desperately try.

Granny didn't really leave us with Grandpa very often. Once Granny and I went to Lubbock with my aunt and left her two small boys with Grandpa. We walked in the house and Grandpa was sitting in the living room. Granny asked, "Where are the boys?"

Grandpa said, "I guess they are in the other room somewhere."

Granny rushed to see what they were doing and found the boys gleefully enjoying all of her makeup—her powder, her rouge, and especially her lipstick. The boys were a mess and Granny's make-up was all ruined. She asked, "Why didn't you go see what they were doing?"

Grandpa said, "Well, they were quiet, so I figured they were all right."

Granny said, "If they are quiet, that should be a sign telling you they are into something they shouldn't be." Granny said Grandpa couldn't babysit anymore.

The farm was lonely for me when my sister went to school. I often longed for her and would stand in the rocking chair, looking over the back of the rocker and out the window, waiting for her to arrive home from school. The bus would drop her off at the end of the road, and she would walk to the house, about one quarter of a mile. It was a beautiful day and I asked Granny, as I often did, "Can I walk down the road to meet Calva?"

She said, "OK, but instead of going all the way to the highway, do you see where that tree is?" she asked.

"Yes, ma'am."

"I want you to stop there and wait for Calva to walk to you. Will you do that?"

"OK, Granny," I said with joy.

I was excited to meet my sister. I began my walk down the dirt road, and in my excitement, I forgot to stop where Granny told me. I walked almost to the end of the road when I noticed a pile of dirt in the field, off the road about twelve feet. I was very curious as to what it was and walked over and saw that the pile of dirt circled a hole in the ground. I wondered what was in the hole so I walked over the pile of dirt and just as I bent down to look into the hole, Granny grabbed me from behind. We fell onto the ground. Granny was hysterical. She hugged me and was almost inconsolable.

"What's wrong Granny?" I asked.

Through her tears she said, "That hole is very deep and I was so scared you would fall in." Grandpa had just dug an irrigation well and they had not capped it yet. "I watched you walk down the road from the window and when I saw you forgot to stop, I ran down here after you." Granny kept hugging me.

I said, "I'm sorry I forgot to stop, Granny."

She said, "It is OK. I should have known better. I'm just so glad I made it down here."

I could tell she was so tired. It was hard for her to run that far. I felt like it was my fault Granny had to run so hard and that she was tired. I would try harder to remember what she told me to do.

We waited for Calva to get off the bus and the three of us walked back to the house.

Sometimes I would wake up in the night scared. My sister and I slept in the same bedroom as Granny and Grandpa. Our big bedroom had two double beds, an armoire, a large dresser, and a sewing machine. When I would wake up scared in the middle of the night, I only had a few steps to get in bed with Granny and Grandpa. The walls were covered with wallpaper that, in the dark, looked like a person peering from behind the door. I would wake up and call, "Granny?"

"What?" she would say.

"I want to get in bed with you," I would answer.

"Come on over," Granny would instruct.

"Watch me," I'd say. I was afraid the "man behind the door" would grab me, so I insisted Granny watch me as I ran to her bedside.

One morning I woke up feeling completely happy, like my heart was singing, because I was in the bed between Granny and Grandpa. How cozy!! Sometimes all four of us would end up in the same double bed before morning.

When I'd wake up in the mornings, I'd call, "Grandpa!" He would come into the bedroom and give me a piggy-back ride, tickling me all the way to the breakfast table. I loved playing with my Grandpa that way!

My Grandpa's sister-in-law was in the hospital in Lubbock and while Calva was in school, Granny, Grandpa, and I went to visit her. We walked into the hospital entrance and I spied a pop machine. We walked down the large hospital hall until we found the right room. Soon I asked Grandpa if I could have the money to get a pop from the waiting room. He handed me the money and I left the room to find the pop machine, as much for fun as for thirst. I was walking down the hall when a really scary woman dressed in all black with a big hat turned the corner and started walking toward me. I quickly turned around and ran back down the hall and through the door to Granny. The scary lady followed me. I clung to Granny as she told me, "Oh honey, this lady is a nun. That is her uniform and they call it a habit. You don't have to be afraid of a nun." No matter what Granny said, I was not completely convinced.

Living on the farm, my sister and I became each other's playmates. Not only did we have our house and a large yard, but also acres of pasture, a barn with ducks, pigs, chickens, and several buildings. Our barn was very large with an area for cottonseed to be stored, an area for chickens to lay their eggs, and an area to store the feed for horses, pigs and chickens. A ladder attached to the inside of the barn led up to the loft. Connected to the barn were fences that housed pigs and a pond that held ducks. About twenty to thirty feet from the barn was a chicken house where the chickens stayed at night, and a fenced area where they roamed during the day. A large equipment shed housed a tractor and numerous plows. We had a small building close to the house, we called the well house, because that was where the pump for the well was located. We had another concrete twelve-by-twelve building where water, at one time, was stored on the top as a cistern, and the bottom floor was used as storage of the equipment needed for the grounds around the house.

There were frequent visits from cousins, but most of the time, my sister and I played together by ourselves. Our dolls were a very important part of our lives. The large utility room was the place we played our favorite "story," which we played everyday for several years. The bench we sat on in the utility room was our make-believe car. We always pretended we were on a trip to California, going to see our great-uncle and great-aunt who had visited us. Since Calva was the oldest, she got to drive, which meant she got to hold the lid to Granny's largest pot, using it for a steering wheel. We would drive, holding our babies when I would suddenly say "My baby is sick and crying and needs to go to the hospital."

We would "drive" to the hospital and my baby would see a doctor who, of course, gave my baby a shot.

We played this story day after day with no changes for years.

But when Grandpa was around, I'd rather be with him than play with my dolls or anything else. My love for my grandpa was so big that I followed him around like a little puppy dog. The only respite he could get from me was when he would go to the bathroom. When I was four-years-old, I was playing with a toy outside the bathroom door, waiting for Grandpa, when he had a major heart attack.

That evening, Uncle Robert took Calva and me to a babysitter to spend the night. We knew Mrs. Green, because she kept the nursery at church. I loved Mrs. Green, but I worried about my grandpa.

Grandpa was my hero and his sickness scared me. I desperately needed Grandpa to be strong and brave. When he came home from the hospital, I hid behind a tree and watched as a man helped Grandpa from the car into the house. My small body shook with fear as he appeared so delicate and fragile. How could my big, strong grandpa look so weak?

My family attempted to get back into our normal routine. One morning I woke up and called, "Grandpa, come and get me."

I was ready for my piggy-back ride to the dining room. He came to the bedroom and said, "You're getting too big for that." I was devastated. No one explained to me that Grandpa had had a major heart attack and perhaps he shouldn't be lifting. I thought he didn't want to love me that way anymore.

CHAPTER SIXTEEN

"With tragedy came the kind and helping hand of uncles and aunts, cousins and grandparents, and a host of friends."[1]

After we got a television, our family life in the evening centered around watching it. Grandpa loved certain television shows like Gunsmoke, Topper and Perry Mason. Since I liked having Grandpa as a playmate as much as possible, it didn't matter to me if he didn't participate. Although I didn't like having my hair set, I loved setting Grandpa's hair in pin curls and adding the occasional barrette. He would sit on the sofa watching television as I walked around behind him making pin curls and sticking a bobby pin or clippy in his hair to hold the pin curl in place. Occasionally he would pull his head away and say, "Oh honey, you're pulling my hair." He never got mad, and I never had to quit until I got tired of playing. Grandpa didn't really seem to notice his new hairdo unless I pulled his hair or poked him with a bobby pin. Obviously, my grandpa had no insecurities about his maleness. In fact, it didn't even bother him if others walked into the house while he was in pincurls and barrettes. Sometimes when my cousin would come, we would both work on his hair at the same time. It was such fun!

It was no wonder that when I was four or five I exclaimed to my sister, "When I get big, I'm going to marry Grandpa!" My love was huge.

The first time I knew I had been in an accident and that I, at one time, had a mama and a daddy was when I was four or five-years-old. I was looking at myself in the mirror when I raised my left arm and noticed something I had never seen before. I saw a funny "thing" on my elbow and was certain it was an "owie" for which I was sure I needed a bandage. I ran to Granny yelling, "Lookie, Granny lookie," with all kinds of concern over my finding.

Granny said, "It's OK. You're not hurt."

"I need a bandage," I squealed with enthusiasm, because I loved tape.

"No you don't. It's just a scar," Granny said.

"What's that?" I asked.

"It's a scar you got in the car wreck," she said.

"What car wreck?" I asked.

"The car wreck you were in with your mama and daddy when they were killed."

My mind was dancing with the thought that I had a mama and daddy, but stopped short with the "when they were killed." I had felt big and expansive when I ran to granny with my new finding. But suddenly, inside I felt like a candle whose flame had been blown out by the words, "when they were killed."

Granny said nothing else. She just continued standing at the kitchen counter preparing lunch. Already at that age, I sensed that I should not say anything more. I turned and walked away, alone with my feelings of sadness.

We went to Hobbs, New Mexico to visit my aunt and uncle and cousin one weekend and my aunt gave my sister and me a little doggie. It was Sunday afternoon and time for us to return to Tahoka, but the sky looked black, and Granny begged Grandpa to wait. But Grandpa was not the kind of man who would wait—even for the weather. He said Calva An, who was in the first grade, had to go to school the next morning.

We left Hobbs and ran into a torrential hailstorm. We were stopped several times by high waters. We had our little doggie in a box on the back floor board and when Grandpa opened his door, water flooded into the car. We slid off the highway getting stuck in the mud. We were pulled out of the ditch several times that night by wreckers. Before the end of the night, Granny put Calva An and me in the front seat with her and Grandpa and covered us with the new kitchen curtains she had bought. She let the doggie ride in the back seat. What normally would be a two hour trip took us nine hours to complete. Granny was a little mad that Grandpa was so stubborn.

If my grandpa liked something, I did too, whether I really did or not. When I was five-years-old, we ate Sunday lunch at a restaurant after church because we were going to visit Grandpa's brother and his wife. I wanted to order the same thing Grandpa ordered to eat. Granny said, "You won't eat all of that." But I wouldn't have it any other way. I had to eat what Grandpa ate.

Grandpa's brother's name was John and his wife's name was Charlene, but everyone called her Charlie. I didn't even know she had another name besides Charlie. It was always confusing to me when we would go see them. On the way to their house, I always asked, "Granny, is John or Charlie the woman?" I could never remember.

One day my grandparents decided my sister and I were old enough to have our own room. Perhaps my sister asked for it, but I certainly did not. Sleeping with Granny and Grandpa was just fine with me. But I didn't protest the move. Instead, I tried to find the comfort I needed from my sister, but sometimes I still slept with Granny and Grandpa.

I often wondered about my mama, especially when other children would talk about their mama. One day I was in the bedroom watching Granny mop the floor in the kitchen. I was unsure of myself because I felt embarrassed and afraid I was being bad, but decided to approach Granny anyway.

"Granny, can I call you mama?" I asked.

The question presented a difficulty for Granny. She stopped mopping, put the mop under her arm, and looked at me. After thinking a minute she said, "I think it would be best if you call me Granny." Sadness welled up inside me because I wanted and needed to call someone mama. I wanted to be like my cousins and friends. I turned and walked away into the bedroom where I could be alone with my sadness. Granny continued mopping.

It would have been helpful if Granny had picked me up and talked with me about my parents. I couldn't remember them, although we had their pictures in the library. I felt sad because my sister and I were the only children I knew who didn't have a mama. It would have helped me if Granny had said she too was sad my parents weren't there, but glad I was with her.

I was left empty-handed and empty-hearted too, as far as my desire for a mama. It appeared to me that no one wanted to be my mama.

In first grade, I had a best friend named Candice, whom I dearly loved. One day I was told Candice was moving. The day came when Candice was to leave school with her cigar box full of supplies. I walked to the car with her and waved goodbye. As the car disappeared into the next block, I watched my friend disappear from my life. I couldn't make the sadness go away.

After lunch in the first grade, we students put our heads on our desks for a rest period. I didn't like to rest, but I liked to talk. One day the teacher saw me talking to another girl during rest period and told me to stand in the corner out in the hall. I felt ashamed and humiliated that I had been bad, and I was obedient and stood in the hall by myself. I needed to be "good" so badly that when the teacher took the class down the hall to see a movie and forgot to include me, I didn't say anything. I wasn't sure my punishment was over. I continued standing in the corner at the end of the hall all by myself. I was scared to be by myself, but more scared not to obey. Before long, my teacher came looking for me, and found me in the corner. She was very nice, apologizing for leaving me there alone. "Why didn't you say something?" she asked. I was too afraid to say anything. After all, I had been bad.

From the age of one, I wore glasses. One day in first grade before returning to the classroom from recess, we stopped at the water fountain. I bent down to get some water and hit my glasses against the fountain and they broke. My teacher said, "I'm going to call your grandpa."

I didn't say anything, but I didn't want her to call Grandpa, because I was afraid he would be mad at me for breaking my glasses. He came to my school room and told me to come with him. He drove me to Lubbock and we got my glasses repaired. He never said anything to me about breaking my glasses and I didn't mention it either. I was glad he wasn't mad.

Grandpa was a "Camel" kind of man and loved to smoke while he sat and watched television with his ash tray beside him. I sat with my box of crayons on the side opposite the ashtray. I chose a crayon for my cigarette and everytime Grandpa put his cigarette in his mouth, I would put a crayon in my mouth. I didn't realize you inhaled the cigarette because it looked to me like he just bit down on it. He told me, "You will never smoke."

"Why not, Grandpa?"

"Because I said so," Grandpa said.

We had company one night, and I was running around and knocked over Grandpa's ashtray spilling all the ashes and butts on the carpet. I was embarrassed and left the room. Grandpa called me back to clean it up. I looked at him from the doorway and said, "I'm going to get a broom."

"I want you to come pick this up," Grandpa said again.

"I'm going to go get the broom," I said peeking my embarrassed face around the door frame.

Grandpa did not like my answer. He came after me, caught hold of my arm and spanked me. He hit me several times. He said, "You need to mind me and when I tell you to come here, I mean right now."

I cried and cried. Mostly I cried because I was scared Grandpa wouldn't love me anymore. Losing his love was more than I could bear. Granny went to the bathroom with me and soothed me. She said, "Honey, you are going to have to learn to mind Grandpa. When he says for you to do something, do it."

In West Texas, the land is flat and there is nothing to interrupt the gaze until it hits the horizon. I loved playing outside. There were several steps coming out of the back door of our house followed by a long sidewalk that led to the barn. The steps were large, and I often set up my house on the second step which was bordered by the cistern. I had my toy stove, refrigerator and washing machine along with my dishes and a few dolls. My sister and I and our cousins loved to make mud pies and would beg spoons off of Granny. Once we made a huge wedding cake. "Be sure and bring my spoons back," Granny would say. But so often, we forgot.

I rarely saw anything upset Grandpa. He was such a strong and controlled man. But when I was seven years old, I was riding in the backseat of our car with

Calva. Granny was in the front seat with Grandpa. He was driving us home from Brownfield, thirty miles away from Tahoka, where we had taken my aunt to catch the bus. It was dusk on a Sunday night and we were on the same highway where my parents had been killed, just a few miles from that fateful site. I was playing with Calva in the back seat, when suddenly Grandpa slammed on his brakes and Granny screamed hysterically. She opened her door and jumped out of the car even before Grandpa had brought the car to a stop. We were out in the middle of nowhere with no other cars in sight. Granny ran down the highway screaming, with her long coat flapping in the wind. I didn't know what was happening. Calva was screaming and Grandpa said, "Hush, sister."

Grandpa would not allow my sister or me to get out of the car. No one could, or would, explain to me what had happened. Calva had seen what happened, but I was so short I was unable to see over the front seat. I went into a state of physical stress, not because I knew what happened, but because I could not figure out what had happened. I knew it was something bad, but the best I could tell was that Granny went "nuts."

Grandpa just sat still in the front seat, while Granny was hysterical in the middle of the highway. I watched Granny out of the back window of the car, but I could not figure out what she was doing. I saw Granny take her coat off and lay it on the highway. I attempted to get out of the car numerous times, but Grandpa always said no, and I was unable to disobey him. Cars began to stop on the highway. A policeman came to Grandpa's window. As the policeman was talking to Grandpa, a very emotional, tearful man walked down the highway to where Granny was. It wasn't until about an hour later when Granny got back in the car, and we were on our way home that I found out what had happened. Granny said, "A little boy ran out in front of our car and when we hit him, we killed him." The tearful man who walked down the highway to Granny had been the boy's father.

I was totally traumatized. I didn't really know that a kid could be killed by a car. I had never heard of it happening before. I didn't know what this would mean, but I knew my grandparents were upset like I had never remembered before, and I felt paralyzed. I needed to do something, but I couldn't do anything. Granny cried all the way home. As Grandpa turned our car off the highway and onto the dirt road towards our house, our car quit running. Minutes later Uncle Robert pulled onto the dirt road and we rode to our house with him. A trucker had stopped at the accident site and Granny asked him to stop by the church and tell Uncle Robert what had happened.

That night many people from Tahoka came to our house. Calva went home with a friend to spend the night. I had an ear ache. At least something hurt. It seemed like everything hurt, especially my heart.

The next morning I went to school. Mrs. Mathis was my second grade teacher, and I was afraid she would be mad at me because of the events of the previous night. I wasn't sure how, but somehow maybe it was my fault. Not knowing how my teacher felt made me feel desperate to know if she was going to be mad. As soon as I walked into the school room, I walked up to Mrs. Mathis and said, "Grandpa ran over a little boy last night and killed him."

She said, "Yes, I know he did, and I know he didn't mean to." My tension eased a little. Thank God, she wasn't mad.

When I arrived home from school, I often found refuge from my worries in my swing. We had a wonderful swing set with two swings, a glider, and a monkey bar. I loved to stand in the swing and go higher and higher.

Granny had a cat that got to stay in the house during the day. The cat was definitely Granny's pet because the cat didn't like me. She would rub up against Granny's leg, but she was not nice to me. She would hide behind Granny's bedroom door and anytime I would walk by, she would jump out at me and scare me to death. I would look very carefully before walking by that door trying to avoid the terror of our house, but somehow I wouldn't see the cat. I hated that cat.

I was eight-years-old when Grandpa's niece was killed in a car accident. She left a husband and two teenage boys. Grandpa and Granny were very sad. The day of the funeral I asked, "Granny, why did she die?"

"She died because she was in a car accident," Granny said.

I sensed not to say anything more, but I had over-heard conversations Granny and Grandpa had with other adults about a drunk driver being involved. I knew that was bad.

The viewing of the body was held in the living room of her parent's home, because her mother, my Grandpa's sister, was very ill. It was the first time I had ever seen a dead person. So that was what a dead person looked like. My mama was dead. I guessed my mama looked like her. She was beautiful! I stood around the casket most of the time we were there. I was unable to take my eyes off of her.

We had lunch and attended the funeral. After the funeral, we were on the way home when Granny said, "Elva Jo, it is not nice to stand around the casket like you did. You go up to the casket once and then you leave and let others have their turn." I felt ashamed of myself and hoped no one else noticed.

Granny was loving and affectionate, but I often needed reassurance of her love. I was afraid I was unlovable, or would do something that would cause her to no longer love me. I needed to know she would love me no matter what. When I was eight, I asked Granny, "Do you love me?"

She answered, "Yes."

I continued asking, "Would you love me if I was bad?"

She said, "Yes."

Then I asked, "Would you love me if I robbed a bank?"

She said, "I wouldn't like what you did, but I will always love you no matter what you do." For awhile, I could relax.

Occasionally, Granny and Grandpa would set aside a Saturday for us to go to Lubbock to shop for school clothes. Since we were thirty miles away from home, we would eat lunch at a restaurant. Grandpa would sit down, look around and say, "Look at all the lazy women in here!" It was reasonable for us to eat out because we were so far from home, but he couldn't conceive of someone "choosing" to eat out. Grandpa definitely had his view of a woman's place in the world! And, he took Granny's cooking for granted.

At the end of the day when we would leave the city of Lubbock to return to Tahoka, we would stop at a drive-in to get something to drink. Grandpa always ordered a root beer, and even though I didn't like root beer, I ordered one too. It didn't matter to me if I didn't like it or if I didn't drink it. What mattered was that I had the same drink Grandpa had.

No matter what Grandpa did, I wanted to do it with him or help him. Being small, I wasn't able to be much help, but I was able to be in his way quite often. I stifled myself when he would yell, "Get out of my way." I just wanted to be his little helper. I grew to hate those words, "Get out of my way," because they made me feel like I was one big bother.

We always had a dog, but the dogs didn't live very long. Living on a farm without the confines of a fence, our dogs would chase the passing cars. One day our barking dog chased my aunt's car as she drove away from the house, and suddenly the barking stopped. I saw our dog lying on the ground, and I knew he was dead. Standing on our front porch, my sister and I cried out loud. My aunt returned to the house telling us how sorry she was. I knew she didn't mean to do it, but my heart was broken and I continued crying. Granny told us if we didn't quit crying, we couldn't have another dog. As soon as we could, we quit crying.

I was busy getting dressed for the first day of third grade. I was selecting a new dress when Granny walked into my bedroom. "Granny, I hope Mrs. Dunagan is my teacher," I said.

"Maybe she will be," Granny said. "You know, Uncle Albert and Aunt Mona are here, and it wouldn't be very nice for me to leave our company here by themselves. I think you are big enough to go to school by yourself today."

"No, Granny. I want you to go with me," I said feeling desperate for her to be with me.

"Do you think it would be nice for me to leave company here by themselves?" Granny asked.

Tears welled up in my eyes, but I didn't let Granny see my tears. I became quiet. I wanted Granny to be with me, but more than that I wanted Granny to be happy and not be mad at me for needing her. I swallowed hard and gave Granny what I thought she wanted. I was afraid if I was needy she wouldn't love me. I gave up what I wanted and needed without so much as a squabble. I didn't beg or cry. I felt unworthy and embarrassed about needing Granny, but behaved as if I was fine. I behaved as if I didn't care that I attended the first day of third grade by myself.

The third graders, along with their mothers, were packed into one of the third grade classrooms. We were told that each teacher would call the names of students that were assigned to her class.

I was afraid to be in Mrs. Fitch's room. Mrs. Fitch was a tall woman with a commanding presence. She was a no-nonsense sort of woman. I was afraid I wouldn't be able to be good enough to stay out of trouble. And, I had heard rumors that she was mean and had an electric paddle.

Mrs. Fitch was the first teacher to walk to the podium. "My name is Mrs. Fitch. If I call your name, you will be in my class. After I call everyone's name we will go into my classroom." Mrs. Fitch looked down at the cards she was holding and said, "Elva Jo Edwards."

Unable to contain my emotions, I burst into tears. "I want my Granny," I cried. Mrs. Fitch was sensitive to my feelings and stopped calling names. She said, "I know some of you have heard things about me, but those things are probably not true. I'm excited about the things we are going to do this year. We are going to have a lot of fun." She looked at me and smiled warmly.

I wasn't completely convinced, but I quit crying. There was nothing I could do about my circumstances. I had no option but to swallow my conflict and behave.

After eating lunch, my sister and I would help Granny with the dishes. Calva An would wash the dishes and I would dry them and put them away. The next day, I would wash and she would dry. Granny would sweep the kitchen and dining room floors. We had fun listening to the radio and working together.

Everyone knew Wednesdays were Grandpa's day to go to Lubbock. He would play roquet, a game similar to croquet, with his buddies at the Mackenzie State Park, and then in the evening go to wrestling. We grandkids never passed up the opportunity to go to wrestling with him, when he would let us. That was usually about once or twice a year. Grandpa would have to forfeit his roquet games when he would take us with him. Of course, we begged to go. For some reason he thought it was more acceptable to take us children if the women or midgets were wrestling. But sometimes we would get to see the big, mean men wrestle, like Dory Funk and his son Dory Funk, Jr. All of them scared the heck out of me, but they never scared Grandpa. He never yelled or carried on like everyone else. He just sat and watched. He was very brave.

We loved it when Grandpa would change the plows on the tractor because sometimes Grandpa would take us for a ride on the tractor. We loved it but Grandpa was always concerned with safety. One day, a little boy in Tahoka fell into a thrasher and Granny and Grandpa were very sad. Grandpa said we couldn't ever ride the tractor again. And, I never did.

As Calva An and I got older, Grandpa and Granny felt we needed more room, so we built on another bedroom and turned our library into a bathroom. Since Calva was older, she wanted her own room, but I did not want to sleep by myself. Calva moved into her own room anyway. I cried. I didn't care about having my own room. I wanted to have someone to sleep with.

It was not uncommon for Grandpa to sit around doing nothing but smoking. He always sat in the same position with his back somewhat straight and his knees far apart. Often each hand would be hugging a knee, even if one had a cigarette in it. If he was at the dining room table, one hand would be on his forehead while the other hand held his cigarette as he leaned forward with his elbow pivoting back and forth from the ashtray to his mouth. Sometimes I would walk by wanting interaction with Grandpa. I would move his arm and sit on his knee. He was somewhat like a statue, never moving. I would take his arm and put it around my waist, but if I didn't hold onto it, his arm would fall toward the floor. I could crawl around on his body here and there, but what I really wanted was for him to put his arm around me and hug me. But it wasn't his nature.

On the way home from church one day, I knew Grandpa was mad because he was the kind of man that you only had to look at to tell. When he was angry, it was as if his whole body was a sore thumb. His anger made me very vigilant, because more than anything I wanted him to be happy. But Grandpa wasn't the kind of man who would tell you what was on his mind. I heard him say to Granny, "I'm going to go see if I can find him."

"Who, Grandpa?" I asked.

"My hired hand." Then I knew he was mad at his worker. This was not uncommon.

A Texas Tragedy

"Can I go with you Grandpa?" I asked.

"I don't care," he answered.

As irritated as Grandpa was, I was afraid the man who worked for him was about to meet his maker. Grandpa didn't have his gun, so I didn't know how, but was convinced, he was going to kill the man. I didn't even know why. I wished I knew how to make things better, but I knew it was best to say nothing. Grandpa drove to a cafe in Tahoka, and when I moved to get out of the car, he said, "Stay in the car."

I was in agony. I could never disobey Grandpa, but how could I stop Grandpa from killing the man if I was in the car? Two minutes later Grandpa returned. He started the car and drove off. I asked, "What's wrong, Grandpa?"

"This is the first time in all of my life I have worked on Sunday," he growled. I felt like an overfilled balloon that just burst. I had been so upset, not by what I knew, but by what I didn't know: why Grandpa was mad. Grandpa was mad because he had to "fight sand." That meant that the life of the new cotton in the field was being threatened by the sand that was blowing. To save that little cotton, Grandpa decided it was necessary to plow the field with a sand fighter. All he wanted was for the man who worked for him to get on the tractor. I was glad Grandpa wasn't going to kill anyone.

Grandpa had taken over my dad's farm, but was getting to the age he needed to retire. His last year of farming was when I was in the fourth grade. My favorite part of farming was picking the cotton. One day that year I came home from school and the cotton-pickers were in the field right beside our house. I ran into the house and got a sack so I could pick cotton, too. I loved being with the Mexicans from Mexico who picked the cotton because they were so nice to me. But, as much as I liked it, Grandpa didn't. He would not allow me to go but about ten feet down the row of cotton and then I would have to turn around and come back. Grandpa was at the end of the row where the scales were. Each employee was paid according to production, or how much cotton they picked. When their sacks were full, they would go to Grandpa and he would put the sack of cotton on the scales and mark down the weight beside their name. I was so excited to have a little bit of cotton in my sack that I decided to ask Grandpa to weigh it. He put my sack on the scales, and the scales did not move. I asked, "How much does it weigh?"

"It doesn't weigh anything," Grandpa said. However, he pulled a dollar out of his pocket, handed it to me and said, "Now go to the house." I was totally defeated. I wanted to be with the Mexicans and I wanted to pick cotton, but I had nothing in me to go against what Grandpa told me to do. Dejected, I walked to the house, mad at myself for asking Grandpa to weigh my sack.

Grandpa became much more available to us after he quit farming. He told me, "the doctor says I could drop dead any minute."

Granny said Grandpa had to quit because he got too mad at the people who worked for him. The doctor was afraid he would have a heart attack. Either way, it meant he was able to be my chauffeur and I liked that.

In the summers my sister, cousins, and I would play outside when one of us would notice that Grandpa had turned off the highway onto the dirt road that led to our house. Within a minute or so we knew he would be parking the car in front of the house. We dropped whatever we were doing, yelled "Grandpa's coming," and ran down the road as fast as we could. Just before the car approached us, we'd stop and put our thumbs out as if we were hitchhiking. He always stopped and let all of us get in the car to ride, at the most, one hundred yards to the house.

Church was always an important part of our lives. In the fourth grade, my sister and I rode with another girl and her mom to a church activity after school on Monday's. That meant I had to stay in busroom. Since we were a small school, the bus would only run once after school. The children in the primary grades stayed in busroom, a sort of free time, to wait about forty-five minutes for our older brothers and sisters to get out of school.

It was a beautiful day outside, so we had recess during busroom and played outside. Minutes before the last bell of the day would ring, I walked a little too close to a classmate who was batting. As he followed through with his swing, he hit me in the temple with the end of the bat. Everything went black. I saw stars. It scared the boy who hit me, and he ran to get the teacher. She sent me to the nurse, but the nurse said it was too close to the eye to do anything. The bell rang and school was dismissed. I didn't know what to do, so I walked on rubbery legs to the car. My friend's mom took one look at my swelling eye and said, "I'm taking you home," which she did after dropping the others at the church.

Granny was horrified at my shiner. It was so swollen I was unable to wear my glasses, which made me miss the next day of school.

Mother's Days were always a mix of missing my mother and loving my granny. Missing my mother felt like something inside of me was missing, like I lacked something, or was deficient in some way and it was my fault. I felt if I only had a mother and a father, I would be a whole human being, a complete person. It didn't mean my Granny wasn't a good mother. But even with my Granny, I felt a loss which I experienced as a deep desire for my mother.

As a little girl I was aware of being different from other kids. One Mother's Day, Granny ordered us corsages to wear to Sunday school and church, and of course, I wanted a red one. Granny insisted I wear a white one which would designate that my mother was dead. Granny was concerned with my showing respect for my mother. I needed to feel like I was like all the other little girls. All of my friends wore red carnations. The outward expression of my inward loss made me feel very deficient compared to the other girls. It was as if I were advertising that something was wrong with me.

CHAPTER SEVENTEEN

*"Lubbock was probably
the bootlegging capital of the world
until the mid-Sixties."[1]*

    The goodness of my grandparents didn't fill the hole in my heart, the ache of missing what others had that I didn't. I couldn't understand the reason I didn't have parents, and needing to have a reason, I accepted the idea that something was wrong with me. I went so far as to think that perhaps my parents weren't really dead. They just didn't want me. So they left. This idea brought up the possibility that, by working really hard, I could become good enough that they would return. It was soothing to me to think I might have the power to have what I deeply wanted, if only I could be good enough.

    Around age ten I wondered if my Uncle Robert was really my dad, but didn't want me. Being eight years younger than my dad, Uncle Robert looked remarkably like the last picture I had of my dad which had been taken shortly before his death. I scrutinized Uncle Robert's face one night when he was at our house. As soon as he left, I ran into the library where my dad's photo was displayed. It never occurred to me that eight years had passed, or that my mother looked nothing like my Aunt Wilma. I compared my uncle's looks with my dad's photo and said, "It is him!"

    Each year the Edwards had a family reunion in Lubbock at Mackenzie State Park where all of Grandpa's brothers, his sister, their children and grandchildren would meet. Everyone brought a picnic lunch and the adults enjoyed visiting and the children enjoyed playing.

    We always looked forward to after lunch when Granny would take us to the amusement park. I noticed none of the other women Granny's age went to the amusement park because all of their grandchildren had parents to take them. Granny always cut her visits short to take us. Sometimes she would even join us on the rides. One time she rode the tilt-a-whirl with Calva and me and lost the grip of her false teeth. We got so tickled! Granny was always a good sport and enjoyed a laugh, even if it was at her expense.

    We never missed Sunday school and church unless we were sick or out of town. One day between Sunday school and church I walked to the back of the church auditorium to get a church bulletin before being seated. As I looked up there was the biggest and most beautiful bouquet of red roses on the alter I had ever seen. I inhaled in awe and stood motionless as I took in the beauty of the flowers. An older lady in the church walked up to me and said, "Do you know who gave the flowers?"

It was customary for a member of the church to give flowers in appreciation of someone or in memory of someone. Each week there was a new bouquet. I shook my head and said, "No, ma'am."

She said, "You did, in memory of your parents."

I said, "Oh." I had no knowledge about it as Grandpa made the arrangement with the florist. Every year around the twenty-first of May, we would provide the flowers.

The woman put her handkerchief to her mouth and said, "It is just so sad," and rushed away from me as if I had caused her some pain. It felt to me like I had done something wrong to her, to upset her, but I didn't know what. How was I, as a little girl, to be with my pain when the adults in my life could not tolerate theirs?

In grade school, I learned to dread the first day of school. Our teachers would talk us students through filling out registration forms with information about ourselves and our families.

The teacher would say, "On the first line, put your father's name." I was the only one in my class who did not have a father.

I couldn't remember the word guardian, so I would have to ask, "What if you don't have a father?" As nice as the teachers were, I was humiliated not to have what others inherently had. Inside the humiliation there was a firm foundation of shame, as if I had done something to cause my circumstances.

"On the next line, write the name of your mother." Would the humiliation ever end? I hated the first day of school.

As I got old enough, I liked to spend the night with my friends. One night I went home with a friend with the intention of spending the night. We were in the kitchen when her mom and dad opened a beer. I had never seen a can of beer before. I might not have even known it was a beer except my friend asked me if I wanted to "taste their beer." I, of course, said no. I knew Grandpa would have a fit. But inside I began shaking, because I knew that any minute the beating would begin. After all, people who drank beer beat their children, and I imagined they also beat their children's friends. People who drank lost their minds and couldn't control themselves. They were mean and scary. At least that was what I had heard. While I was at my aunt and uncles in Hobbs, a neighbor girl had run to my aunt for refuge because "my daddy is drinking and he is going to beat me." Secretly, I was glad when my plans fell through with my friend and I had to go home to spend the night, but I never spoke to anyone about my feelings.

One evening when I was ten, I was sitting in a movie theater with a friend when Uncle Robert came in and knelt down beside me. He said, "Granny is sick and in the hospital."

I said, "What's wrong?"

He said, "The doctors don't know yet, but she is pretty sick. She threw up a lot of blood. Do you want to stay with your friend or come with me?"

There was absolutely no question. "I want to go with you. I want to see Granny."

We left the theater and went to the hospital. I had never seen Granny look so bad and I was afraid she was going to die that very night. She was so weak and so pale. She didn't even have the energy to raise her head from the pillow. I was allowed to be with her one scary minute when she held my hand and said in a faint voice. "Honey, be sweet." I stood beside her bed speechless.

The nurses made me leave the room. That night Calva and I went to a friend's house to spend the night after going to our house to get clean clothes.

Granny was transferred that night to the hospital in Lubbock and was there for two weeks. They examined her and tested her in many different ways. One day the family gathered in Granny's room to wait for the doctor's report. He came in and reported what was wrong with Granny, but I didn't understand a word of what he said. Suddenly Aunt Freda started crying and threw her arms around Granny. Granny started crying, too. All I knew was, if an adult cried, it must be very bad. I couldn't tolerate my overwhelming feelings and ran from the room crying. Uncle James, Aunt Freda's husband, followed me out into the hall and talked with me, "Granny is going to be OK."

Through my tears I asked, "Well why are they crying if she is going to be OK?" I didn't know whether to believe him or not.

He said, "They are crying because they are happy." It didn't make any sense to me, because I didn't cry when I was happy. But, he calmed me down. We walked down to the nursery and looked at the babies and when we returned, everyone in Granny's room seemed to be happy. It took some time before Granny regained her health, but within a year, you would never have known she was sick.

About a week after Granny came home, she was in bed recuperating and I was playing outside when Uncle Robert and Aunt Wilma drove up and got out of their car. I could sense something was wrong. I ran up to them, "What's wrong?"

"Nothing's wrong. We just wanted to see Granny. Go ahead and play outside."

They said everything was all right, but my inner sense told me something was definitely wrong. I couldn't stay outside for long. I entered Granny's bedroom where everyone had gathered and saw Granny crying and wiping tears from her eyes. "What's wrong, Granny?"

Granny said, "We had some bad news. Grandpa's sister-in-law, Aunt Charlie died." I cried, because I loved her too. But most of my tears were because I couldn't tolerate Granny hurting physically or emotionally.

Every summer Grandpa would plant a large garden. At least they called it a garden, but it was actually acres and acres of black-eyed peas, green beans, and corn. They planted smaller quantities of other vegetables. Calva An and I helped Granny and Aunt Mona shell peas and snap beans. We would do it all day long. Granny would say, "you are a big help." I thought it was a lot of fun, too.

Calva was a better helper than I was, because she would help with the corn, too. I tried to help Granny once, but a worm got on me and I almost had a heart attack. I had quite a worm and snake phobia, so Granny said not to worry with the corn. She would do it without me.

Sixteen-millimeter movie cameras were all the rage when I was very small. My dad, wanting to record the lives of my sister and me, bought one and enjoyed using it.

After my parents' deaths, the movie camera wasn't used for awhile. But as life became less hectic and more routine for my grandparents, they would take our pictures at special occasions like Christmas, birthdays, and so forth. Uncle Robert would come to our house on occasion and show the movies for us. He would show the recent movies and then show some of the old movies, like the one where I was breast feeding. During those movies, I knew I too had a mama and a daddy. I could see them. I liked watching the movies, but it made me sad and aware again of missing my parents.

When I was ten years old, Uncle Robert was showing the movies and my sister and I and our cousins were laughing and enjoying seeing ourselves on the screen. Uncle Robert put on an old movie, one with my parents in it, and as we were watching it, I heard this painful outburst of crying I had never heard before. I didn't know what happened. I ran to see what was happening and was sent back to the living room by Granny. She said, "It is ok. Go back and watch the movie."

I asked, "What's wrong?" as I could see Grandpa hiding his face, crying at the dining room table. I wanted to go to him, but Granny blocked my path.

Granny said, "Grandpa thought he could watch the movie with Calvin in it, but he just can't. Go on in the living room and watch the movies." I realized Grandpa had never watched the movies. He couldn't without crying, and he wasn't the kind of man who was comfortable with his tears. I was sad for Grandpa because I could see he was suffering. As far as I know, he never looked at another picture of my dad.

In the summer time, my sister and I would take the Greyhound bus to Hobbs, New Mexico to visit Aunt Mona, Uncle Albert and their daughter, Mary Nell. We usually spent a week with them, then they would return us home, or Granny and Grandpa would come and get us. We got to buy funny books for entertainment on the bus. For two country girls, this was big stuff.

Uncle Albert and Aunt Mona would always show us a wonderful time. They took us roller skating, to minor league baseball games, and to the VFW bingo games. I often won a game of bingo winning ten dollars, which was a lot of money to me. But I didn't say anything to Grandpa, because he considered it gambling and I didn't want him unhappy with me. Once Aunt Mona let us sell poppies for the VFW. My sister and I had never experienced so much excitement in all our lives.

The first time I witnessed a female expressing her anger, I was visiting Aunt Mona in Hobbs. They lived in town which was a whole new experience for a country girl like myself. I wasn't used to someone living right next door. I rode Mary Nell's bike down the alley and upon my return was hit in the arm with a rock. I started crying and ran inside to Aunt Mona.

She could see the red place on my arm where the rock hit me. She stormed out onto her back porch and started yelling at the boy across the fence. Soon his mother was standing on their porch, and the two women were yelling back and forth at each other. It scared me to death. I had never seen Granny do anything like that. Granny said, "We have to act like ladies and turn the other cheek." But Aunt Mona was comfortable expressing her anger and had no problem defending the rights of a child.

Granny kept two of her other grandchildren while their mother worked. In the winter, they would come home with us from school. In the summer, their mother would bring them in the morning and return for them in the evening. They were both boys and were two and three years younger than me. I loved them, but I was jealous of them.

On summer days when we sat down to eat lunch, my sister, my cousins, and I watched Grandpa. He would say the blessing, and then begin eating. We loved the way Grandpa ate because he didn't have any teeth. We were mesmerized. In fact, we all imitated the way he ate. He was, of course, oblivious to what we were doing, or at least it appeared that way. Granny would let us eat "like Grandpa" for a minute or so and then say, "OK, stop that and eat the way you are supposed to." Grandpa had false teeth, but one day decided he wasn't going to wear them anymore. That was a typical "Grandpa" way of doing things.

I was envious of my cousins, because they had a mama and a grandma, too. I felt Granny treated them special when I wanted her to treat me special. I was taught when I had company, I needed to let the other person have his way. But, my cousins were there every day, and I didn't think of them as company. When we came in from school, we all wanted to watch comedies, but we wanted to watch different stations. I would complain, "Granny, I don't want to watch that station."

She said, "Well, they are little and they don't know how not to have their way." I resented that because I definitely knew how not to have my way.

Times like that I thought, "Things would be different if I had parents." The only difference I could see in us was that they had parents and I didn't.

I loved going swimming in the summer, and Grandpa was the one who took my sister and me as well as my cousins. Grandpa would sit on the bench watching us with sweat running down the front of his shirt. He never seemed to mind sweating.

We took swimming lessons as soon as we were old enough and could touch the bottom of the pool. Grandpa put us in swimming lessons because as he said, "You'd hate for me to have to come in and get you." I don't think Grandpa could swim.

I would hold onto the side of the pool and maneuver down to the deeper part of the pool. I didn't think Grandpa could see me, because my head was below the cement that surrounded the pool. But he would walk to the side of the pool and say, "Get back down to that end," pointing to the shallow end. I obeyed immediately. I wanted so badly to be in the deep end, but not so much that I'd risk Grandpa being unhappy with me.

Grandpa always let us stay in the pool for two hours and I loved every minute of it. I was never ready to leave, but when Grandpa said, "Let's go," I knew he meant right now.

Although I had bad allergies to the chlorine and my eyes would swell, I wanted to go back the next day.

One summer day of my fifth grade year, we wanted to go swimming. Actually we wanted to go swimming every day. My sister, cousins, and I would get together and decide who would ask Grandpa today. I was the chosen one and when Grandpa was walking across the front yard, I caught up with him and asked, "Grandpa, would you take us swimming today?"

"Not today," he said. He didn't sound mad but like he had plans to do something else. Going swimming that day was the most important thing in the world.

But I knew when Grandpa said no, he meant no and not to ask again.

I went back to my sister and cousins and reported that Grandpa said he wouldn't take us today. One of the boys said, "Well, I'm going to go ask him," as if he was not willing to settle for a no. I would never have asked a second time. I had never known him to change his mind.

My cousin returned in about two minutes and said, "Grandpa said for us to put our swimming suits on." I was devastated. I felt like Grandpa didn't love me. Why did he say no to me and yes to my cousin? I felt I was lacking something that my cousin had. Whatever that was, it made Grandpa love him more than me, because he said yes to him, when he had said no to me. The obvious reason I could think of that he would love him more than me was because he had parents. And I was unable to do anything about not having parents. If Grandpa loved my cousin more, there was nothing I could do. I was deeply crushed, but I never said anything. What was there to say? Anytime I compared myself to other children, my glaring deficiency was that I didn't have parents. I felt that any slight that came my way must have been because of that.

I was rummaging through the closet one day when I found the newspaper articles reporting the death of my parents and grandmother. That evening I sat on the couch reading the articles. Granny was sitting on a love seat and Grandpa was sitting in "his" chair. I read the articles, softly crying and wiping my eyes while they watched television. It made me so sad to read about myself, and my loss. It made me miss my parents tremendously and at the same time I felt I had to stifle my feelings as much as possible, because I didn't want to upset Granny and Grandpa. The same photos were in the paper as we had in our library. I didn't sob out loud, only cried softly, as tears ran down my face. I wiped them with a tissue. Neither Granny or Grandpa said anything. I didn't feel I could say anything to them either. I put the articles back in the closet and went to bed feeling very alone with my painful loss.

Since church was a big part of our lives, in the summer I would go to church camp. It usually lasted three days which was long enough for me to be away from Granny. We usually had a good time, but once I was on a hike with several other girls and a counselor when all of a sudden a rattlesnake was coiled right in front of me on the trail. I screamed at the top of my lungs and we all ran down the mountain as fast as we could. That was the last time I ever went on a hike at that camp. Snakes terrified me.

When our church had a revival, the men had breakfast every morning at the church. Boys were obviously invited, but the girls in the church wanted to go with their dads, too. So on Friday, the girls went with their dads, and of course, me with my Grandpa. One Friday morning as Grandpa and I were leaving the breakfast, we were walking down the long hall to the outside door when Grandpa started lightly hitting on his chest. He said, "I need my pill."

I was petrified. I jumped in front of Grandpa and put my hand in his shirt pocket and pulled out his nitroglycerin pills. I started opening them, and he said, "Not that."

Then he pulled out his Camels. He wanted a cigarette. He laughed thinking it was funny. I was trembling inside. I didn't think it was funny at all.

CHAPTER EIGHTEEN

"Lawyers awarded him (Pinkie) a Liberty Bell as the non-lawyer who best upheld the tradition of American Justice."[1]

As my sister got older and did not want to play with me, I recruited Grandpa for games of checkers. He built me a checkers' board out of plywood and painted in the spaces. Grandpa would laugh loudly after my jaw dropped because he double jumped me. I was awed by how smart he was, because I never won a game.

I spent vast amounts of time in the trees in our backyard in the summer. If I got mad at my sister, cousins, or Granny, I would go outside and climb one of the two trees I found comforting. Nobody would bother me and I wasn't a bother to anyone else as long as I was up a tree. The tree was my sanctuary. I could tell the tree all the things that would be different in my life if I had parents. The tree was the only one I could talk to about such things.

While in Lubbock one day, Grandpa said, "We are going by the architects." I didn't know what an architect was.

"What's that?" I asked.

Granny said, "When you build a house, an architect has to make the plans."

I was so excited. I had been begging Grandpa for us to move to town so I could ride my bicycle with my friends. "Oh boy, we're getting a new house."

"Well, no, we aren't," Granny said.

"Who is?" I asked, confused.

"You're going to pay for it," Granny said, "but Robert is going to live in it."

"Why?" I asked.

"Well, he farms your land, and you have to provide a house for him," Granny said. My uncle farmed the land that my sister and I inherited from my great-granddad upon his death the year after my parents were killed.

"He has a house," I argued.

"Yes, but it is not a very good house, and he needs a new one," Granny said.

"But I want to live in the new house," I said. The subject was dropped. I knew not to say more, but I was mad.

It wasn't long after that conversation that the house was built for my uncle and his family. They moved in and the house was beautiful, and I was jealous. I wanted to live in "my" new house.

One day Granny and I were at their house and I was playing with their daughter, who was two years my junior. We were playing in her room when she said something about "her new house."

I said, "It isn't your house. It is my house."

She said, "No it isn't." When I nodded my head that it was, she said, "I'm going to go ask my mama."

We went into the kitchen where Granny and my aunt were sitting. "Is this her house?" she asked.

My aunt said, "Yes, it is her house, and we are living in it."

On the way home, Granny admonished me for saying it was my house because it made my cousin feel bad. Her words made me feel guilty for saying anything. But, I wondered, who was concerned about my feelings? I was the one who had been begging Grandpa to build a new house in town.

When I was in the sixth grade, Grandpa had surgery for kidney stones. I was only twelve and you had to be fourteen to be allowed to visit patients. But I desperately needed to see my grandpa. Uncle Robert agreed to take my sister and me to see Grandpa if we walked upstairs, avoided walking by the nurses' station, and we didn't stay too long.

Before walking into the stairwell Uncle Robert said, "Now Grandpa doesn't look like he does at home sleeping. He is moaning and groaning and carrying on. He has a hose coming out of his nose. But he isn't hurting. Honey, he won't even remember this when he gets home."

We walked up the stairway and sneaked into Grandpa's room. It was a frightening sight to see him. He was moaning and groaning as if he was having a really bad dream. I was scared to death. There was nothing to do but look at him, so I only stayed a few minutes. I had so much anxiety when Granny or Grandpa weren't well. It made me feel so helpless and accentuated my need for them.

I always knew my job was to please adults. Granny wanted Calva and me to look nice and be nice. When we would leave the house to go somewhere, she would remind us to be on our best behavior. She said, "Now I want you to be nice. Remember, people in town will see how well you behave and decide if I am a good mother for you girls."

"We will behave," we would say. And, for the most part we did behave very well. I didn't want anyone to think Granny wasn't a good Granny. I knew she wouldn't like that. But protecting her image made me feel very self conscious about how I looked and made me feel I needed to behave perfectly.

Grandpa was always interested in my showing respect to my elders. I had a teacher at church who wanted us to call her by her first name. All the kids did.

Once I said the woman's name, Reno, in front of Grandpa and he said he didn't want to hear me call her that again. I was to call her Mrs. Riddle. "But Grandpa, she wants me to call her by her first name," I insisted.

"I don't care if she does," he said, "I want you to show her respect and call her Mrs. Riddle."

So, from then on I called her Mrs. Riddle when I was in front of Grandpa. But I thought it was so cool to call a grown woman by her first name that, in her presence, I did. And, I always felt guilty about it. I felt in Grandpa's eyes, it would be unforgiveable.

Although my grandparents always wanted me to do my best in school, they were not obsessed with my bringing home A's. Usually when I brought my report card home, I would put it on the buffet or dining table. Granny would usually say, "You did real well."

But it was more important to me what Grandpa thought. I would notice, from a distance, when Grandpa was looking at my report card. If he said nothing, I knew he thought it was acceptable. When I was in the fifth grade, Grandpa was looking at my report card and called, "Elva Jo."

I went to him immediately. He said, "The left side of the card tells me how you are doing on your school subjects. And your grades are fine. The right side of the report card tells me how you are behaving in class. You have a B- in talking. I don't want to see that next time. It is more important to me what you make on the right side of your report card than what you make on the left side."

I liked talking and giggling. I wanted to have fun. But, I vowed to bring that grade up, because I couldn't bear Grandpa being disappointed in me. If I could only find a way to make myself quit talking.

Calva and I would sometimes ride the school bus to school or home from school. The younger kids like me were not allowed by the high school kids to sit on the back three rows of the bus. But one day when I got on the bus, there was no place to sit except on the third row from the back. Calva and I were the first two students to be dropped off by the bus that day, but before we arrived at our stop, a boy in the seat behind me, pinched me on the arm and neck because I was sitting on one of the back three seats. I yelled out and started crying. My sister came to my defense telling him to leave me alone. When he talked back to her, she went straight to the bus driver and got him in trouble.

While I was at school, sometimes I would hear the fire whistle. I would immediately feel anxious. What if Grandpa and Granny were in the house and it was on fire? I worried about them and would look out toward the farm to see if any smoke was visible. If the house were on fire, they would need me to help them get out of the house. I didn't know what would happen to me if something happened to them. Grandpa would have said I was "borrowing trouble."

In the sixth grade, my teacher taught us about the cold war with Russia. I was petrified with visions of the Russians coming. It seemed to start a nightmare I had every night for two years.

I dreamed I was at home with Granny and Grandpa and my sister on the farm. Suddenly overhead, there was a helicopter from Russia. With all the people in the United States to choose from, the Russians wanted us. A rope descended from the helicopter along with numerous Russian soldiers with guns. They corralled us and made us climb up the rope into the helicopter to take us back to Russia. I was first and my sister second. Then they made Granny climb up the rope. I was watching down from the door of the helicopter because I was afraid the climb would be too much for her, but she made it. Then I watched as they made Grandpa start up the rope when suddenly he grabbed at his chest in pain. At that point I woke up with a start. Sometimes I would sit straight up in bed scared to death about Grandpa.

I learned to hate that dream. I told Granny about it and she assured me it was just a dream and that the Russians weren't on their way over. Sometimes I would cry before having to go to bed. I didn't want to go to bed because I knew what was coming. And, even though I knew it was a dream, every time it seemed completely real.

Calva and I flew to California the summer after my sixth grade year because my Granny's brother and his wife invited us to visit the magical wonderland of the Los Angeles area. That was the first time I was ever on an airplane. Calva and I were introduced to the big city and all of the wonderful things it had to offer. My aunt and uncle really went all out to show us a wonderful time taking us to Disneyland, Marineland, Knott's Berry Farm, and many other tourists sights. Calva and I had not been around them since we were very small and we did not remember them. Granny's brother was nothing like her. I liked him, but he was not warm and fuzzy like Granny. And neither was my aunt. All day I would have a great time with them, but at bedtime I needed Granny. Calva and I would lie in bed and I would softly cry for Granny. Calva would comfort me by saying, "Don't worry. It will only be a few more days and you will be with Granny."

I was with Grandpa one day when he was driving on the road between Lubbock and Tahoka and I was riding shotgun. I was about thirteen years old. We passed the 'Strip,' which was well-known by anyone in Lubbock or Lynn county and actually had a great following from people in many counties on the South Plains. It was the only area where packaged liquor was allowed to be sold in

Lubbock County. It was a small area south of the city of Lubbock and only on the east side of the highway. The law allowing packaged liquor sales had just passed so all the buildings were new.

As Grandpa drove by Pinkie's bright new liquor store that had Las Vegas type lighting, Grandpa growled with an attitude of contempt, "I guess he thinks he's awful smart."

I did not understand why he said it. But having been raised to always be nice and polite, I said, "Grandpa!" in a reprimanding way. I knew we shouldn't talk like that about anyone.

He responded in a loud, gruff voice, "Well, he's the reason Calvin and Pearle are dead." There was silence.

I was shocked! I had never before heard that. I didn't know who Pinkie was, but I had been told that my parents were killed by bootleggers. I wanted to ask more, but it was obvious Grandpa was angry. I had been told if Grandpa got too angry, he could have a heart attack. That fear was enough to silence me. When my parents were mentioned, Grandpa would leave the room or grow silent. It was obvious he didn't want to talk about them. More important than hearing about my parents was my desire for my Grandpa not to be upset. We continued our car ride in silence.

My friends started getting contact lenses when I was in the eighth grade. I had worn glasses since I was one-year-old and found them to be a big annoyance. I was always protecting my glasses or hitting them and getting them out of shape. As I watched my friends lose their glasses and sport contacts, I decided I wanted contact lenses, too. I knew Grandpa would think contact lenses were "foolishness," so I felt it would be best to ask for them as a Christmas gift. All I wanted for Christmas was contact lenses, and had no reason to think I wouldn't get them. There was one small package under the tree for me and I assumed there would be a picture of eyes or contacts, because obviously, the contacts would not be in the box. On Christmas day, I opened the box and found a watch. My jaw dropped. It was pretty. It just wasn't what I wanted. I said, "Thanks," and put it aside.

The following day, Granny said, "You didn't act very appreciative of the watch Grandpa and I gave you yesterday."

I said, "I asked for contacts, not a watch."

Granny said, "You should appreciate anything you get."

But I didn't. I asked, "Why couldn't I have what I wanted?"

Granny didn't say anything, but I knew Grandpa just couldn't see how contact lenses were important.

The following summer Grandpa went with me to have my annual eye exam. When we were in the examining room with the doctor, I said, "I want contacts."

The doctor gave us instructions for how to proceed with getting contacts from his prescription. Grandpa said, "Lord Geminy," as we left the office, and I knew he wasn't happy, but I wanted contacts. Suddenly I wondered if I could adjust to contacts in my eyes. I knew whether I liked the way they felt or not, I'd be wearing them.

I was staying after school one day in the eighth grade to work on a class project. I walked to the door of the classroom and looked out into the hall at six of my friends: Lexi, Debbie, Arlene, Richard, Doyle, and John. All of them stopped what they were doing and looked at me. It is a moment etched in time. I felt so much love from all of them and for all of them. That moment transformed my self image. It was at that point that I pivoted my attention. From that point on in my life, I didn't place my attention on feeling deficient for not having parents, except under extraordinary situations. Instead, I focused on what I had instead of what I didn't have. I loved being a teenager, had many friends, loved my grandparents, and was in most of the activities at school and church. That moment of contacting my love shifted my attention. That was a moment of grace. And I needed grace. That experience shifted the way I interacted in my world of friends and family, making my outer experience happier. But it also supported my not getting the help I needed to recognize the many inner feelings, conflicts and hurts that would run my life.

CHAPTER NINETEEN

"His adopted hometown of Odessa, the rowdy West Texas oil mecca, honored him (Pinkie) as its outstanding citizen."[1]

In high school Granny never cared if I had a friend spend the night as she never had her own plans. Her schedule was her family. In a certain way, she had no life of her own. Granny always said if we children couldn't go, she didn't need to go either. She was in many ways the ideal "grandma" as her identity was centered around caretaking. All of her life was about caring for her husband, children, and grandchildren. After washing clothes, ironing, cooking, mopping, vacuuming, and doing other chores in her seventies, I doubt that much energy was left to pursue her own interests. But I don't remember her complaining.

Granny trained me to consider death. As a teenager I would be leaving the house to drive the car and she would say, "Be careful."

I would respond with an attitude in my voice, "Granny, I will."

She would say, "OK, but that's what Calvin always said."

My heart would melt and I would tenderly say, "Granny, really, I will be careful." She knew she had gotten my attention. My feelings were more for her losing her child, than for me losing my father. I could see her pain from losing her child, but was not self-reflective enough to see how the loss of my parents affected me.

At Christmas each year it was always important to Granny that we all be together because, as she would say, "We don't know who won't be here next year." I always took that to mean she was afraid she wouldn't be because her health was precarious. As I matured I realized she meant exactly what she said. Her message was true: life was uncertain.

We always went to church as a family. There was never a question of "Are we going to go to church today?" On Sunday, that is what we did. When I was in high school, Grandpa stopped going to church, because he suffered from narcolepsy. He would fall asleep and the snoring would begin. His faith never waivered, but he could not stay awake.

That was when our tasty Sunday lunches ceased. Granny was a wonderful cook, but in Grandpa's older age, he decided to do a little cooking. Most of the time it wasn't very good, sometimes it was really bad, and on occasion hysterical.

One day Granny and I walked in from church and as I opened the door, I asked, "What is that smell?"

Grandpa was sitting at the table eating. I went straight to the kitchen and opened the oven. I said, "What is that in the oven?"

Grandpa said, "I don't know. I put some bread in the oven on a cookie sheet and when I went back to get it, the cookie sheet was gone." I couldn't help but laugh. Grandpa had not used a cookie sheet but the plastic cover for a nine-by-eleven-inch cake pan. The plastic melted and it looked like we had stalactites in the oven, reminding me of Carlsbad Caverns. I spent the rest of the afternoon laughing and using a hammer on the oven racks trying to break off the melted plastic. That was life with Grandpa.

Grandpa's more eccentric side was often available for observation. One day I was walking through the kitchen and Grandpa was at the stove stirring something. It was uncommon for Grandpa to do much in the kitchen, and when he did, it was often a sign I wanted to go get a hamburger at the drive-in. I stopped to see what he was up to.

I looked in the pan and there was something I didn't recognize, small pieces of white stuff. I said, "What is that Grandpa?"

"Radishes."

"Radishes," I exclaimed. "I've never seen them cooked like that."

"I just wondered what stewed radishes would taste like," he said.

"Yuck!" I didn't say anything more, but walked away knowing that I would not be tasting Grandpa's latest concoction.

Calva had more tolerance for pushing Grandpa's boundaries than I did. While riding around in town she would wait until the last moment before curfew to go home. This always created anxiety in me because I didn't want Grandpa to be mad. One night we were in town and as we rushed home, attempting to arrive home by curfew, Calva passed a car. The man in the car she passed took this as a personal affront and zoomed past us, slamming on his brakes in front of us and pulling onto the shoulder of the highway. After we passed him, he did the same thing again, requiring us to pass him again. He pulled over at the dirt road which we needed to turn down to go home. Calva couldn't turn in. What were we to do? He was scaring us. Calva didn't mean anything personal by passing him. We were just trying to make our curfew.

Calva drove past our farm to the next farmhouse, which is where the sheriff happened to live. Calva pulled off the road and into his driveway allowing the maniac in the car to pass. After we were sure he was gone, Calva backed out of the driveway and we went home.

In a small town like Tahoka, the teenagers just drive around town to have fun. One night Calva went to pick up a girlfriend and they drove around town. Of course, this gives the boys and girls an opportunity to flirt with each other. They flirted with some guys that night and when it was time for Calva to come home, her friend wanted to get in the car with the boy.

We were asleep that night when the mother of Calva's friend rang our doorbell about two o'clock in the morning. The next thing I knew this woman was in Calva's bedroom screaming at her, "Where is my daughter?"

I was afraid the roof of our house was going to come off that night. Granny played interference between the mother and Calva, while I worried and shook with fear that something bad was happening. Grandpa took the opportunity to sit on the side of the bed and have a smoke. Finally, the mother left and I could find out what was happening. Calva's friend had not returned home that night and her mother was frantically trying to find her. She was only a junior in high school.

We didn't find out until the next day, but Calva's friend had eloped that night with the boy she had gotten in the car with. I asked Granny, "Was it Calva's fault?" Granny said, "No, it wasn't. Calva couldn't make that girl get back in the car with her. Calva wasn't her boss. She knew what time she was supposed to be home just like Calva did." I was glad it wasn't Calva's fault. I felt bad for Calva because it would have scared me to be yelled at like that.

But Calva didn't mind getting yelled at as much as I did. Several times Grandpa yelled plenty about his disapproval of her boyfriend. If it had been me, I would have dumped him, just to make Grandpa happy. No boy would have been worth Grandpa's being mad. But my sister didn't see it that way.

Calva got married the summer after she fininshed high school. She and Kenny, her husband, moved to the Houston area where they lived for several years. It was never anything personal, but Grandpa felt he was too old for Calva. When she was sixteen-years-old, the eight years' difference in their age was too much difference in Grandpa's eyes. Grandpa learned to like, even love, Kenny. Once they were married, Kenny was family.

During their first year of marriage, they came home for a visit, and Grandpa asked Kenny what highway they had traveled. Kenny tried to explain to Grandpa, but when Grandpa didn't understand, Kenny said, "Here, let me show you on the map."

Kenny placed the opened map on the table and pointed to the route he had driven, giving a verbal explanation as well. Grandpa looked at the map and said, "The map is wrong. There isn't a road there." He turned and walked away. That was the end of the conversation. Kenny had the funniest look on his face, as if he had never heard anyone talk like that. Kenny soon learned that when someone in our family was being stubborn, which we usually referred to as being hardheaded, we would say, "You're just like Grandpa."

Granny and Grandpa went to Houston to visit Calva and Kenny. Calva wanted them to experience some of what they had missed living in a small town. She drove about an hour to a very nice restaurant on the coast that had a beautiful view so they could enjoy a leisurely lunch. But Grandpa was a simple man who couldn't be bothered with luxuries or indulgencies. He would often refer to anything more than the most basic of necessities as, "That's a bunch of foolishness."

Seated in the restaurant, he looked at the menu and noticing the exorbitant prices, he refused to eat as he was not going to pay such ridiculous prices for food. Paying money for ambiance or a view would be considered "foolishness." When the waitress approached, Grandpa ordered french fries. Granny and Calva got tickled, but knowing there would be no way to change his mind, Calva cancelled the order of french fries and they left the restaurant without eating.

I went to visit Calva and Kenny, too. One time I was there with a friend and I asked Kenny if we could take his beautiful red car to get a Coke. We were tickled when he gave me the keys. We were at a drive-in when I put the car in reverse as we were going to leave. A man had pulled his fancy car about one inch behind me to get out of the way of traffic. He was parked in a place that wasn't really a parking space, but behind the parking space I was in. When I put the car in reverse, I hit him. I was shocked, but he was mad. He walked up to the side of my car, put his hand through my window, caught me by the collar of my shirt and tried to pull me through the car window. But someone stopped him. I called Calva and Kenny and they came and rescued me. They never gave me a hard time about it either.

In high school, I was popular and well liked. My junior year I was crowned band sweetheart. The Thursday night before the Friday night game, we were practicing for the crowning event that would take place on the football field during half time. Two other candidates and I were riding on the back of a car around the field, when the man driving floor-boarded it. The three of us were thrown up in the air and landed directly on our tail bones. We could hardly walk the next day.

When the evening arrived, Grandpa's car was parked at the end of the football field. A high school boy escorted each candidate onto the football field for the crowning ceremony. After I was crowned queen, the boy escorting me, kissed me. Music was playing and celebration was in the air.

The next day, Granny said, "It is a good thing Grandpa was in the car where he couldn't see that boy kiss you, because he wouldn't have liked that."

Neither grandparent handled budding sexuality very well. Granny used guilt to control me. She told me she would rather that I die than have a child out of wedlock. That was a heavy-duty statement. Needing my grandparents' love so much, curbing any sexual feelings in order to maintain their love was a small sacrifice. I felt no support for being a sexual person. I was ashamed and embarrassed instead of being curious and excited about my development.

During my senior year in high school, Grandpa told me if I went to college at Baylor University, I'd probably need a new car. But, if I went to Texas Tech University, I wouldn't. Grandpa told me he wanted me to have the Baptist influence. I really wanted to go to the University of Texas, but I mentioned it just once and Grandpa said, "Absolutely not." I knew there would be no further discussion.

I decided to go to Baylor, so in the spring of 1968, I got a new car. It was a beautiful green super-sport three ninety-six. I liked it, but as Grandpa said more than a few times, "Your foot is too heavy." In August, before attending Baylor in September, I had my little cousin in the car with me when I had an accident. My car was hurt pretty badly, but my cousin and I were not visibly injured. An older cousin happened to drive by the scene, stopped, and said he would go find Grandpa.

Grandpa was a man of few words, and didn't say anything even though the blame for the accident was shared. The woman in front of me had her left blinker on, but the blinker light wasn't working. I passed her as she turned into me. It shook me up, especially because my cousin got scared and started crying. Previously, I had a fender bender in town which I never even mentioned, but felt guilty about, because I wasn't paying attention. I was waving at a friend as she came out of a store and I didn't notice that the car in front of me stopped. I rear ended him at a low speed. Of course, the accidents were my fault, but at that time, I had no understanding of how heavy our early imprints could be.

That was just the beginning of my many car accidents. I was on a date with a boyfriend one night when he drove onto an exit ramp off a highway. A man rammed into the front of our car as the man entered the exit, which of course meant he was driving into oncoming traffic. The driver of the other car left the scene of the accident, and since my boyfriend's car wouldn't start, we hitched a ride to the police station. The man who hit us was driving without a license, while drunk, going on a one way the wrong way, and left the scene of an accident. My boyfriend's parents were out of town, so I called Uncle Robert to come and get us. Grandpa was in bed and Granny didn't have a driver's license, and I knew she would be upset.

I was a very sheltered young lady preparing to go to college. One day I was in my bedroom when Grandpa called, "Elva Jo."

I went to the dining room where Grandpa was and he handed me a newspaper article and said, "Read this." The article was about the death of a young University of Texas coed. According to the article, she had gone for a run and then to her boyfriend's apartment where she took a shower. Then, her boyfriend killed her.

I said, "That is terrible, Grandpa."

He said, "It is her own fault she is dead. She should never have gone to her boyfriend's apartment. Don't ever do that."

I said, "OK," and left the room. My head was swirling with his words, "It is her own fault she is dead." Those words echoed in my head for years. I wondered, was there anything for which a man could be held responsible?

CHAPTER TWENTY

"A former state whiskey regulator praised him (Pinkie) as 'an outstanding citizen, a great character, a dear friend and the kingpin of the liquor business in Texas for many years.'"[1]

In the fall of 1968, I went to Baylor University and loved it. But I was so attached to my grandparents, as well as a boyfriend, that I didn't involve myself in the school like I had wanted. I went home almost every weekend.

While I was growing up in Tahoka, all of my friends knew about my parents' deaths and that I lived with my grandparents. We never talked about it, not even once. In fact, my sister and I never talked about it either. I suppose my friends' parents had told them about my circumstances, and they simply accepted it. When I went to college, it was a new experience for me to have to tell people, "My parents were killed when I was nineteen-months-old." They often had a look of disbelief on their faces and became very compassionate and said something like, "That's terrible." To avoid falling into that deep abyss of pain that had never been acknowledged by others or myself, I put a smile on my face and attempted to relieve their discomfort, as well as my own, about the tragedy I endured. I attempted to take care of them by telling them that what I had gone through was OK, because I had my Granny and Grandpa whom I simply adored. But the truth was that though I loved and adored my grandparents, I had a hole in my heart where pain and suffering resided from the loss of my mother and father. Many of my feelings were hidden, even from me, in my subconscious and in my body. But what suffering I was aware of, I felt I had to keep to myself.

I was very sick at Baylor and at spring break, I had my tonsils removed in Lubbock. I came home from the hospital and that afternoon my boyfriend came over to take me to the drive-in. My cousin went with us, and as we went through the one stoplight in Tahoka, someone ran a red light, going at a high rate of speed, hitting us on the driver's side. I was sitting in the middle and hit my leg on the gear shift. My leg immediately started to swell and turn black. My boyfriend's parents insisted I go to the doctor. My leg wasn't broken, but turned black all the way around the knee. It looked disgusting.

By the end of the second semester at Baylor, I had decided to transfer to Texas Tech for my second year, because Grandpa was sick and Texas Tech was one of the top schools in the country for my major.

My sister and her husband had moved to San Diego, California, and she was expecting a baby. My sister had no family in California. Granny couldn't leave Grandpa as he needed her, so I went to California to be with my sister for her delivery. I arrived a day before her due date, but the baby decided the due date was wrong. Two weeks later, my family called and said I had better come home because they didn't know what was going to happen with Grandpa. He was bad, and they were afraid he was going to have to have surgery. I flew out of San Diego and on the way home from taking me to the airport, my sister began her contractions.

Grandpa resorted to surgery, although the doctors had told him that with his heart condition, he had a fifty-fifty chance of living through the surgery. He was seventy-six years old, but I had not seriously considered that he wouldn't make it. He didn't seem that old to me. I was sitting with Grandpa after his surgery while several family members were eating in the cafeteria. Grandpa raised his fist to his chest, and I thought he was signaling that he was in pain. I went to the nurse's station and requested her to come check him. She took his vital signs and told me he was fine. However, she left the room and called his doctor. Several of my family members came through the door minutes later, just about the time the doctor arrived.

They moved Grandpa to another area in the hospital to monitor him. We gathered in the lobby of the hospital while Grandpa was alone in his room. In the middle of the night, someone came out and told us he was gone. He had died one week after my niece was born. I couldn't comprehend that he was dead. What? We just go home without him?

Granny and I left the hospital with my aunt and uncle. As we walked to the car, the sun was rising. How could the sun rise when Grandpa's life had just set? How could things go on?

I went to bed when we arrived home. I was asleep when someone put a hand on my arm and woke me up. It was one of my best friends from high school. Our eyes met and suddenly all of the events of the night came crashing into my consciousness. Grandpa was dead! I just cried.

My job, as I saw it, was to be strong for Granny. She was a woman of her era who relied on her man. She didn't even have a driver's license. How would she get by without him? Being strong for her, to me, meant hiding my feelings and not "carrying on." In other words, to the best of my ability, limit my crying and other expressions of grief. After all, I couldn't not cry. Some just leaked out. But I was a trained veteran of hiding my inner feelings.

Grandpa's funeral was on the first day of my sophomore year in college. It was one big blur to me. The next day, I went back to college. My major was not lenient on missed classes, so I had to meet with the dean before I was allowed into the classes that I had missed. She was very sweet and understanding, and I had no logistical problems returning to school.

Much of my time in college was spent being pulled between taking care of Granny and her feelings by giving her comfort, and being a college student. Even at college, I hid my sadness, because it appeared to make my friends uncomfortable. I had learned so well to be alone with my feelings of sadness as a child, that it wasn't hard to stifle myself once again. Then came the frantic activity of classes and a busy college life. Activity kept me from paying attention to my inner feelings and grieving the big loss I had experienced.

At Texas Tech, I became active in the Baptist Student Union. I had many good times with friends I made through that association. In fact, I met a boyfriend through the BSU. This was the boyfriend I eventually married.

I was on a bus trip to Fort Worth with the Baptist Student Union when I was involved in a Greyhound bus accident outside of Fort Worth. Two people were killed and many students were injured. I injured my back and was taken by ambulance to a hospital. I waited for hours to be x-rayed. I knew I didn't want Granny to get up the next morning and hear about my being in the hospital on the news.

The accident had completely overwhelmed a small town hospital and its staff. The local pastors came to help. One approached me and asked if I wanted him to make a call for me. I asked him to call Uncle Robert, as I didn't want anyone to call Granny after midnight with news I had been in an accident. I was afraid she couldn't handle it. I couldn't move, and I didn't know what was wrong with me. I was shaking on the inside, terrorized I would never be able to walk again.

Uncle Robert and Aunt Wilma went by Granny's house and gently woke her up by calling to her outside her bedroom window. Granny dressed and they drove to Jacksonville where I was hospitalized. They had no idea what injuries I would have and were relieved to see me.

In the accident, I had been lifted up out of my seat and my body was thrown against the luggage rack on the other side of the aisle with my hip taking the impact. Although no broken bones were found, I could not walk. Drugged, I returned to Tahoka the following day with my family and to college a week later. But, I suffered with back pain for years. That was a small price to pay, as two people died in that accident.

My last year in college I was home for Easter break and Granny was ill. My aunts and uncles were at our house one evening and were planning to take Granny to the doctor the next morning. Before Uncle Robert left, he said, "If you need us, give us a call." I assured him I would.

Granny passed out during the night when she got up to use the bathroom. I called the ambulance and then called my aunts and uncles. I only said, "She's real sick. Come." They arrived before the ambulance.

When the ambulance attendant arrived and put Granny in the ambulance. He said, "Why don't you ride in the back with her."

I said, "No, I can't. Aunt Mona, you ride with her." I was paralyzed with fear that Granny would die in my presence. She seemed so near death when they put her in the ambulance. Granny recovered, but after that incident I was aware of how I feared death and especially her death. I began a search and some time later read Elizabeth Kubler-Ross's books. They changed my attitude about her impending death. I realized what a blessed moment it would be if I were with her when she died. After working through that process, I always told her, no matter what health challenge she was facing at the time, we would face it together.

The month I graduated from Texas Tech University, I married a man whom I thought I could trust with my life. We moved to Denver, Colorado, where I taught school in a rough school district. My husband traveled three weeks out of a month so I was alone most of the time. For six months I was blissfully happy. Then, I discovered he had lied to me, and it broke my heart. But, I felt I had to make my marriage work. Besides, I loved him.

I wasn't left on the farm alone, and I had never lived in a large city. In fact, the first time I ever stayed alone was when I was eighteen, and Granny and Grandpa went to town to vote. They were only gone about twenty minutes, but I thought I was going to have a heart attack before they returned. I was very unworldly and quite the country girl.

With my husband traveling so much, I was alone a great deal. I was petrified of being alone at night and felt someone was watching me. My comment was "I feel like I'm in a fishbowl." I spent many nights with the lights on and no sleep, all out of fear.

We had been married less than a year when I came home from teaching one day, and my front door was wide open. My husband was out of town. At first I thought that the wind had blown it open, and then I thought better of that idea. My neighbor walked into my house with me, and we discovered my house had been ransacked.

When the policeman arrived he said, "pull yourself together." The scene was so disturbing, I couldn't. The burglar had even taken food out of the refrigerator and placed it on the floor and had gone through all of my bedroom drawers. I spent the night at a friend's house, and she helped me clean up the next day. My bedroom looked the worst. The contents of the dresser drawers were thrown across the room. Just as I was putting one drawer back in the nightstand, I noticed the molding around the closet door was gone. The burglars had pulled the molding from the wall and taken it with them as it was nowhere to be found.

I recalled a visit we had from a woman about six weeks prior to the burglary, with an outlandish story about having paid three hundred dollars down toward buying our house to a man living in our house nine months before. But our house had been empty before we bought it, so we knew the story was not true. In fact, our house had been broken into while empty, which led me to wonder if someone had planted some items in our house in the molding, and the burglary occurred when they came back for them. The woman could have approached us to see if we had a dog, basically sizing up the place for a burglary. I believe my premise because after the burglary, I was no longer scared. I no longer felt I was being watched and was able to stay alone without being fearful, beginning the very first night after the burglary.

After being married for two years, after many lies and various women later, I packed my husband's bags and left them for him at his work. That night he almost broke our front door down. He promised me he would do whatever it took to keep our marriage. He called a therapist and made us an appointment. But he knew how to talk a good line, and I wanted so badly to believe him that we didn't stay in counseling for more than a few sessions. Naive as I was, I thought he would and could change. Instead, he got somewhat better at hiding his indiscretions and his deceptions. There were so many lies, it was impossible to ignore, but I had to work up the strength to leave again.

I had lunch with a friend who worked as a psychiatric nurse. I confided in her about my painful relationship and that I was trying to get the courage, again, to leave him. I loved him and just couldn't see not having him in my life. She said, "Elva, I think he is a sociopath."

I had never heard of that and asked, "What is that?"

She explained to me that a sociopath has a personality disorder. I had never heard of a personality disorder. "There is no help for these people," she said. "They would rather lie when the truth is easier."

"That is my husband," I said.

"There are a lot of sociopaths in jail and psychiatric wards," she said. "They can be on the wrong side of the law or get addicted to sex, gambling, or something else. When they go to a counselor, they manipulate the counselor. They can lie with a straight face because they have no conscience."

"I know that one," I said.

"These people can be very popular. People love them. Just think about it, Elva. You could get anyone to love you if you could say anything they wanted to hear and walk away and forget all the promises you made, and not even feel guilty about it."

I appreciated her information and her honesty. I had no idea if he was a sociopath or not. And it didn't really matter. I knew he lied, and it appeared he wasn't going to stop. I was more certain than ever that I would have to leave.

One day, after we had been married for five-and-a-half years, the last straw was broken. It wasn't the biggest lie he had ever told me. But, it was the last one. It was the lie that convinced me it would never be any different. I finally accepted that I would never be his first priority. We filed for a legal separation, and I moved back to Texas.

My heart was broken. Even though I left, I couldn't turn off the faucet of love for my husband. But with distance between us, I began to get a clearer view of the hell I had gone through and changed the legal separation into a divorce.

I moved in with my grandmother for a few months until I could find a place to live in Lubbock. My uncle suggested I get a job in Lubbock to keep my mind occupied until I found a place to live and put in applications for an appropriate job for my skills. I took a job working from four in the afternoon until twelve-thirty in the morning with Texas Instruments.

After working only about a week, I was driving home one night after work and had pulled onto the country dirt road heading toward Granny's house when I noticed car lights behind me. It was after one o'clock in the morning! The road was not a private road and sometimes cars would go around our house to their destination, but I didn't want to be foolish at that late hour of night. I pulled onto Granny's cement driveway, but did not open the garage door. I sat there waiting for the car to drive on around the house, but instead the car stopped, shining its lights on me. The car was behind me about thiry yards. We both sat there for about twenty seconds when I put my car in reverse and started backing up. The other car backed up, too, but stopped again when I stopped. My anger rose to the surface. I wanted to kill him because he was scaring the life out of me. I turned my car around and started chasing him. I drove fast and so did he. I followed him all the way into Tahoka.

He pulled into a gas station at the red light and jumped out of the car and walked over to a gang of about twelve high school boys. I pulled in right behind his car and wrote his car license number on a piece of paper. The gang of boys started walking toward me in a threatening manner. I put my car in reverse, and with tires squealing, turned out of the gas station and drove straight to the police station.

I walked in and a policeman met me. I asked him, "Do you know who drives this car?" and I showed him the license number.

"Yes, I think I do," he answered.

I told him what happend and that I was plenty hot about it. "What was he trying to do? Scare me to death?" I asked. "My grandmother is usually at the farm by herself. Tell him I had better never find him on my property again or I will sue him for trespassing."

I had no intention of Granny finding out about the night's incident, because I didn't want her to be afraid. I assumed the police would handle the teenager. But the next day, as I was walking out the front door with Granny, a young man got out of a car parked in front of our house. He walked up to the door and introduced himself. "I want to apologize for what I did last night. I am really sorry."

I just wanted him gone, but Granny said, "What is he talking about?"

I looked at the boy and asked, "What were you thinking?"

With cowboy hat in hand he said, "I don't know. I've never done anything like that before."

"OK, just don't ever do it again." He assured me he wouldn't and left.

But Granny wanted to know what was going on, so I told her. I would try, like this time, to save her from pain or upset when I could. But I had never lied to her, and I wouldn't start now.

Within days, I found myself in the hospital for a ten day stay due to bronchitis.

CHAPTER TWENTY-ONE

"We'll never know the extent of his (Pinkie's) contributions or philanthropy."[1]

January 1979

After recuperating, I moved to Lubbock, built a new house, and lived there for four years. I first worked as a caseworker for the mentally retarded who lived in the community. One client was a six-year-old little boy who desperately needed firm discipline. He would take new puppies onto their raised porch and drop them to the ground. I felt so badly for them, I took one of the puppies home. I began to wonder if perhaps he had brain damage, because I couldn't train the dog.

I had all new plants and bushes in my back yard, and the dog ruined them. I wondered if perhaps he would be happier if I bought him a dog house. One Saturday morning I looked through the newspaper for a doghouse, called, and drove to a place outside Lubbock where a man was selling dog houses. I pulled into the business that was surrounded by a wire fence, but was somewhat uncomfortable as it was out in the middle of nowhere. There was another customer, so I thought it must be OK.

The man who made the dog houses waited on me after the other customer left. I decided on a dog house and the man put it in my trunk. I was twenty-nine years old, and he was at least sixty-five, if not more. He made several flirty remarks about how he sure would like for me to be his wife. I responded as if he were teasing. Surely the man wasn't serious, but I was becoming uncomfortable with his remarks. Then he said, "If you will marry me, I will take you anywhere this side of the Mississippi for a honeymoon."

I was dumbfounded, but attempted to keep it lighthearted and said, "I've always said my next husband will have to take me to Europe for a honeymoon."

He said, "I can't go that far, but I will buy you a new car to drive around town, and I will give you plenty of money to spend."

This man was beginning to scare me. I didn't even know him. I wanted to put an end to it, and said, "I wouldn't be interested, thank you. How much do I owe you?"

I was writing my check to him when he said, "Do you need some money?"

Born dense, I didn't even understand what he was talking about. I said, "No," because I just wanted to disconnect and get away from him.

He had his wallet out and let me see many hundred dollar bills. He said, "I will give you two hundred dollars to spend a couple of hours with me."

I was mortified! I wondered if I was going to be able to get out of his place. I said, "No."

"Don't you need some more money?" he asked. "Young women usually do."

At that point my anger rose to the surface. "No, I have more money than I could ever spend," I said with my anger noticeable. I handed him the check and quickly jumped in my car and drove away. As I drove out of the fenced property leaving dust behind me, he yelled after me, "You're beautiful and you know it."

Driving back toward Lubbock, my nerves were shot. I felt like I had a firm hold on an electric fence. I didn't know if the man was mentally off or just a dirty old man.

I worried over having given him my check with my address on it. Once home, I went to my next-door neighbors' and told them what happened. "If you see a strange vehicle at my place, please come help me," I said. We had a good laugh, but inside I felt terrorized.

I was in my late twenties, single, and loved parties. There were at least a hundred people, if not more, at a party where we celebrated something falling from the sky in 1979. It was as good an excuse as any to have a party. I found myself in the backyard talking with a man who was about my age. We had previously worked at the same place, but in different departments. We flirted with each other and kissed numerous times in the course of a couple of hours. He told me another couple was coming to his apartment to play backgammon and wanted me to come with him.

"I don't know how to play backgammon," I said.

"That's OK," he said.

I paused, looking at him, then said, "Look around. There are lots of people here. It is fine with me if you want to invite someone else to your place, because I want you to know that if I come over to your place, it doesn't mean I am going to spend the night with you." I wanted to be clear so there was no misunderstanding.

"I think you know me well enough to know that is OK with me."

Soon we left the party and went to his house. We had a small glass of wine and we talked. I still thought his friends were coming over. He wanted me to massage his back and I did. He started being more physical, kissing me and touching me. I liked him, but attempted to stop the progression, as I had no intention, as I had stated, of being intimate. But, things got out of hand, and he took liberties over my protests. I was getting fearful, but what could I do? Actually, at twenty-nine years of age, I had never found myself in such a compromising place. I said no and he paid absolutely no attention to my words. I had never had that happen before. I said, "No!" once again.

His response, as he leaned into me and on top of me was, "I know when a woman says no, she really means yes."

I was stunned, as if I were a deer on a highway looking at headlights. I had never heard that comment before. The only way my mind could understand what was happening to me was to assume this man was a psychopath and what was happening was just a prelude to being killed. I was paralyzed, but his unkind gestures were painful and I screamed, "Stop. You're hurting me!"

He did not stop. He did not make any attempt to show any concern about my pain. I had never had a man treat me this way. It was total confirmation, in my mind, that this man was a nut case. But my mind revisited my grandpa's remarks, "It's her own fault she is dead. She should never have gone to his apartment." I took my focus from my body, which felt like a knife was being plunged into it repeatedly, and placed it on how he was going to kill me. My concern was how my grandmother would hear of my death.

But, finally, he was through, and rolled off of me.

I jumped up, grabbed my purse, and left. I drove home, and showered. I kept trying to console myself, until I gave up and called one of my best friends. She came over, at three-thirty in the morning. For about a week, she stayed with me.

I couldn't call the police. After all, I had gone to his apartment. I had kissed him. It was Texas. I simply had to take it.

Because, at one time, we had worked together, I did take the liberty of calling the personnel director of the place we worked and told her what happened since he still worked there. "I can't believe it," she said.

"I know what you mean," I said. "I couldn't believe it either."

"But he is so mild mannered," she said.

"I know. But he did it."

She was completely taken by surprise, but no more than I was.

As time passed, I realized that I needed help to overcome this ordeal. I decided some counseling would be the answer. I went to the counseling department at Texas Tech University, where I started seeing a counselor who was a student, but seeing patients under a supervisor.

I saw him numerous times. I told him my story. I felt guilty that I made the mistake, again, of trusting the wrong kind of man. I also felt guilty for having done what my Grandpa said to never do: go to a man's apartment. I felt so betrayed by the man who raped me, not only because he was a jerk, but because he was a counselor. He knew what a heavy mark he left on me. He hurt me by choice. I just couldn't come to grips with the fact that a man who would take the time and energy to become a counselor, would do that to me or any woman.

After one of my counseling sessions, we were attempting to make another appointment around our schedules. My counselor said, "I got a job." Instantly in my heart, I knew.

"Where?" I asked.

"At the half-way house."

I looked my couselor right in the eyes and said, "The man who runs that house is the man who raped me."

Without skipping a beat he said, "That's OK with me, if it is OK with you." I was stunned. How could it be OK with me? I never went back.

That experience made it difficult for me to ever speak of being raped again, because I felt there would be no compassion for me. I felt the only choice I had was to simply suppress my feelings.

I turned more and more of my attention toward Granny. She said she was enjoying her life more than ever before. After a few years of mourning Grandpa's death, she blossomed. She had her own friends, especially other widows, and spent a great deal of time on the telephone. Uncle Robert would try for long periods of time to call her on the telephone, but would continue to get a busy signal. Becoming concerned, he would drive to the farm, walk in the front door, and see her talking on the telephone. She would say to her friend, "Oh, Robert is here. I've got to go." However, her arthritic hand had been in one position, wrapped around the telephone, for so long my uncle would have to pry her hand from the telephone receiver. Of course, he would tease her and she would say, "I just couldn't get off the phone."

I would occasionally have Granny spend the weekend with me. She was in her eighties and when we went shopping, she would sometimes choose to stay in the car while I ran in a store to make a purchase. I wanted to leave the keys in the car in case she needed to turn on the air-conditioner or heater, but Granny insisted I take the keys with me as "someone might jump in the car and drive off." This was years before I had ever heard of car-jacking.

It was uncommon for a woman in her eighties to be living on the farm by herself. She always kept the house locked and the windows covered to avoid crime. But sometimes I know she worried. Having trouble sleeping, she consulted her doctor and was given sleeping pills. She refused to take them because she "didn't want to get hooked on drugs."

She was living on the farm by herself and each morning Aunt Wilma would call her to make sure she was well. One morning Aunt Wilma called several times and Granny never answered. About eleven o'clock Aunt Wilma decided she must go check on her and drove the eleven miles to do so. She rang the doorbell and called out to Granny by her bedroom window, but there was no answer. Aunt Wilma ran around the house to the well house where we kept an extra key. She was nervous and wondering if she would find Granny dead. Returning to the front door with the key, she unlocked it and walked into the house calling "Granny," but there was no response. Turning the corner into Granny's bedroom, Aunt Wilma saw her lying in the bed. Instinctively, Aunt Wilma yelled, "Granny!" and threw the covers back. Granny sat straight up in bed, shocked. Her emotion soon changed to shame as any self-respecting farm woman should be up with the chickens. Unable to sleep, she had decided she would try a sleeping pill about two in the morning. After this incident she vowed she would never take another sleeping pill, even if she couldn't sleep, and to my knowledge, as long as she was responsible for her own medication, she didn't.

I recognized that I had been foolish in regards to money while I was married, so I sought a professional to help me determine how to wisely invest my money. Our relationship was some months old when he approached me about buying a bed-and-bath shop. After some consideration, I decided to buy it. I went to market and ordered what we would sell in the store.

One night there was a knock at my front door. I opened it to find a person from my past, someone I had known minimally during my teenage years. I invited him in and in the course of the evening, he bared his soul to me. He said his accountant, who was selling me the bath shop, told him he had found a "sucker" to buy the store. I, of course, was the sucker. He told me the financial adviser I had trusted was getting a big compensation for dumping the store in my lap.

It completely stressed me out. I felt as if my body was being held against an electric fence. He said he trusted me to do the right thing, because he was risking his financial future by telling me this information. If the accountant found out, he could ruin him. I wanted to confront the financial adviser, but felt I couldn't put my friend at risk, so I simply retracted my buy offer for the bed-and-bath shop. It cost me over six-thousand dollars to do so. The financial adviser was not pleased with me, and we ended our professional relationship. He never really knew what happened.

To make a long story short, the "friend" I found at my door that night wanted me to go into a real estate deal with him. I did. I assumed he had kept me from being used previously which earned him my trust. I gave him money to put into a real estate "deal" that never happened. When I finally realized I was being taken for a ride, I approached his parents and told them how their son was cheating me. I realized that the story about my financial advisor was not true, but had been used as a ploy to get me to give him my money instead of buying the bath shop. One more con man in my life!

The next time I saw him, he was furious with me. He said, "If you have anything to say, say it to me. If you approach my parents behind my back again, I will kill you. And, don't think I won't either. I broke a man's legs who messed with me, and don't think I wouldn't kill you."

I was terrified. I got out with my life and some money.

In nineteen-eighty-one, I was teaching school in Shallowater, a small town outside Lubbock. I took a weekend class called Touch for Health. It was my introduction to becoming interested in health and healing and the energy connections in the body. I was fascinated by the technique and wanted to become an instructor.

But the next week, Granny became ill with shingles, and it ravaged her body. At one point the doctor said that everything that had ever been wrong with her before was wrong with her now. She was in the hospital for two months, and we were finally told to take her home and do the best we could with her. She was throwing up six to eight times a day, but they could find nothing wrong. My aunt and uncle took her home with them while I spent two weeks becoming an instructor in Touch for Health. I returned home and Granny came to stay with me for the summer as she was still unable to care for herself.

I worked on Granny using the energy techniques I had learned in Touch for Health, and she quit throwing up—that day. I was a bit awestruck by her results from the treatment. My friends knew I was house bound for the summer so they visited me and gave me the opportunity to practice my Touch for Health on them. The end of the summer meant returning to teaching, and I recognized how much I loved doing body work on people. I gave myself until Christmas to decide if chiropractic school would be my next pursuit.

It was that school year when Aunt Wilma called me in the middle of the night, "Granny's in the hospital in Tahoka in critical condition, and the doctor doesn't expect her to make it through the night."

I said I would be there right away, but Aunt Wilma was afraid I would be too upset to drive so she sent Milton, her son, to pick me up. Milton and I arrived at the hospital in Tahoka, but before we got out of his pickup, he looked at me and put his hand on mine and said, "Now Elva, we don't know what we're going to find in there."

I said, "I know," and ran into the hospital. Entering the hospital we found our eighty-six year old Granny had made a miraculous turn around in an hour!

It never occurred to me that Granny would never regain her health or live alone again. Aunt Wilma tried to prepare me several times with comments she would make, but I wasn't willing to hear it.

My inner life was being torn apart. I wanted to go to chiropractic school, but how could I leave my sick and ailing Granny who had changed her whole life to be there for me when I needed her? Through tears of grief, I managed to find the strength at the age of thirty-two, to go towards my heart's desire and move to Portland, Oregon, and enter chiropractic school. Except for the decision to leave my ex-husband, that choice was the most difficult and heart-wrenching decision I ever made in my life.

Of course, there were many times Granny was in and out of the hospital. At one point, she even had to have a colostomy.

Chiropractic school was a huge adjustment and it took all of my time. I had never been so challenged! One day I got a notice from my insurance company in Texas that since I had moved out of the state, I needed to purchase car insurance in Oregon. I asked a neighbor what kind of insurance she had, and, because time was a big factor, I looked in the yellow pages to find the closest office selling the insurance my neighbor suggested.

The agent explained that I would need to come to his office to fill out the paperwork and pay certain monies that would secure the insurance until they had a chance to process my paperwork and send me a policy.

I walked into his office, and as disorganized as I have been, his desk looked worse. But I had my own irons in the fire and needed to be expedient: do the paperwork, pay the man, and leave.

"You will be receiving your policy in the mail in about a month," he said. I thanked the man and left and put the insurance out of my mind since he assured me I would receive a bill in the mail for the remaining amount I owed.

About six weeks later I was filling out an application for a student loan and it asked for my car insurance policy number. Suddenly I remembered I had not received anything from the company. I called the agent and spoke with him on the telephone telling him I needed a policy number for the application.

"The insurance company is behind on the paperwork," he said. "I think they are about a month behind and this isn't uncommon. Don't worry about it."

Such was life when dealing with large companies! I didn't have time nor inclination to worry about it, but about a month later, I realized I still had not received anything from the insurance company. I called again.

"I still do not have a policy from the insurance company," I complained.

"Oh, well, there were some problems," he said.

"What kind of problems?" I asked.

He fumbled around for the right words and finally said, "They didn't accept you."

"Why not?" I asked. He beat around the bush until I got angry. "What reason did they give you for not giving me insurance?" I demanded in my most commanding voice.

"It isn't like they didn't accept you, but more like they didn't accept me," he said.

"What in the world are you talking about?" I yelled.

"They aren't accepting me as an agent," he said.

It felt like my hair stood straight up off my head. "Do I have insurance or not?" I demanded.

"No, you don't," he said.

"Do you mean to tell me I've been driving around for over two months without any insurance?" I asked.

"Yes," he said.

"When were you planning on telling me?" I screamed.

"I'm sorry," he said.

I was irate. "You had better have my money in the mail to me by tomorrow," I said and hung up the telephone. I was shaking at the thought of not having car insurance and ever so thankful I had not been involved in an accident.

I immediately called the insurance commissioner in Oregon. I told him my sad story, through a few tears, and he was very kind. He told me to send him a copy of my canceled check, a copy of the paperwork and he would get to the bottom of it.

I was dumbfounded. I had planned on driving to Seattle the next day to spend the weekend with a friend, but didn't dare leave until I had some insurance. Therefore, I spent the next morning on the telephone calling and getting estimates for car insurance. One man I spoke to had me in tears. He asked, "Do you have insurance now?"

"Well, I was supposed to but," I answered.

"But do you?" he interrupted.

"No, but it isn't my fault," I insisted.

I was not familiar with Oregon law, and frankly did not know the law in Texas about insurance, because I had always had insurance. He said, "If you buy insurance after letting your insurance lapse, you have to pay a large penalty."

"Why?" I asked.

"Because it is irresponsible to let your insurance lapse," he said.

"But I told you I was supposed to have insurance and this man.."

He cut me off again, "But you don't have insurance and that's the law."

I was so frustrated from being hammered by him I started crying, which I hated, but I could not contain myself. I hung up.

I found the number for the insurance commissioner again and immediately called him. He was so nice to me. Through my tears of frustration, I told him what I was up against trying to get insurance.

He said, "I'll tell you what to do. Find the person you want to do business with and if they have a problem with it, tell them to call me. And, when I get your paperwork, if I find that all you have told me is true, you will not be penalized for not having insurance."

I drove to the nearest insurance office and asked the receptionist if I could speak with a woman agent. I told her my story and what the insurance commisnioner had said. She nodded and sold me insurance. What a fiasco! I didn't have the time or energy to deal with these kinds of problems. I was more concerned with what was happening back in Texas.

After five-and-one-half years of having someone stay with Granny on the farm to take care of her, we could no longer find anyone appropriate to do the job. Granny knew how heavy our hearts were with the imminent decision, so she said, "I think it is time for me to go to the nursing home." We all thanked God for her courage and strength to do what we all knew was necessary, but what we didn't want to have to do.

Although a nursing home would be no one's first choice, Granny had numerous family members who visited and took care of her on a daily basis. The roles of grandmother and granddaughter had been reversed many years before. I felt more like Granny was my child. I'm sure Calva felt the same way. Under normal circumstances, most people are approaching middle age before they must take on the demands of aging parents. But for Calva and me, life was always different that way.

CHAPTER TWENTY-TWO

*"He (Pinkie) helped chisel out
a rollicking chapter of state history."*[1]

Portland, Oregon, 1984

I parked my car on a tree-lined parkway and walked inside the two-story brick building for my 5:30 p.m. appointment with Denny Johnson. My study partner in chiropractic school had told me Denny Johnson had an uncanny ability to look into a person's eyes and tell them what experiences were imprinted in their psyche. I thought I knew my own history, but this sounded so interesting, I wanted to experience it.

I entered the building and a secretary escorted me into a small waiting room. I sat there a bit uneasily, feeling some uncertainty and apprehension. A few moments later a tall, slender man with curly, brown hair entered the room. He was casually dressed in a dark brown sweater. Smiling warmly, he offered his hand and said, "Are you Elva?"

I felt immediately at ease with him, and replied "Yes, I'm Elva. It's nice to meet you."

He offered a handshake and said, "I'm Denny Johnson. It's nice to meet you." He led me into a small room and gestured for me to be seated.

He stood before a light box and withdrew from a brown envelope a set of photographs of my eyes, taken the previous day. About thirty seconds passed in silence as he studied the photos. Then he spoke, with assurance but without drama. "When you were one-and-a-half-years-old, the worst thing that could ever happen to anyone happened to you."

My mind went into a long spin. His subsequent remarks simply did not register. Although I sat there for an hour while Denny explained his interpretations of the markings in my eyes, the only words I could recall were, "When you were one-and-a-half-years-old the worst thing that could ever happen to anyone happened to you." Those words echoed in my mind like a recording that was stuck in a groove and constantly replayed. An hour later, moving in a daze, I managed to thank Denny, pay him, and walk to my car. There I sat for a few minutes collecting myself emotionally. It was the first time anyone had ever said something happened to *ME*.

Driving home, I knew I had to spend the weekend studying instead of taking the time to contemplate and integrate my experience with Denny the way I would have preferred. With the goal of finishing chiropractic school foremost in my mind, I feared if I dropped the studying for even a weekend, I'd lag behind. I was competent at stuffing the feelings that began arising about my childhood, as I had done it all of my life. It wasn't difficult to do one more time, but I could not forget what he had said. Something had happened to *ME*.

I returned to Texas several times a year. I would try to get all my "business" taken care of while out of school, so I wouldn't have to think about it while I was in school. I was in Lubbock and went to visit my CPA. She had just remarried and had a nine-year-old boy from a previous marriage. I was in her office, and we were catching up on each other's lives. When I asked her how her marriage was for her child, she said, "He really likes him. My son is wanting to call my husband dad and I don't know what to do about it."

I said, "The boy knows good and well who his natural father is. But his natural father lives in Oklahoma. What he wants is to be able to say to his friends, 'My dad this and my dad that.' He just wants to have someone to call dad like all the other kids."

CHAPTER TWENTY-THREE

"It took him (Pinkie) no time at all to learn that hotel guests would pay handsomely for booze in a dry town, a lesson he took to heart."[1]

1986

I graduated chiropractic school in June 1986 and spent the summer taking state boards. I had met a chiropractor from Houston at a seminar in Colorado, who said he would like for me to work for him, but he didn't know any women chiropractors in Texas who had passed the board the first time. He reminded me that it was "good-ol'-boy country" down there. When I called and told him I had passed the board, he and I were both excited about the new possibilities that achievement afforded me.

I moved from Oregon to Texas and took two months to clean out my grandmother's house. She would obviously not be back, so I had to clean through years of our family history. That house had originally belonged to my grandmother who was killed in our car accident. She and her husband had lived there for many years. Then my parents had lived there for thirteen years, followed by Granny and Grandpa who lived there for more than thirty years. It was a large house, with a couple of small sheds around it, and the largest cellar I've ever seen. It took a full two months to go through everything and decide what to keep and what to save. It was emotionally wrenching as well as physically exhausting.

It was a relief to arrive in Houston to start my career as a chiropractor. I had the greatest respect for the man I worked for, and he taught me what it would have taken me years to learn in practice. My appreciation for him has never waivered. It was with a great deal of sadness for me when our time together ended. It worked out well for two years, and then it no longer worked out at all. Uncle Robert and Aunt Wilma had helped me move to Houston, and when the time came for me to move again, I called Uncle Robert and asked, "How is your truck running?" He helped me move to Denver, Colorado, where I had originally intended to go, when the proper time came to start my own practice.

I was not a business person and it took some time for me to put myself and my practice together. While I was in transition, I substituted for other doctors now and then. I was at another doctor's office when Uncle Robert called me, "Granny is in severe pain. I don't know what to do. She is ninety-three years old, and they don't know if she would make it through the surgery or what kind of shape she would be in if she made it through. If we don't do anything, they say she will die."

"What do you think?" I asked.

"I don't know. I can't just sit here and watch her suffer and not do anything about it," he said. "I'm calling because I want to know what you think I should do."

"I don't know. I'm not there and you are," I said. We talked a little more and I said, "I trust you to do the best by Granny you can. You decide and I will stand by you."

When I called later, I could hear Granny screaming in the background as if someone was hurting her. I was assured no one was. She was having a bad reaction to some medication. I spoke by telephone several times that day to my family, and we opted for exploratory surgery for Granny even at her advanced age. I arrived in her hospital room about three-thirty in the morning the day her surgery was scheduled. I found Uncle Robert sitting up with her in the hospital. She had finally calmed down just hours before I had arrived. For three days and three nights she had screamed at the top of her lungs. The nurses had not even been able to take her vital signs for three days.

When it came to Granny, our family could get close really fast. We all loved her. Her fragility made us all want to protect her in whatever ways we could. We never left her at the hospital alone because we always monitored all medications. As shifts would change, we left notes for each other as to how she was doing, what the doctors said, and what to ask the doctor the next time he was in the room. We all sacrificed for Granny, just as Granny had sacrificed for each and every one of us.

Once again, Granny recovered. Actually, recovered is not an apt description because, although she was out of pain and suffering in that area of her body, she was old and she suffered with a worn out body and a mind that was more and more like a child's.

I opened my private practice in Denver, and although I never became a business model to copy, I provided a needed service to many patients and, in the process, enjoyed my practice. It was a wonderful road of maturation as I learned more and more about the body, adding to my skills along the way. I not only used chiropractic, but incorporated vitamins, minerals, and herbs, as well as a long list of natural products. I loved acupuncture and took a year long class to become certified. And, to quote another chiropractor, Dr. Scott Walker, "you don't have to work with people very long to discover the emotional aspect in healing." Dr.

Walker was the innovator of a system called Neuro Emotional Technique™ whereby practitioners could remove from the body an energetic distortion that had been created by an emotion. It wasn't a talk-it-out kind of therapy, it was easy on the patient, and it resolved many problems where emotions got stuck in the body. It wasn't uncommon to find people's lives being run by the distortions of energy created by holding a certain emotional pattern in the body. Many of my patients have said, "I think there is an emotional element to what is going on with me."

My response was, "There almost always is. We are emotional beings and the mind/body connection is huge." I was beginning to understand how much this was true for me. My body was trying to tell me something I needed to know. I learned that doing what I could for the body often included using the technique I learned from Dr. Walker.

I looked at health as a triad where all three aspects, structure, chemistry, and energy, needed to be addressed. The structural aspect I dealt with through my chiropractic skills. The chemistry aspect I supported through proper nutrition and supplements, such as vitamins, minerals, and herbs. I used acupuncture, the Neuro-Emotional Technique™, flower essences, and other natural methods to address the energetic aspects of health.

I studied and went to many classes to learn for my patients as well as for myself. As many have said, we are attracted to a field because we need it ourselves. And I needed chiropractic.

One day a patient was distressed over the pain she was experiencing because she had been in a car accident and I said, "I really do know how you feel. I know because I've been in fifteen car accidents."

She said, "My gosh. You are a testament to chiropractic."

We both laughed, but it was true. I was.

I learned that the physical work of chiropractic adjustments and soft tissue manipulations, necessary supplements and the Neuro-Emotional Technique™ were all vital to my body. Through being worked on by other chiropractors, I learned just how much my body had been affected by my many traumatic experiences, including all of my car accidents. The most important trauma by far was my first accident and the quick and sudden death of my parents. From a child's point of view, it was pure abandonment. Since I was never encouraged to grieve or to talk about my feelings, I suppressed them and my body and my psyche were affected.

CHAPTER TWENTY-FOUR

"But it's not the end for the two little girls."[1]

October 1991

I didn't really have an inkling of the magnitude of the influence the death of my parents and grandmother, and the accident itself, had on my life. My feelings stayed frozen at an inner depth until one day something happened, and it broke the dam. The fortress I had built inside to protect myself from the sadness of my early experience began tumbling down Halloween weekend of 1991.

It was a great October day with the sun shining on the plains of West Texas. I was home, in Tahoka, Texas, for a visit. I'd learned to love and appreciate the beauty of West Texas and life on the farm in a way that wasn't possible for me until I moved away.

Returning to the farm, I had learned to appreciate a night that was pin-dropping quiet and stars that popped right out of the big Texas sky. I had rarely noticed the exquisite beauty before I left West Texas. Even though I hadn't lived in Tahoka in over twenty years, I still called it home.

When in Tahoka, I divided my time between sitting with Granny at the nursing home and visiting my extended family and friends. Granny would anticipate my visits, and we would do things she normally didn't do. As her mind became affected by dementia, she didn't care so much about my visits. At that point it was my desire to reconnect with her that spurred my visits, even if she was the shell of who she once had been.

Uncle Robert and Aunt Wilma invited me to lunch on Sunday, my last day in Tahoka before returning to Denver, where I could visit with my aunts, uncles, and cousins. We brought Granny to the occasion because I liked being with her. My love for her was not dependent on the brilliance of her mind. She was now at the point of being happier if we just left her alone. I could leave her alone, but I couldn't leave her out.

Aunt Wilma was a great cook and the dinner was tasty and the conversation friendly. Aunt Wilma and Uncle Robert, who lived on my late great-granddad's farm ten miles north of Tahoka, had been married forty-five years and had two children, Milton and Donna. Milton was one year my senior and like his dad, a farmer. Single for some years, he had married Mary Ann when he was about thirty-five years old. Donna, two years younger than I, married Dan, a farmer, and they had three children whom I adored.

My dad's sister, Aunt Freda, also lived in Tahoka with her husband Wayne. Aunt Freda had married Wayne when I was in high school, and the word Uncle never seemed to get attached to the name Wayne. Aunt Freda had three children from a previous marriage who were grown and lived away from Tahoka and were not at the gathering. I was close to all of my cousins, because we all grew up together.

Our conversation was about the latest happenings in our lives.

"It was scary," I said, referring to a recent break-in at my house.

"Exactly what happened?" asked my cousin.

"I left my house and went to a little strip mall that wasn't far from home. When I returned, I walked up to my front door and it was open. I ran over to Mike and Shirley's, only about two blocks away. We called the police and then we went back over there," I said.

"Did you see anyone leaving your house?" my cousin asked.

"No. Shirley and I tried to slow Mike down because he took along his bat as a weapon. Shirley and I wanted the burglars to be gone before we returned. We weren't there long when the police arrived. They searched my house, but the burglars were gone, thank God."

"Did they take anything?" my cousin asked.

"They took my television. They messed up my house some, but not nearly as much as they did the first time I was burglarized." I was the only one in my family that had ever been burglarized, and several times at that.

After lunch the women cleaned off the table and put the dishes in the dishwasher while the men found their place in front of the television to watch a football game. At this point Mary Ann pulled me aside and said, "I was just wondering if you had seen the *Lubbock Avalanche-Journal* recently. They had a series of articles about Pinkie."

I simply replied, "No." Living in Denver I would never see the *Lubbock Avalanche-Journal*, the daily newspaper from Lubbock, unless I was visiting or someone sent it to me.

She continued, "They painted a picture of Pinkie as some sort of hero."

That seemed preposterous to me. In West Texas his name was synonymous with alcohol.

Mary Ann said, "I think I upset Robert. Milton and I were here for dinner Sunday after the articles appeared in the paper. I just casually asked Robert if he had seen the articles about Pinkie. He was cold as ice and said, 'I glanced at them,' and walked away leaving me with the distinct impression that I shouldn't say anything more." Mary Ann paused momentarily, then continued, "I didn't understand his attitude, but I dropped the subject."

I asked, "What exactly did the articles say about Pinkie?"

Mary Ann gestured with her hand, "It said he was a civic godfather and philanthropist, and it even mentioned how the politicians privately sought his counsel."

Wrinkling my brow, I asked, "What do you mean 'sought his counsel?' Sought his counsel about what?"

"Basically, how the politicians could give Pinkie what he wanted without alienating their constituents," Mary Ann said, her dimples shining when she smiled. "They said it was hard to get a liquor bill passed in Austin when Pinkie was walking the halls."[2]

I was feeling confused because Pinkie was the bootlegger, not the lawmaker. "Tell me more," I said.

"The articles talked about how he spent his life outfoxing and befriending the sheriffs, the Texas Rangers, and the liquor control agents, for fun as well as profit,"[3] Mary Ann said.

"Is Pinkie still alive?" I asked.

Mary Ann replied, "No, he died a couple of years ago. His wife said he died a lonely man."

"Isn't that too bad," I said, in an uncaring tone of voice. "I can't seem to conjure up much compassion for him."

Mary Ann took a sip of the iced tea she was holding and continued, "The articles said his wife confronted him one night and they had an argument. She asked him, 'Have you ever killed anyone?'[4] and guess what his answer was?"

"I don't know, what did he say?"

"He said, 'That's an unfair question.'"[5] Mary Ann smiled at the coldness of such an answer.

"You've got to be kidding," I responded as goose bumps covered my arms. In disbelief I said, "Can you imagine crawling between the sheets with someone who answers that question that way?"

Mary Ann continued, "The articles were full of information about Pinkie and the way he made money legally and illegally by bootlegging. Even the men who worked for the liquor control board laughed about how Pinkie out-maneuvered them, about how he got by with his illegal activities."

"You must be joking," I said.

"No, that's why I thought you'd be interested in the articles. It talked about how historically Lubbock was bone dry except for the private clubs." Mary Ann took another sip of iced tea. "I suppose the creation of the Strip ended the era of

Lubbock being the bootlegging capital of the world."⁶ The 'Strip' was an area outside Lubbock where beer, wine, and liquor would be sold.

"I remember when the Strip was built, but you know, I was pretty young," I said realizing I did not know too much about the situation.

"The articles said that for Pinkie, life was a game that he played to the hilt. And of course the game involved politics, and he played by his own rules,"⁷ added Mary Ann. She paused as if waiting for me to speak. I was silent so she continued, "They said Pinkie had the smartest drivers and the fastest cars, that he was a special breed, and that his legacy would be with Texas for a long time."⁸

Sarcastically I said, "I can't believe someone would have the audacity to talk about Pinkie's legacy in a favorable way!"

"You know," Mary Ann said while her thumb and index finger played with her earring, "I am new to this family, and I had never been told the whole story about your parents. All I knew was that they had been killed in a car accident. On Monday I dropped by here to pick something up after work, and I guess Robert had been thinking about the articles, because when I came in, he started talking about your parents' accident. It just rolled out of him. He said, 'Someone should write the newspaper and set them straight.' I told him I would send a letter to the editor, which I did, but it was never published. I've heard that if someone writes anything bad about Pinkie and the paper publishes it, the next week that person's business will burn down, by an act of God, of course."

"Really?" Feeling guilty for not helping in the kitchen and wanting to get away from the feelings that were arising in me, I said, "You know, we better help with the dishes, but I would appreciate it if you would send me a copy of your letter," and she agreed as we walked back into the kitchen to help clean up.

The afternoon went by quickly and the time arrived for me to return to Denver. It was difficult to leave my Granny as I felt she was close to death, a feeling I'd had much of my life.

CHAPTER TWENTY-FIVE

"Stevenson insisted that Pinkie could drive better in the dark than in daylight."[1]

I arrived back in Denver and began my usual routines of taking my morning walks with my best friends, Mike and Shirley, and going to work. Several days after arriving back in Denver, I received a letter from Mary Ann. Opening the envelope, I found the copy of her letter to the editor of the *Lubbock Avalanche-Journal* which she had promised to send me.

"October 22, 1991
Dear Editor:
   Sunday as I had lunch at the home of my in-laws, I asked my father-in-law if he had read the newspaper article on Pinkie. He said that he had glanced at it, then he just walked off. I knew I had triggered a nerve so deep that he really didn't even want to discuss it.
   Forty years ago, Calvin and Pearl Edwards, and Pearl's mother, as well as two people in another car were killed by one of Pinkie's drivers who was cutting through the back roads of West Texas trying to evade the police on Monday evening, May 21, 1951. The driver was crossing the main highway between Tahoka and Brownfield at the West Point Gin. His lights were not on, and he never even slowed down for the stop sign, let alone the traffic on the main highway. The ensuing collision left five people dead, orphaned ten children, and devastated the lives of many people. Pinkie's driver survived. You can read the details of what happened in the Lubbock Avalanche-Journal. There were several articles in the newspapers published after May 21, 1951.
   Calvin and Pearl's two girls survived the wreck. One was three years, the other only nineteen months old. The girls were taken by Calvin's parents who reared them. They were very loving people, who provided a wonderful home for the children. But even in recent years, I have seen both girls, now in their forties, with tears in their eyes somewhat haunted by the past they can't even recall, a past they had no control over, but that controlled them.

> *It must be very hard for my father-in-law to read the head lines and the stories that seem to glorify the deeds and life of someone whose dealings dealt such a hard blow to him early in life.*
>
> *I'm not trying to make Pinkie's dealings any worse than they were, but it is very disheartening to read articles that glorify those dealings and make a hero out of someone who was even afraid that his picture might appear in a newspaper.*
>
> *Time has a way of healing old wounds and a way of making heroes out of those who never were heroes during their lifetimes; so why now?*
>
> *I know this family could have done without the articles that opened old wounds laid to rest many years ago.*
>
> *Very truly yours,*
Mary Ann Edwards"[2]

My tears began to flow, unleashing years of grief. Sadness was not something I was comfortable with, and I couldn't tolerate it for long. Years of habit led me to quiet the intolerable grief with anger. Anger would bring me the strength for action. At least it led me to think I could do something that would take away the sadness, because sadness left me in a place of powerlessness, and powerlessness was intolerable.

My personality style was to be agreeable and a peacemaker. Basically I avoided conflict. However, when I was pushed far enough, my anger would rise to the surface and spurt out in ugly ways, especially in defense of my grandparents or my parents. Defending myself was more difficult.

After reading Mary Ann's letter, I sat down at my computer, boiling with anger, and wrote a scathing letter to the editor of the *Lubbock Avalanche-Journal*, admonishing him for printing articles that praised a bootlegger. Furthermore, I accused him of minimizing and discounting my personal pain from being orphaned by Pinkie and suggested, that, if he had more compassion, he would call me. I gave the date of the accident so he could look up the articles printed at the time of the accident when the people at the *Lubbock Avalanche-Journal* had more compassion for Pinkie's victims.

Writing and mailing the letter silenced a portion of my body reactivity which was triggered by being so emotional. Anxiety was on the prowl.

As I prepared for bed, my memory slipped to the sadness I had felt as a child because I didn't have parents and the ache of missing what others had that I didn't. Even at forty-one years old, I couldn't help but cry.

CHAPTER TWENTY-SIX

"Perhaps the last of his special if not always noble breed, Pinkie is gone but his legacy will be with Texas for generations to come."[1]

Three days later

The editor of the *Lubbock Avalanche-Journal* called me after getting my letter. "Ms. Edwards, my name is Jon Hunt and I'm the editor of the *Lubbock Avalanche-Journal*. I received your letter and wanted to call and talk with you."

My heart started beating loudly. I had asked him to call, but was surprised that he did. I felt defensive and argumentative and my response was a tart "Yes."

"Well, I checked the newspaper back in 1951, and I can't find anything to corroborate your accusations that bootleggers were responsible for the deaths of your parents. And, I read nothing connecting the accident to Pinkie."

Angry, I spit out a reply, "Well, the information is there because I've read it."

"Well, I can't find it," Jon Hunt responded.

I suddenly realized that perhaps it wasn't the *Lubbock Avalanche-Journal* I had read. Mr. Hunt was a nice man and calmed me down momentarily by saying, "I'm new to this job, and I'm not a Lubbock native. I don't know the history of this area. However, I can't find anything to back up your accusations about Pinkie." My anger started mounting again as he finished with, "But, I want you to know that the *Lubbock Avalanche-Journal* didn't do that story."

I cut him off. "You did print the series of articles didn't you?"

"Yes, we printed them, but the *Lubbock Avalanche-Journal* did not send a newspaper reporter out to do a story on Pinkie. Mike Cochran is a reporter for the Associated Press, and the story ran in newspapers all over the state of Texas, not just in the *Lubbock Avalanche-Journal*."

Dripping with sarcasm I replied, "Well, aren't the citizens of the state of Texas fortunate."

I was too full of anger to concern myself with my presentation. Hiding my pain with anger was not a new way of coping for me. Perhaps I had learned that from my grandpa. If I didn't hide it, I might just break down and cry, and I had many defenses in place to keep that from happening. Behaving angrily kept me from going past the anger to the deeper feeling of hurt. My emotional defense had been perfected over the years and was firmly in place.

Mr. Hunt said, "Ms. Edwards, it isn't useful for you to be angry with me. I don't know anything about what happened in 1951. I'm calling you as a courtesy."

I realized he was right. He didn't have to call me, and I did appreciate the call. His words touched a chord in my body and soul that allowed me to relax, at least momentarily. My anger dissipated as I listened to him talk. Inside, moment by moment, I vacillated between wanting to be nice to him and feeling like directing my anger toward him.

"Even if you couldn't validate my information, I can't believe the *Lubbock Avalanche-Journal* would print articles making a law-breaking, bootlegging criminal like Pinkie out to be some kind of hero." His compassion allowed me to feel softer. My eyes began to tear and my voice began to crack. During our conversation I realized that I didn't really know what had happened in our accident!! At forty-one years old, I was having an epiphany! I felt like a kaleidoscope that was in the midst of a change. There was no focus, and then suddenly a very clear focus. I was completely curious about the facts around the death of my parents. This kind of intense curiosity was a first for me in regards to our accident.

"You aren't the only person we've received negative letters from about our articles on Pinkie. I wish we had never printed those articles in the paper."

I liked Mr. Hunt. Of course, it helped that he felt the way I did about the articles about Pinkie. I told him that perhaps the articles I referred to were from the *Lynn County News* as opposed to the *Lubbock Avalanche-Journal*. Our conversation created a great many questions for which I had no answers.

Mr. Hunt continued, "I'm willing to print any article you write, but it has to be one that will keep us all out of court. I can't jeopardize the newspaper, and I think you might want to reconsider jeopardizing yourself. You made a lot of accusations that I'm unable to substantiate."

"I understand, and I will write a letter for you to publish. And, I will find the articles I'm talking about and send them to you. I realize I have a lot of questions that no one has ever answered."[2]

Mr. Hunt agreed to send me copies of the articles about Pinkie, so I could see for myself just how much Mr. Cochran had insulted my family. As I hung up the telephone, I was grateful to Mr. Hunt for bringing to my attention that I DID NOT KNOW the details of the events surrounding our accident in May of 1951!!

I was stunned! As a child, I had asked a few questions which were answered in such a way that I felt it best not to ask more. When I was older, I asked Granny numerous times why no one was ever prosecuted for the death of my parents and she always replied, "We had other things to do, like raising children." I would say no more realizing they had their hands full. There were wounds for everyone in my family, not just myself. It seemed difficult for them to talk about anything that brought up hurtful or painful feelings and I became like them. The pain was too much, so we avoided it. We were no different from most other families, living according to the pain and pleasure principle: going toward pleasure and away from pain. If anyone talked about my parents and it became apparent someone was in pain, the subject was dropped. To say something that would elicit a tear would be seen as mean or abusive. My family would say, "there was no call for it." Since nothing could be done to bring my parents back, what would be the point of bringing a person to tears, especially a child. A child is supposed to have a carefree life, running, playing, and being happy. My grandparents wanted that life for me, but that dream ended for me before my grandparents entered the picture.

When I was grown, why had I not tried to discover the facts? I knew it had something to do with protecting my family, as well as myself, from the pain. I felt differently now, and I made myself a promise. I would investigate and find out the details around our accident in 1951. I wanted to know for myself. And, I vowed not to let anyone make light of my parents' deaths, even if they did write for the Associated Press.

CHAPTER TWENTY-SEVEN

*"He (Pinkie) drove us crazy.
But I couldn't help but like him."*[1]

It had been years since I'd looked at the newspaper articles written about our accident. I couldn't remember if Pinkie was mentioned or not, but I thought Pinkie was involved. After rummaging through my bookshelves and finding the articles in one of my scrapbooks, I sat down and reread them looking for any meaningful information.

One article, written in the *Lynn County News* said, "Investigation by officers revealed that Roy Monroe Maxey, driving a 1951 Lincoln, coming from 'somewhere south' en route 'somewhere north' stopped at Sand, on the Dawson-Gaines county line, between 7 and 8 p.m. and picked up Mr. and Mrs. Riley. It is said Mr. Maxey and Mr. Riley are cousins. The three are believed to have been riding in the front seat of the Lincoln. As the Edwards neared the intersection of a farm road with U.S. Highway 380 at West Point, suddenly from the south the Lincoln drove out into the highway. The tracks showed that Edwards had applied his brakes, but the two cars crashed on the paving, veered to the right, and came to rest about thirty feet apart at the northwest corner of the intersection. The Edwards car, after the impact, crashed head-on into a telephone pole and the Lincoln rolled over on its top."[2]

It didn't say anything about alcohol or Pinkie. I continued reading, "Maxey was pinned behind the steering wheel in the Lincoln. Mrs. Riley, still alive, was wedged against him. Mr. Riley had been thrown out of the machine, and the car had landed on top of him. His head was crushed."[3]

Was it necessary to be so graphic in their description? But I had to remind myself I wanted to know all the details. Even though I didn't remember the accident consciously, my body recorded all traumas. Anxiety was traveling throughout my body. Nothing was wrong with my body in the sense of getting sick, but my body was remembering in its own way through bodily held tension.

"Around the gory scene, covering a wide area, whiskey bottles and beer cans were strewn. Evidently the back seat of the Lincoln had been removed and the car was packed with liquor. Though many of the liquor bottles were broken, two cars and a pick-up truck were required to bring that liquor and beer which was not destroyed by the crash into town."[4]

Mr. Hunt was right about there being no mention of Pinkie. Why had I thought Pinkie was involved if he wasn't?

I continued to read, "The Rileys are survived by 10 children, three of whom are grown and seven of whom are small: five sons, Orville, Jesse J., David Earl and J.W., all of Sand, and Billy Don of Stephenville; and five daughters, Doris Jane, Donnie Ruth, Dorothy Nell, Dora Marie, and Dela May, all of Sand; and two grandchildren."[5]

Oh my goodness!! Look how many lives were tragically altered in this one accident! I had focused on my sister and myself since we were the ones in the accident. Now I began to wonder what had happened to those other children. No matter what had happened to them, I knew we shared the same hole in our hearts, the same loss of our parents.

When I was teaching high school, I studied the negative effects of alcohol and discovered that one in three people are in some way significantly negatively impacted by the use and abuse of alcohol. This one accident changed the primary family structure for many people. There certainly was a rippling effect.

As I read an article written by Jerry Hall for the *Lubbock Avalache-Journal*, my eyes filled with tears. "...A watch found on Mrs. Riley's arm was smashed at 9:20 p.m. That was the fatal moment. But it's not the end for the two little girls. Calva An and Elva Jo are young. They do not realize what has happened. With tragedy came the kind and helping hands of uncles and aunts, cousins and grandparents, and a host of friends.

The girls will wonder many times why they do not have a father and mother. And its going to be hard to explain. But time will help.

For those who survived it will take a long time to forget . . .

And if it were possible to talk, five of those involved in the accident might have the comment —'We didn't think it would happen to us . . .'

But it did . . ."[6]

CHAPTER TWENTY-EIGHT

"Jerry Hall of Austin...says Pinkie's whiskey fleet in Lubbock included false bottom cattle trucks, taxis and even a hearse."[1]

I often went next door to the convenience-store from my chiropractic office to get a cup of hot tea and say hello to the employees. One day I wanted to take a break, and as I walked across the driveway that divided my office and the convenience-store, I saw a man lying against the outer brick wall of my office. I continued my walk and said hello to the convenience-store employees, got my cup of tea, and walked back to my office. I stopped beside the man lying against my office building and wondered if he was drunk or dead. He appeared to be homeless, because he was dirty, disheveled and had a backpack lying beside him. I wanted to check for a pulse, but restrained myself. I went inside my office and called the police. When I explained the situation, they advised me not to touch him because, if he had passed out from alcohol, he might become violent. They told me to leave him alone and they would handle the situation. A few minutes later I saw a police car pull up. They put the man in the police car and advised me that he was on his way to detox. It was sad to see what alcohol could do. Did he have a wife and children somewhere? He was someone's son. It was frightening how many ways alcohol could tear a life apart. It certainly tore my life apart, but in a way that looked much different.

I left my office at noon and went home for lunch and to check the mail. Jon Hunt had sent the newspaper articles promptly. He included a letter reminding me that he was willing to review another letter to the editor if it had fewer legal pitfalls for the newspaper.

Grateful to him, I glanced at all five pages before I began reading. I stopped and focused my attention on one page with a picture of Pinkie. So that was what he looked like! A balding and chubby guy, he appeared friendly and approachable. He did not appear a handsome man, but seemed, even in a photograph to have a certain charisma. I realized that every time I thought of Pinkie, I saw a "Pinkie's Liquor Store" sign because I had never had a face to connect with the name.

Pinkie was described as a "...shy, gentle, stuttering, freckle-faced, enigmatic hulk who grew up dirt poor and made a fortune bootlegging whiskey and founded the most far flung, Byzantine liquor store chain in all of Texas."[2]

I wondered why everyone referred to him as Pinkie, a nickname, when his legal name was Tom Roden?

I continued reading the articles and every few paragraphs I found something that tore at my heart, so I had to stop and cry a few tears. I did just that after reading a comment made by a former Governor of Texas, Preston Smith, who said, "I would class Tom Roden as one of the top ten people I know. The state and the community have lost a great man."[3] I couldn't believe he made such a comment about a bootlegger! My mind couldn't grasp it.

The time I had scheduled for lunch was over. Although I loved my work, and it was the most satisfying aspect of my life, this was one afternoon I was anxious to conclude with my last patient so I could go home and finish reading the articles.

CHAPTER TWENTY-NINE

*"To label Pinkie a visionary or an entrepreneur
would not be straining the truth:
his actions speak for themselves.
With West Texas ripe for the taking, he took."*[1]

Arriving home shortly after six in the evening, I changed my clothes and sat on the couch devouring the articles. "When Prohibition was repealed in 1933, Pinkie went semi-legitimate, opening his first liquor store the following year in Big Spring, west of Sweetwater.

That's not to suggest that Texas was suddenly awash in legal whiskey.

At the time, vast stretches of West Texas were dry, and would remain so for years to come. Across thousands of square miles, Prohibition was not dead or even gravely wounded.

Those wanting to purchase legal whiskey often had to travel a hundred miles or more. Even today, large sections of the region remain dry except for scattered tiny and remote crossroads where beer and liquor are sold.

To label Pinkie a visionary or an entrepreneur would not be straining the truth: his actions speak for themselves. With West Texas ripe for the taking, he took.

The Big Spring store provided a facade of legitimacy and an early base for what would become a multi-million dollar enterprise, both legal and otherwise.

And West Texans always were a thirsty lot with a lusty affection for cold beer and good, bad or bootleg whiskey.

'Pinkie never considered bootlegging a crime,' joked one of his old cronies. 'He considered it a public service.'

Pinkie roamed his kingdom endlessly, meeting people, mapping routes, scouting potential store sites and almost always befriending bankers and making loans or deposits."[2]

I had to take a break. My mind was overwhelmed with questions and my heart felt burdened. They thought it was funny that I was orphaned? I couldn't see how bootlegging could be considered so funny. I could feel a rip in my heart as if someone had stuck a knife in it. Losing my parents had been bad enough, but to read this article making Pinkie out to be some kind of folk hero, made me feel wounded all over again. I found a box of tissues before I continued reading the articles.

"Legislators created the Texas Liquor Control Board (LCB) in 1935 to regulate the industry and ride herd on the bootleggers, who were prospering in the wide open spaces of West Texas.

From his corner hotel suite in Big Spring, Pinkie used binoculars to keep an eye on the local LCB office down the street, notifying his runners when agents were in and out and on the prowl.

His gifts of holiday hams, turkeys, steaks and liquor would come later.

Dan McCarty, a weekly newspaper publisher in Glen Rose, would one day maintain that 'Pinkie's clout with the LCB was almost mystical,' but his spell was not universal.

'If he had an unfriendly sheriff,' Gene Garrison said, 'he wouldn't drive through his county. But he would send in gifts to make friends.'

Pinkie showed up one day in brother Bill's office and said, 'I've got to find a way to drive from Big Spring to Lubbock without getting on a highway,' a distance just over 100 miles.

In Bill's single engine airplane, Pinkie scouted out every dirt road between the cities, but could not figure a way to get around a small town.

'He finally found a rancher who gave him a key to his gate,' Bill said."[3]

"In the mid-1950's, the Texas House Crime Investigating Committee convened in Amarillo to look into bootlegging activities in West Texas, particularly Lubbock. Then the biggest and wettest dry town in Texas, Lubbock was a tempting 120 miles north of Pinkie's Odessa base.

The Houston Post, in a series on bootlegging, reported:

'Testimony, telephone calls and other records showed beyond a doubt that a multi-million dollar syndicate, controlled by one Tom (Pinkie) Roden of Odessa, sold most of the liquor which ended up in Lubbock and other dry West Texas cities.

'A single store called The Farm near the Ector County line on the Odessa-Andrews highway sold $47,266 of liquor within three days after it opened. Its monthly sales thereafter...ranged from $279,310 to $93,639, and never lower.

'And that for a country store 25 miles from a city.'

In reality, the country oasis was not that remote but it most likely was a legal entity created for a nefarious purpose, namely to service a network of bootleggers.

'It was a fantastic store, sittin' out there in the boonies,' says Gabe West, who once ran the operation for Pinkie. 'There wasn't nothing else out there.

'You'd have to see it to believe it.'...

'A single Lubbock bootlegger bought whiskey at wholesale for $47,000 in 30 days from one of the 10 stores,' the Post reported. Pinkie's unusual blend of legal and illegal whiskey dealing was a law enforcement nightmare...

On occasion, he lobbied state liquor officials to replace troublesome agents with more compliant colleagues. But he probably used less subtle methods of persuasion, too.

In at least one instance, Pinkie was suspected of sending an aide to fire a warning shot through the window of an uncommonly aggressive investigator.

No one was hurt, but the bullet narrowly missed the agent's wife and the infant child she was holding."4

I stopped reading and felt inside how scared that woman must have been for her life as well as for that of her newborn. It was hard for me to understand just how much Pinkie got by with hurting other people. It wasn't just that he did those illegal things as many people do. Jails are full of them. What bothered me were the statements by the highest elected state officials and even the people who spent their lives chasing Pinkie. I had to ask 'why' as I read:

"At his death in 1989, Pinkie's long-time friend John Ben Sheppard, a former state attorney general, declared:

'We'll never know the extent of his contributions or philanthropy. He let others take the bows, and he did the work and paid the bills.'"5

I found it incredible that the state attorney general would be a good friend to the most powerful bootlegger in West Texas. But the story became more incredible as I continued to read.

"'Pinkie wrote an awful lot of liquor law in Texas,' says his friend Gene Garrison. 'I'm a buyer, not a seller, and I don't understand it all.'

Pinkie helped found the Texas Package Stores Association and for three decades was a major force in the organization although, by choice, he never served as president.

He and fellow liquor kingpins Sidney Siegel of Dallas and James Leggett Jr. of Fort Worth comprised the group's legislative committee and soon became known as 'The Three Musketeers' of the industry.

They were powerful and popular and a familiar sight at the state Capitol when the Legislature was in session.

Texas Beverage News, a trade publication, sent a reporter to Austin once for a story on a legislative controversy involving the package store association and another retail group. The reporter asked the lobbyist for the opposition to assess his chances.

'Well, I tell you,' he replied. 'Sometimes when Mr. Roden and Mr. Siegel and

Mr. Leggett are prowling the halls of the Capitol, it's just mighty hard to move a liquor bill.'"[6]

I found myself wishing for a private conversation with the former governor of the state of Texas, as well as the head of the liquor control board. In fact, as I kept reading, I found myself wanting to address the whole legislative body of Texas. Was I the only person who found this insane?

But instead, I walked to the kitchen and made a cup of tea to settle my stomach. Reading these articles had literally made me sick.

CHAPTER THIRTY

"Friends called him Pinkie, 'The Wizard of the West.'"[1]

I couldn't stay away from the articles for long. They pulled at me. The articles spanned the early years and the later years with the dividing dates being somewhere in the mid-Sixties. The articles continued, "Pinkie master-minded a stunning, incredibly profitable scheme to incorporate a tiny precinct totally surrounded by Abilene, the so-called Buckle on the Bible Belt.

Its name: Impact.

With a 1960 metropolitan population of 120,000, Abilene, in the very heart of a dry area, was a prime target for whiskey merchants of whatever stripe.

"Project Impact involved 50 or so people in a tiny, isolated, largely overlooked or ignored part of Abilene. In effect, they quietly voted to incorporate, then legalized off-premises sale of alcoholic beverages."

By no means as simple as it sounds, Impact was the forerunner for any number of similar booze-related schemes across the state.

As always, Pinkie spurned the limelight, though privately pulling the political strings. A colorful local figure named Dallas Perkins, Impact's first mayor, got the credit but Pinkie and Abilene attorney Beverly Tarpley got it done.

'Dallas was the originator of Impact but Pinkie had the expertise of liquor laws and politics to make the operation successful and keep it running for a long period of time,' Ms. Tarpley said."

According to James Leggett, Pinkie didn't give Perkins much choice in dealing himself into the Impact caper, declaring:

'I've been selling liquor in Abilene all of my life and I intend to keep selling it.'...

On weekends and holidays in particular, motorists lined up for blocks to buy beer and booze, and Pinkie and Perkins made millions, tax figures showed.

'All it took to defeat it was for Abilene to go wet, but it took a long, long time to do it,' Ms. Tarpley said.

Abilene's churchgoers and Pinkie, their unlikely ally, saw to that.

When the city did vote wet, presumably dooming Impact as an oasis, a reporter telephoned Pinkie for comment.

'Will this break you?' the reporter asked.

'It would have, had I not long ago prepared for it,' Pinkie replied grandly.

'But thanks to the good Christians of Abilene, I will die a wealthy man.'

Perhaps the last of his special if not always noble breed, Pinkie is gone but his legacy will be with Texas for generations to come. Like no other, he shaped the crazy-quilt laws governing how, where, what and when Texans buy and drink their booze.

Liquor wise, Lubbock was, is, and may always be peculiar, thanks in part to Pinkie.

Historically bone dry except for private clubs, Lubbock was probably the bootlegging capital of the world until the mid-Sixties. That's when a precinct on the southern tip of town approved the sale of beer and liquor for off-premises consumption.

"Pinkie was probably the first liquor baron to open a store on the milelong 'Strip,' so-named for its similarity to the neon glitter of Las Vegas.

Owners paid handsomely for the lucrative leases, and to protect their investments they vigorously resisted efforts to legalize liquor in Lubbock, either by the drink or the bottle.

Hotels, restaurants and others obviously wanted to sell mixed drinks.

Eventually, insiders say, Pinkie realized that a compromise might be the best bet. He joined forces with liquor-by-the-drink advocates in exchange for preserving the off-premises sanctity of the Strip.

To this day, Lubbock's 185,000 residents can drink freeely in clubs or restaurants but must drive to the 'Strip' to buy liquor by the bottle or six-packs of beer.

And they sometimes pay the highest prices in Texas."[2]

Reading this excerpt, I began to recall the day when I was with Grandpa as we were driving by the Strip, and he said, "I guess he thinks he is awful smart." He was referring to Pinkie. Grandpa's words echoed in my head, "He is the reason Calvin and Pearle are dead."

CHAPTER THIRTY ONE

*"A guy (Pinkie) who spent a lifetime outfoxing
or befriending Texas cops, sheriffs, Rangers and liquor agents,
as much for fun as profit."*[1]

I kept reading until I had read all five articles. I had a box of tissues beside me and, when I finished reading the articles, there was a big pile of used tissues on the floor. I picked them up and carried them to the waste basket in the kitchen and then I put water on the stove for a cup of tea. I had a wide assortment of teas from which to choose. I knew I used the hot cup of tea to soothe my psyche and my body, but I felt I needed it. This was a typical way I substituted an activity, like drinking tea, for feeling the emotional pain. The activity took me away from the intensity of the feelings. I needed to numb myself to all of the feelings that arose from all I was learning.

With the newspaper articles about Pinkie around me, as well as the newspaper articles about my parents' accident, I called my sister, Calva, in San Diego. It felt like only she could understand how these articles had affected me.

"I got the articles from the *Lubbock Avalanche-Journal*. You just won't believe what they said about bootleggers. The articles started with 'some of the most honorable people in the world are bootleggers.'[2] Can you believe this guy? And then the second article starts with 'the days of the wild West may be over, but the legacy left by the bootlegging "Wizard of the West" may never fade.'[3] We've certainly lived a legacy from bootlegging." My voice started to crack. "I just can't understand why they're so proud of that, or as Grandpa would say, 'why do they think that is so cute?'"

"That's pretty incredible, huh," Calva said.

"Listen to this Calva," I said, continuing to read to her from the articles, "'For those who knew Tom 'Pinkie' Roden knew that he singlehandledly shaped the crazy Texas quilt-like laws governing how, where, what and when Texans could buy and drink their booze."[4]

"Pinkie was a tough, shrewd, hard-drinking gambler and bootlegger who spent half his life breaking laws and the other half writing, reshaping, defending and upholding new ones.'"[5]

"It is hard to believe they would print that," Calva said. "I want you to send me a copy of the articles."

"When I talked with Mr. Hunt, I realized I didn't really know what happened around our accident and I'm going to find out."

"How are you going to do that?" she asked.

"I'm not sure, but I'm going to investigate it. In one of those articles about Pinkie, a man by the name of Jerry Hall was mentioned, and it said he now lives in Austin. I got the newspaper articles out from 1951 about our wreck, and it was Jerry Hall who wrote the articles for the paper. I think I'll call him and ask him if he knows whether Pinkie was involved with our accident." I paused, waiting for her opinion.

"He may remember the accident, because it was a big story at the time," Calva remarked.

"Yes, and he was the one that wrote in the paper at the time of the accident—here let me find it—oh here it is: '... But it's not the end for the two little girls.'"[6]

"Yes, I remember that article," she said.

"Listen to this Calva. I'm reading from the articles written by Mike Cochran. 'Pinkie showed up one day in brother Bill's office and said, "I've got to find a way to drive from Big Spring to Lubbock without getting on a highway."'[7] That was the road they were traveling when we had our accident! I can't believe they would think all of this is wonderful." My voice cracked and tears rolled down my cheeks.

"I know, Elva," my sister said.

"What really hurts is that it sounds like all these people who are talking about Pinkie and the bootlegging business are laughing. It's a great big joke. It's never been a joke to me that I didn't have parents." I continued to cry because I couldn't tolerate people laughing about what had been so deeply painful in my life. It felt like they were laughing about what we had gone through and how our lives were changed because of bootlegging. I took it personally because that's how it affected my life—in a very personal way. I knew the articles didn't mention the wreck, but did this author, Mike Cochran, think it was possible for Pinkie to do all the things he mentioned in these articles without many innocent people being hurt? Those innocent people didn't seem to matter to Mike Cochran.

"Did you know Pinkie spent some time in jail?" I asked Calva.

"No, I don't really know anything about him, except that he was involved in the alcohol business," she replied.

"His wife said, 'He was only in for three months. He wasn't supposed to have gone at all. It was suppose to have been fixed.' The article said she was hinting at political hanky panky. It says Ma Ferguson was governor of the state of Texas at the time and she got him out, hinting that he didn't stay his full time. Then he adds, 'Ma was a business lady.'[8] I feel like I'm in a western movie and I am getting the good guys and the bad guys all mixed up, you know?" I asked with a tension in my voice. "How many governor's of Texas and legislators did Pinkie control?"

"You have to remember," Calva reminded me, "those people probably never even knew about our accident."

"Maybe yes, maybe no. What difference does it make? The people we are talking about are supposed to be trusted public servants. Pinkie felt fine about running illegal alcohol and illegal gambling, so why would he care if a few good people were killed or orphaned along the way? It's obvious Pinkie had no scruples, but I'd like to think these other elected officials did," I said.

"I know," Calva said.

"I have to wonder how those people could not have known about our accident? I guess you could say we were little more than casualties on Pinkie's playing field. I guess we were expendable annoyances."

"It certainly seems that way," Calva said.

"I'll let you go. We can talk about these articles better when you have a copy. I'll send them to you tomorrow. I'm going to call Jerry Hall."

"Good luck," Calva said.

CHAPTER THIRTY-TWO

*"Pinkie was a tough, shrewd,
hard-drinking gambler and bootlegger
who spent half his life breaking laws
and the other half writing,
reshaping, defending and
upholding new ones."*[1]

After bidding my sister goodnight, I immediately dialed information in Austin, Texas, and got the number for Jerry Hall. The article written by him after our accident in 1951 was right beside me. I took a deep breath and dialed his number. A woman answered and I asked for Jerry Hall. About fifteen seconds later, I heard a distinctive Texas man's voice on the other end of the line, "Hello."

"Hello, is this Jerry Hall?" I asked. I couldn't help but be a little apprehensive and glad to have the gift of gab.

"Yes, this is Jerry Hall."

"I'm sure there's more than one Jerry Hall, so I want to make sure I have the right Jerry Hall," I said, realizing this must sound strange to him.

He seemed a bit amused, chuckled and said, "OK."

"Are you the Jerry Hall that was a reporter for the *Lubbock Avalanche-Journal* in the early 1950's?" I asked.

"Yes, I am," he replied.

"Well, then, I am a flash from your past. I have no idea if you will remember me. My name is Elva Jo Edwards, and I was born in Lubbock and raised in Tahoka," I said, and then paused to give him a moment to comprehend my statement.

"Oh, yeah, I'm familiar with Tahoka. It's just south of Lubbock," he replied.

"That's right, and back in May of 1951, there was a bad car accident between Tahoka and Brownfield where five adults were killed. I was only nineteen-months-old at the time, and I survived the accident along with my sister. You wrote an article about the accident and I have it here in front of me," I concluded, waiting for him to remember.

"Oh, yeah, I remember you," he stated. "That was a real sad thing. I remember going up to your hospital room. You and your sister were in the same hospital room. Now which one are you, the older one or the younger one?" he asked, giving me confidence that he did, indeed, remember us.

"I'm the younger one," I responded. Continuing, I said, "I now live in Denver, and my sister lives in San Diego. How long have you been away from Lubbock?" I asked.

"I worked at the *Lubbock Avalanche-Journal* just out of college, and I haven't lived there in a long time. I'm the Chief of Staff for John Montford here in Austin," he said.

"Well, I called you because I was wondering if you saw the series of articles about Pinkie in the Texas papers back in October?"

Mr. Hall chuckled and said, "Yes, I saw them."

"Well, I'm wondering, since you were a reporter at the time, if you remember Pinkie being involved or implicated at all in the accident that killed my parents?"

"Well, you know, that was a long time ago. Let me see. I don't remember his name ever being mentioned in connection with that accident. No, I sure don't," he said with certainty.

"Well, I couldn't believe those articles. They made him out to be some sort of hero," I said, changing the subject slightly.

"Yes, they did. He was something else." Again, he chuckled. I liked Mr. Hall. His voice and mannerisms reminded me of my Texas roots.

I ended the conversation expressing my thanks for his time. I hung up the telephone feeling really confused. He would have known, wouldn't he, if there had been any connection between the bootlegging car and Pinkie?[2]

CHAPTER THIRTY-THREE

*"The state and the community
have lost a great man (Pinkie),"
said Texas Governor Preston Smith*[1]

Later the same evening

I made a pot of tea. I suppose if I had been inclined toward alcohol or drugs, they would have been the object of my compulsion. My upbringing was so deathly against alcohol and since my family was killed because of alcohol, I was not drawn in that direction. Drugs had not been attractive to me for numerous reasons. It almost felt like tea was my drug of choice. Most of the time I actually drank the tea, but I often found full cups of tea sitting around my house. It seemed that the mere act of preparing the tea was enough to numb part of my anxiety.

With tea in hand, I walked back to the sofa and sat amidst the articles about Pinkie. I took a sip of tea and sat the cup on the end table. I picked up the articles and attempted to sort them. When I originally read the articles, I had underlined important sentences or key phrases. As I quickly scanned the articles, my attention was drawn to the word Montford. He was one of Pinkie's "contacts" in Austin.[2] Wasn't he the person Jerry Hall had just said he worked for? Thoughts ran through my mind, and they weren't very nice thoughts.

I was needing someone to bounce ideas off of to help me decide a direction for my investigation. Polly and Wilson Edwards came to mind. Even though I didn't know them very well, they had always been willing to talk to me about my parents, so I called.

"Yes, this is Polly. How are you doing, Elva Jo?"

"Well, I'm upset." My voice started to crack. I really didn't want to cry while on the telephone with her, but I could no longer hold my tears back. "Did you and Wilson see the series of articles about Pinkie in the paper back in October?"

"Yes, we did. They were just terrible. Wilson threatened at the time to write a letter to the editor, but he didn't."

I told Polly about writing the letter to Mr. Hunt, his calling me, receiving the articles, and calling Mr. Hall.

Polly said, "Now Elva Jo, it was the talk of the town the next day about how that was Pinkie's driver, and they were running from the liquor control board. I don't know why the newspaper reporter didn't know it." She paused, then continued with, "You know, it was a big, big deal and that is all anyone talked about for days."

"Polly, I want to find out what happened," I said. "Writing that series of articles and making this common criminal out to be some sort of hero is like someone spitting on the graves of my parents. They're not here to defend themselves, so I'll do it for them. He wrote so much good stuff about Pinkie. My God, he even made bootlegging and outfoxing the police seem as if they were accomplishments. Could this writer not know that, in all of Pinkie's criminal activities, a lot of innocent, good, and decent people have been hurt?"

"Well, I'd be just like you. I'd want to know what happened, just for my own peace of mind."

I appreciated Polly's support. "I'm going to write a response to the articles and the editor of the *Lubbock Avalanche-Journal* promised me he'd print it. But, I want to find out more about what happened in regards to the accident. You know, Grandpa had some reason for thinking Pinkie was responsible. In my letter to the paper, I won't mention Pinkie's name, but I am going to investigate until I find out what I want to know! I'm embarrassed that it's taken me this long to realize I don't know the particulars about something that was such an important moment in my life. You know, it just never set too well with my family if I asked too many questions, so I think I simply did what would make everyone happy—say nothing. But this pushed me too far."[3]

CHAPTER THIRTY-FOUR

*"It would be difficult to fault Tom "Pinkie" Roden's
choice of political cronies, since one,
Bob Bullock, is arguably the most powerful person
now in state government. He liked to say
he opened every campaign in Odessa
with his friend Pinkie at his side."*[1]

Living close to my office allowed me the convenience of stopping by the office after hours or on the weekend. With the sun fading over the mountains on a Saturday afternoon, I stopped by the office to pick up a deposit to take to the bank before meeting friends for a movie. I opened the door and immediately locked it behind me so I wouldn't be surprised by unwanted guests. While sitting at the front desk, I decided to return a patient's call, and as we were visiting, I heard a hard knock on the glass front door. I looked up to see a homeless man standing on the other side of the door looking at me. Putting my patient on hold, I went to the front door and, without opening it, I asked, "What do you want?' I recognized the man as he had visited my office before, and his odor indicated an obvious alcohol problem. He was the kind of person the police had told me to avoid.

Gently and beseechingly he pleaded, "I want you to let me in. I want to take a nap."

"I'm sorry, I'm closed," I responded. I felt compassion for his plight, but I couldn't put myself at risk. I returned to my phone call. He continued beating on my door and, in an effort to acknowledge him, I went to the door four more times and told him I couldn't open the door. After the second time, I ended the conversation with my patient and called the police. I was unable to get him to move away from the door, and I wanted to leave.

Suddenly he became violent, beating the door and screaming curse words at me. I was afraid he was going to break the door down. Suddenly, lights flashed on the homeless man. He and I both looked to see where the lights were coming from. I wanted to think the police were responding, but instead a man drove up in his pickup and parked directly in front of my office. He saw a man yelling and beating his clenched fist on my door.

As the driver got out of his pickup, the homeless man fled running down the street to another business. The driver of the pickup walked up to my front door and looked in to see why the man was so agitated. I opened the door, thanked him, explained the situation, and told him the police were on their way. He had parked his pickup in front of my business in order to go to the business next door.

That drunken man brought home to me the incredibleness of the statements in those articles about the bootlegging 'hero' of West Texas. Didn't Mr. Cochran know that Pinkie's actions, his way of living in the world, and his disregard for human life was hurtful to others? That poor man suffered from alcohol addiction. No, it wasn't Pinkie fault but I'm sure there were plenty of alcoholics in West Texas who suffered from Pinkie's bootlegging.

Feeling spent, I gathered my things and went home. Changing my plans, I decided to use the evening for writing the letter to the *Lubbock Avalanche-Journal*. After an hour of fussing over my words, I proofread my letter.

> *"Dear Editor,*
>
> *What is the purpose of making a person like Pinkie Roden out to be some sort of folk hero? I did not read anything that impressed me.*
>
> *What good did he do for his fellow man? Oh, yes, he gave money to charity. So what? Most people who have money give to charity. Besides, money made from bootlegging is illegal money anyway—money that I wouldn't want to be associated with if I were a politician!*
>
> *I hope no impressionable young people read the series of articles as they may get the idea that to be a hero they need to be like Pinkie—breaking the law while laughing in the lawman's face.*
>
> *I have my own beef with bootleggers. My mother, father, and grandmother were killed in 1951 in an accident with a bootlegger, leaving my sister and me orphans when I was one year old. The wreck claimed five lives and left twelve children orphans. I do not consider that a public service.*
>
> *I do not know of any person who has become a better person through the use of alcohol. Not one. And yet, I know many people whose lives have been impacted in some negative way through alcohol.*
>
> *Pinkie simply believed the end (money, greed, and power) justified the means (bootlegging.)*
>
> *If Mr. Cochran wants to write articles about people who are heroes, perhaps he should meet my grandmother, Nellie*

Edwards, who is now ninty-six years old, living in the care center in Tahoka.

While Pinkie was busy making money bootlegging, my grandmother and grandfather were raising two little girls whose lives were shattered when their parents lives were taken in an accident.

While Pinkie was hobnobbing in Austin, making the proper political connections, my grandmother was in her 60's and 70's washing clothes, ironing, getting kids off to school and participating in extracurricular activities when she rightfully should have been enjoying her golden years with short visits from grandchildren and delighting in their presence.

As Mr. Cochran said, "Pinkie's legacy will be with Texas for generations to come." I will live my life with the legacy a bootlegger gave me...never being able to call anyone Mom or Dad. As Jerry Hall, formerly of the A. J. wrote about the accident and its impact on my life. "The girls will wonder many times why they do not have a father and mother. And it's going to be hard to explain."

Pinkie died of a broken heart and lonely. My grandmother, on the other hand, has a loving family to see her through her most difficult hours. Her family is devoted to her—in sickness and in health—as she has been devoted to her family. My grandmother will die while being surrounded with love.

I feel her contribution to society far outweighs Pinkie's. And yet, there is no series of articles written about her, as hers was a labor of love, not one of greed and power.

As for me, I am glad I come from a long line of love instead of a long line of bootleggers.

Elva Edwards"[2]

I was pleased with the letter and put it in an envelope and sent it to Mr. Hunt the next morning.

CHAPTER THIRTY-FIVE

"Pinkie lived and breathed politics."[1]

During my morning walk with my best friends, Shirley and her husband Michael, I told them about the response I had written to the articles about Pinkie. Then I continued, "You know, I've been thinking about our accident, and I'm going to write two attorneys who would probably know what happened. Since Calva and I were wards of the state, Grandpa had to have a guardianship and be under bond. I know this one guy was our attorney and he might know something. What do you think, Mike?"

Mike was an attorney, too. "Well, you can always write a letter and find out," he said.

"I think this attorney lives in Lubbock now. His family moved from Tahoka my senior year. He has a son who was one year ahead of me in school, and his wife was my first grade teacher. The other attorney became a judge when I was in high school and was a conservator of my great granddad's estate. I'm going to write both of them. I'd still like to know why no one was ever prosecuted. Granny always said they were too busy raising children, but Michael, wouldn't it be the state's job to make the charges?"

"Yes, the state is the only one who could file criminal charges. Your grandparents could not have filed the charges even if they had wanted to," Michael replied.

"Well, I'm going to see if these two attorneys will tell me about the accident."

At the end of our walk together, I turned to say farewell, and asked Michael, "So, who are you going to sue today?" We laughed because I asked him that question at the end of each walk. What a great way to start my day, because I was totally energized and ready for a day at the office after my morning walk.

Within the week I wrote each lawyer a letter. I wondered if they would remember me? I was sure Truett Smith, the judge, would remember me because he watched me grow up while we attended the same Southern Baptist Church. I wondered how to approach this subject forty years after the fact. My request was simple: what happened? I wanted details. Was anyone prosecuted for the accident? If not, why not? I was embarrassed to ask questions to which I felt I should know the answer. It was as if I had been asleep to my own history all these years and suddenly woke up. I would be satisfied just to know the truth and was hoping that forty years later, I could still find it.

"11-22-91
Dear Truett,

I hope this holiday season finds you and Lucille happy and well.

I am writing to you for some information. I have a feeling you probably know some of what I want and I am asking you to please tell me.

Recently a series of articles were written in the Lubbock Avalanche-Journal about Pinkie. They praised the way he trained his runners to go the back roads with their lights off to bootleg alcohol to Lubbock. I personally am appalled with the articles. As you know, my parents and grandmother were killed by such bootleggers. I wrote a letter to the editor of the AJ and am in process of writing one that will be printed.

Frankly, here it is forty years later and I do not understand what happened. A few times I've asked my family why someone wasn't prosecuted for that accident. Five people were killed. Twelve children were orphaned. Their reply to me was they had more urgent things to do like raising children. But it was not the responsibility of my family to prosecute but the responsibility of the state. I do not know who was D.A. or Chief of Police in 1951, but wouldn't it have been their job to prosecute? It was the responsibility of the state. I've heard a rumor that someone was paid off to keep it out of the courts. I also heard it was in court. What did take place?

I am not out for revenge. What's done is done. I am asking you for this information to further my own healing process. I don't ask you to understand what I am going through, just to help me piece together what happened.

Grandpa always blamed Pinkie. He said the driver was Pinkie's driver. None of the newspaper articles mention his name. Do you know? Is there any documentation? Do you know of any court action? If so what happened? If not, why not? Do you know if someone was paid off or silenced in some way? What were the rumors you heard?

I would really appreciate your dipping into the past and letting me know. Writing this article to the AJ has brought up a lot of questions I realize I do not have the answers to. You are one of the few people I feel I can ask who would know. Thank you very much.

Fondly,
Elva Jo"[2]

CHAPTER THIRTY-SIX

"From his corner hotel suite in Big Spring, Pinkie used binoculars to keep an eye on the local LCB office down the street, notifying his runners when agents were in and out and on the prowl."[1]

The articles had shaken me to the core. Yet externally I was more settled and sedate than ever in my adult life. I lived a simple life of getting up each morning at six, taking a walk, doing a meditation, going to work, enjoying friends, visiting my Granny and extended family in Texas three or four times a year, and visiting my sister and niece in California about once a year. I was a lifetime student interested in many healing techniques, and incorporated them into my practice. I had become a student on a spiritual path that recognized the importance of our psychological development in relationship to our spiritual development with the emphasis on maintaining a connection to our Being, or essential self, as we lived our ordinary lives. I saw my teacher once a week and he helped me deal with the feelings that surfaced from my investigation, while also developing my capacity to experience my essential nature. It was this teacher who helped me begin to understand how my life had been imprinted and the connection of the early accident to the other negative events in my life.

I found intimate relationships difficult and didn't seek them, although God knows I would have loved a great, low-maintenance relationship with just the right man. However, it never happened. My marriage had left me feeling used both emotionally and financially. When I loved someone, my heart opened and my brains appeared to go on a sabbatical. I wouldn't know how it felt to be treated well in a love relationship. Fear of another disappointment in the people I loved kept me from being able to be vulnerable in that realm. I saw the dysfunction, but it wasn't as if I could just be different. It didn't seem to work that way.

Walking into my house, I noticed the mail on the floor and in full view was an envelope with a return address from Truett Smith. As I picked it up, I opened the letter and read:

> *"Dec. 4, 1991*
> *Dear Elva Jo:*
> *In reply to your letter about the facts of the death of your parents and grandmother, I could not recall all of the information. So I called the county and district clerks in Tahoka*

and was given the following information:

From County Clerks office. Tahoka, Texas case filed in Lynn County No. 2862. Styled: "The State of Texas vs Roy Maxey" for negligent homicide, filed Oct. 9, 1951. Tried before a jury of six jurors. Verdict of Jury and Judgment of Court: 2 years in jail. Another case in County Court Lynn Co. No. 2855 Judgment $1000.00 Charges possession for purpose of sale in a dry area. Mitchell William's was Co. Attorney.

From District Clerk's office, Tahoka, TX. Case No. 1989 on civil docket of District Court Styled: Elva Jo and Calva An Edwards acting by their guardian, Carroll Edwards and by their attorneys Calloway Huffaker and Truett Smith vs. S.F. Wells Jr., Roy Maxey, and Tom Roden for death of parents of minors (meaning you and your sister) for the sum of $160,000+. The defendants were represented by Little and Little of Big Spring, TX. and Crenshaw, Dupree, and Milam. A settlement agreement was entered into in February 1954, signed by Carroll Edwards and Calloway for the plaintiffs and J.H. Milam, one of the lawyers for defendants for $12,000.00.

I have given you the case numbers so that if you want to see the original papers, you can go to the offices of the respective clerks and tell them the numbers and they will show them to you. I do not recall who was District Attorney at that time and did not check on that.

Of course we all knew the agreement as to damages and punishment was not adequate, but you must understand that we did not have one witness, except 2 small girls who were too young to testify. The vehicle was in the name of S.F. Wells Jr. and was driven by Roy Maxey. If we had gone to trial in the civil suit, with no evidence against Tom Roden (Pinkie) the court would, under the law, have instructed a verdict against us for we could not prove Tom Roden had any connection with the case. The vehicle was in the name of S. F. Wells, Jr., who had no property in his name and we understood that if a judgment was had against him, he would take bankruptcy and we would get nothing. The latter part of this paragraph applies to the civil suit only.

I am positive no one was paid off to avoid any court action. I hope this information will be helpful to you.

Sincerely,
Truett Smith"[2]

Unbelievable! How come I had never heard of this before in my life? I felt betrayed by my family. Why hadn't anyone told me? Tears rushed down my cheeks. I called the one person who would understand. I called Calva. She was also surprised as she had never heard about any trials. It felt like I had been deceived by people I had always known. All of the old timers in Tahoka had to have known. My family had to have known. My tears reminded me how painful the death of my parents had been for my family to even speak about. I was learning in my spiritual work that understanding and honoring my feelings was what was needed. I was learning to cry when I felt like crying. I was learning to stay present with the intolerable feelings that started in my early childhood. It sounded simple and yet was so hard, especially since my pattern of stuffing my feelings was so ingrained. I would simply go numb.

A recent telephone conversation I had with my uncle was the only hint I ever heard of a trial. I was asleep in bed when the telephone rang.

"Hello, darling. It's Uncle Robert. Mary Ann said you wanted to talk to me."

I pulled myself up into a sitting position. "Yes, I did want to ask you a few questions about my parents' accident. I'm wondering what happened and why no one was prosecuted." All these years later I was still unconscious to the fact that it was "our" accident, not "my parents" accident. I normally spoke about it as if I was not involved.

"Oh, honey, it was such a long time ago. The man driving the car was supposed to go to jail, but he never did. He was pretty bad off physically and had lots of health problems. I think he was in the hospital for over a year. I know he lost a leg, and, I think an arm." Uncle Robert paused, then continued, "But what are you doing all of this for?" he asked, sounding aggravated.

"I'm doing it because I want to," I said with a stubborn edge to my voice. Even though I didn't want to be defensive with him, I was. I continued, "For Pinkie to be made into a hero by that man who wrote those articles published in the *Lubbock Avalanche-Journal* doesn't set well with me and, since my parents are not here to defend themselves, I'm going to do it for them." I knew I sounded like I had my back up, because I did.

"So what are you going to do about it?" he asked.

"Nothing, there is nothing to do about it. It happened forty years ago. Nothing can be done about it." Again, I didn't want to have an attitude, but I could feel it in my body and hear it in my voice.

Softened, my uncle said, "I really wish you wouldn't."

I could sense a concern on his part for my well being. Changing my tone, I asked, "Why?"

"I just don't want you to get hurt."

I knew that was true. But, couldn't he see that I was already hurt? It reminded me of the times people had said, "You were so young you never even knew your parents," implying that I couldn't have been hurt by their death. People who had that view were wrong. When I was nineteen-months-old, my mother, father, and grandmother were all I knew. How could it have been otherwise?

So, it came down to the fact that a child's pain was not viewed as important. Since I couldn't voice my concerns, it was as if my concerns didn't exist. As I looked back, I wondered if people making those remarks were attempting in some way to make it permissible in their own mind that I endured such a devastating loss. That was the only way I could understand it.

CHAPTER THIRTY-SEVEN

"Oilmen, lawyers, politicians and Texas cops would call on Pinkie when they needed money, jobs, donations, legal advice, political clout or maybe just a good bottle of whiskey."[1]

December 1991

Every year I had my picture taken sitting on Santa Claus's lap and sent it to my Granny for a laugh. I was doubtful she would enjoy it this year because of her failing mental condition. A little shopping area in Denver on Gaylord Street had a Santa Claus walking down the street, so I took advantage of a photo opportunity by asking Shirley to take my picture while I sat on Santa's lap. We continued shopping and finally called it a day when I dropped her off at her house. I stopped by my house to change clothes before meeting a friend for dinner. As I walked in the house I picked up the mail and found a letter with the return address from the law office of Mitchell Williams. I quickly opened and read the letter which confirmed all the information Judge Truett Smith had reported to me in his letter. Mr. Williams informed me that he was the county attorney and since it was his first case, our family attorney, Truett Smith assisted him in the prosecution.

He also added, "under the law as it existed at that time and under the facts that were available, the maximum crime involved would be negligent homicide of the second degree against the driver of the vehicle involved whose name was Roy Maxey. It was obvious that he was a driver for Pinkie but there was no evidence tying him in with Pinkie and the car could not be traced to Pinkie. You must also realize that the two people riding with Mr. Maxey were killed in the accident. You and your sister were the only survivors.

Nevertheless, based upon the circumstantial evidence such as skid marks and other physical evidence at the scene, and a statement made by your father before he died to the effect that the driver of the other vehicle had not stopped at the stop sign, we did file a charge against Mr. Maxey for negligent homicide of the second degree, and he was prosecuted in the county court before a jury. The jury rendered a quick verdict for the maximum punishment for negligent homicide which was two years in the County Jail. Mr. Maxey appealed the decision, but it was affirmed by the Court of Criminal Appeals in the case entitled Maxey vs.

State, which for many years was considered a landmark decision concerning negligent homicide of the second degree. The same fact situation under today's law would be a felony, I understand.

I might mention that even though Mr. Maxey was convicted, he never had to serve his term, because he contracted some type of osteoporosis from the accident and his leg was amputated, I understand. The county judge and the district judge, Mr. Walter Mathis and Louis B. Reed, both now deceased, ordered that he not be confined to the Lynn County Jail since the county would then be responsible for his medical expenses and might be amenable to a law suit. I was County Attorney at the time, and I was not in favor of this procedure, but it seemed there was nothing I could do."[2]

Interesting! I had never heard of anyone not going to jail when they were convicted. But it did remind me of a statement I read in the articles by Mike Cochran. He said, "If he (Pinkie) had an unfriendly sheriff, he wouldn't drive through his county. But he would send in gifts to make friends. Gifts of holiday hams, turkeys, steaks and liquor would come later."[3] I guess I shouldn't be surprised at anything I read about Pinkie.

The attorneys' responses to my letters were very compassionate. I appreciated their assistance more than they would ever know, especially since it was forty years after the fact. Knowing I would go to Texas for Christmas, I decided to get copies of the legal cases Judge Smith spoke of so I could read, first hand, the information that was available.

CHAPTER THIRTY EIGHT

*"She (Mrs. Roden) said he (Pinkie) did indeed
have state liquor agents transferred
when they crossed him."*[1]

Tahoka, Texas, Christmas week, 1991

I arrived at the nursing home about nine o'clock to spend the morning with Granny. Time with her included combing her hair, giving her a manicure, or simply sitting with her and holding her hand. Sometimes I would take her to the dining room and play the piano and sing. If Calva or Donna were there, they, of course, would play the piano, because they played very well. We all took years of piano lessons, but they excelled where I did not. But if Calva or Donna were not at the nursing home, the residents didn't seem to mind if I hit wrong notes. They enjoyed any activity.

Depending on her ability at the moment, Granny and I talked. I sat with her until she went to lunch and then requested the staff to put her down for her afternoon nap. I'd have lunch with my family or friends and return to Granny about three-thirty in the afternoon and stay with her until dinner time. In the evenings I was free to spend time with friends and family. It was easy to feel torn about where I should be and what I should be doing. As Granny slowly deteriorated before my eyes, it was easier to leave the nursing home, since she didn't seem to care if I was there, and sometimes even preferred that I leave. As she aged, she seemed to be more content if we simply left her alone. Over the years I learned to be attuned to what was best for her. I had always included her in our family dinners, but as time went by, I could see it was in her best interest to leave her out of the confusion when our extended families got together, especially when children were involved. There was too much noise and activity which made her nervous and agitated.

The woman whose home was always open to children could no longer tolerate them. Some of my sadness was that some of her great-grandchildren saw this gripy old lady who was critical of them, and I was afraid they would be unable to see what a great and wonderful woman she was in her prime. I wanted them to know the Granny I knew and loved—the Granny of days past. I supposed each passing generation felt that way.

A few days before Christmas, Calva and I were in Lubbock doing last minute holiday shopping when we decided to go by Mitchell Williams' law office. His office was located on our way back to Tahoka from Lubbock. We walked in his door and within a few minutes, Mr. Williams appeared. I had not seen him in over twenty years. He looked older, but was still a handsome man. After becoming reacquainted, we talked for a few minutes about the appearance of the articles in the *Lubbock Avalanche-Journal*, about Pinkie, about my response to the articles, about such a big case being his first case, and about dirty politics. He told us that the driver of the bootlegging car, Maxey, said he was not driving. I was shocked! He said that the evidence pointed to Maxey being the driver because he was pinned behind the steering wheel. He said my father's death-bed statement that the bootlegging car did not have its lights on was instrumental in the guilty verdict of vehicular homicide in the second degree.[2]

One day during my Christmas visit in Tahoka, I put Granny to bed for a nap and went to meet some of my family for lunch. Tahoka, a town of approximately 3500 people, provided limited luncheon possibilities, so we decided to meet at the Dairy Queen. I would also see friends who lived in the community, many of whom I'd known all of my life.

This particular trip home many people commented about the letter I had written to the editor. One person, Melvin Burks, my high school counselor, approached me in the Dairy Queen and said, "I saw the letter you wrote about your grandmother in the newspaper." He continued, "You know, I only had one experience with Pinkie. It was before I came to Tahoka when I was a school counselor in another small town east of Lubbock. One of my student's father was a runner for Pinkie and was in jail for bootlegging. The student asked me if I would go to court and be a character witness for his father. I said I would for the boy's sake. There was a pre-trial meeting for all of us who were going to testify, and Pinkie was there. We met in a lawyer's office and after awhile Pinkie stood up and said he was going to buy everyone lunch. We went to a restaurant and ordered our meal. Pinkie didn't stay to eat lunch, but on his way out he stopped by me and leaned down and said, 'We really appreciate what you are doing.' Then he pushed a hundred dollar bill into my shirt pocket. You know, in the 1950's that was a lot of money!!" Mr. Burks chuckled and said, "The funny thing was I never heard from them again. I guess they dropped the case."

"Yeah, Mr. Burks. Money talks and you may not be the only person who got money," I said. "Why do you think the case never came to trial?"[3]

Was there no end to what that man could buy? I suppose there wasn't. In the newspaper articles, even the law officers interviewed laughed about how Pinkie controlled things—even the law. None of his law breaking, paying people off, and controlling the laws around liquor seemed to matter at the end of his life when his wife said he died lonely and of a broken heart. His money, power, and greed couldn't hold his hand or sit by him on his death bed.

CHAPTER THIRTY-NINE

"He (Pinkie) died of a broken heart."[1]

Christmas Day, 1991

I've always enjoyed Christmas, especially when I'm around little children whose eyes dance with the magic of the season. I loved spending Christmas in Tahoka with my aunts, uncles, sister, niece, cousins, and their children. Because some of us lived away from Tahoka, it was possible not to see each other from one Christmas to the next or longer. In a year's time, the children grew so much in stature, as well as maturity. Reconnecting with them allowed me to see what I'd missed by not having children of my own. It isn't as if I never wanted children. I always assumed I would have a couple. It just never worked out that way.

With the wound of not having parents, becoming a parent felt like the largest kind of commitment. I felt I needed to solve all of my problems before participating in parenthood. I remember a conversation I had with Granny about waiting until things were better in my married life before having children and her reply was, "If you wait for your life to be perfect, you won't ever have any children." But Granny never really knew the depth of problems in my marriage. For me, it was vitally important to bring children into the world in a good situation or not at all, which I've come to understand comes, at least in part, from my reaction to my early loss.

For me, I needed to have a committed relationship that was stable both emotionally and financially. I wanted a husband who would support my staying home with the children during their earliest years. None of those things ever materialized in my marriage.

After divorce, I assumed I would find a man with whom I would have a family. But I was left with a lack of trust in men and a lack of confidence in my ability to make a good decision in choosing a mate. Instead, I fell into a few more difficult relationships with men that left me wanting an intimate relationship deeply, but needing even more to protect myself from hurt. I have lived in that emotional place most of my adult years, and I'm certain that I created that protective pattern as a child.

Our family's Christmas feast was about one o'clock on Christmas day. Of course, there was always more than enough to eat. The Edwards' family is not short of good cooks, so the food always tastes great. My aunt prepared buffet style where everyone could choose their favorite foods. There were so many desserts they wouldn't all fit on the kitchen cart. The typical complaint after eating was, "I ate too much." It seemed we never learned.

The women, including my aunts and cousins, sat at the large dining table and filled out our calendars for the new year, while the men retired to the living room for an afternoon full of football's vicarious pleasures. My sister got our family started on calendars some years back. She bought everyone a calendar for the new year, and we filled out the important dates of the coming year like birthdays and anniversaries. As we sat at the table, Uncle Robert walked by, and I took the opportunity to ask, "Uncle Robert, how come no one ever told me or Calva An about the court cases stemming from my parents accident?"

Uncle Robert said, "Oh honey, you knew about it. You just forgot."

"Oh, no, I didn't. I never knew there were any court proceedings," I exclaimed.

Aunt Freda spoke up, "I didn't know there were any court proceedings."

I said, "Well there were two trials and a law suit."

Aunt Freda was flabbergasted. "There were," she exclaimed. "Well, I don't remember anything about it."

Uncle Robert said, "Yes, they fined the guy who was driving for bootlegging. Then they convicted him —I can't remember the exact charge—but he was supposed to go to the pen for two years, but he never did. He was really bad off physically. Honey, it was such a long time ago it is hard to remember."

"Uncle Robert, Wilson told me Granddad Pierce wanted Calva An and me to go to an orphanage. Is that true?"

He nodded his head yes.

"Why?" I asked holding back my tears.

"Well, you have to remember back then, everyone thought the Baptist orphanages were pretty good places."

"It is hard for me to imagine anyone wanting a child to go to an orphanage," I exclaimed. "The newspaper clippings said the Rileys had ten children. Do you know what happened to them after the accident?"

Uncle Robert scratched his head trying to recollect and said, "I can't really remember. I think some of them were old enough to be on their own but it seems like I remember some of them went to an orphanage."

"I just have a hard time with the fact that I am forty-one years old and have never known the information about our accident," I said. "I asked Granny many times why no one was ever prosecuted and she always said 'they had other things to do, like raise children.'"

Uncle Robert concluded, "Well, honey, I didn't know you didn't know it."[2]

That was true because we each suffered alone. Our family didn't talk about hurtful things. I remember the time I became truly aware of how little my family talked about the really important things in our lives. I was about eighteen, and Aunt Mona was at our house for the weekend. Grandpa, Aunt Mona, and I were in the dining room. The conversation led to Grandpa's telling the story of how I learned about the death of my parents. That was the first time I had heard about being told my parents were dead by my not-yet-four-year-old sister. I asked Grandpa, "How did Calva know our parents were dead?"

He said, "I don't know."

Aunt Mona spoke up and said, "I told her. After you brought them home, I took Calva An in the other room and told her that her parents were dead and wouldn't ever be coming back."[3]

I was shocked! My family didn't even discuss how to talk to us and who should talk to us about the most traumatic of events? My aunt didn't feel any need to inform my grandparents of her conversation with my sister? No wonder I was confused.

When I read in Ann Lander's column "The Elephant in the Room," I identified with it strongly. That was the way my family dealt with the death of my parents.

"The Elephant in the Room"

> There's an elephant in the room.
> It is large and squatting, so it is hard to get around it.
> Yet we squeeze by with "How are you?" and "I'm Fine"...
> And a thousand forms of trivial chatter.
> We talk about the weather.
> We talk about work.
> We talk about everything else—except the elephant in the room.
> There's an elephant in the room.
> We all know it is there.
> We are thinking about the elephant as we talk together.
> It is constantly on our minds.
> For, you see, it is a very big elephant.
> It has hurt us all.
> But we do not talk about the elephant in the room.
> Oh, please, say her name.
> Oh, please, say "Barbara" again.

Oh, please, let's talk about the elephant in the room.
For if we talk about her death,
Perhaps we can talk about her life.
Can I say "Barbara" to you and not have you look away?
For if I cannot, then you leave me
Alone...In a room...
With an elephant.[4]

Each of us suffered silently. We walked around this big elephant in our living room— each of us alone in our own pain and grief.

CHAPTER FORTY

"I (Mrs. Roden) was married to a gangster."[1]

January 1992

January was a cold month in Denver, Colorado, and sometimes it was difficult to get out of bed to meet the dark and cold. The colder it was outside the better my hot bath felt at the end of our walk. As I washed my hair in the shower, I was hoping today would be the day I'd receive my photo copy of the depositions Truett said would be available to us. In case they arrived, I reserved my evening for reading.

At the office, I treated patients who came in for various complaints such as neck pain, digestive problems, allergies, and low back pain.

One of the reasons I became a chiropractor was so I would have the knowledge to determine what happens to my body. I never wanted to be at the mercy of someone else physically. I needed to have the proper information and expertise to make my own decisions if I experienced any health challenges. I learned that, in part, this was my reactivity to my early experiences of having had no control over the overwhelming events in my life and their effect on my body.

I left work and arrived home after six in the evening. Opening the door with anticipation, I found the large package of depositions waiting for me. I was surprised at the large volume of material. I situated myself comfortably on my couch to read what had happened in the courtrooms in Tahoka after our accident.

In October of 1951, Mr. Maxey was charged and fined $1000 for possession with the purpose of selling in a dry area, better known as bootlegging.

He certainly deserved the conviction. By his own assertion, he drove it six days a week. But it is one more time when the little guy took the fall for the greater criminal. Pinkie Roden knew how to cover his tracks really well, and he had the power and money to do it.

I'm not certain if Roy's problems started when he quit his job in the oil field to work in the bootlegging business, or if it was the day he was introduced to Pinkie Roden by his brother-in-law. Either way, bootlegging was the beginning of the end for Roy Maxey.

Roy's bootlegging days started two or three months prior to working for Pinkie. He worked for another, smaller bootlegger. One day while he was living in Lubbock, he went to Big Spring and left a message for Pinkie to contact him.

When Pinkie came to Lubbock a week or so later, about seven or eight months before the accident, the manager of Pinkie's operation in the Lubbock area, D.C. Turner, called Roy and told him to come over to the Camp Joy Service Station to see Pinkie about work.[2]

"Hello," Roy said to Pinkie and D.C. when he arrived at the Camp Joy Service Station.

D.C. said, "Let's get in the car." He was making reference to an Oldsmobile that was parked beside the service station.

D.C. drove, Pinkie rode shotgun, and Roy sat in the back seat. There was silence for about three-quarters of a mile when D.C. pulled over as if he was going to turn around. But instead, he stopped.[3]

Pinkie turned half way around and asked, "Roy, you want to go to work for me? You left word for me to contact you."

Roy answered, "Yeah, I need a job. I don't have a job now."

Pinkie said, "Well, I could use you. If you go to work for me, you will take all of your orders from D.C. Turner." Pinkie paused and said, "I will pay all bills. Regardless of what happens, you will be taken care of."[4]

Pinkie agreed to pay Roy one hundred dollars a week, and provide him a furnished house to live in as well as a vehicle in which to haul whiskey.[5] Pinkie said, "You will either be hauling whiskey or delivering whiskey in town, but you will take your orders from D.C."[6]

D.C. Turner had little to say that day except that they would need to set Roy up in the Brophy Courts, a motel, until they could rent him a house and furnish it.

The next day Roy moved into the Brophy Courts. He and D.C. went to a local store and selected a house full of furniture and D.C. paid for it. For a vehicle, Roy was provided a Cadillac-Ford, which meant it was a Ford with a Cadillac engine. He never knew who owned the car.[7]

Roy drove that car until one day, about four or five months before the accident, D.C. said, "I have another car for you."[8]

Roy didn't know who owned that car either, nor did he ask. That was the way it was in the bootlegging business. Ask no questions and keep your mouth shut.

One day while Roy's car was being loaded up with whiskey by the boys in the warehouse, Pinkie bragged to Roy saying, "You know, I am the first man to map out this road going north to Lubbock. I think it is a safe road to run on."[9] And run on it, Roy did. He made that trip six days a week hauling beer and whiskey from Big Spring to Lubbock.

In the early spring of 1951, Roy moved to a small sixty-acre farm outside Ropesville, about twelve miles outside of Lubbock. There was a farmhouse, a large barn and a dairy barn included in the lease. Of course, they used the farm to stash, under lock and key, the beer and whiskey they bootlegged into the dry area. D.C. told Roy to write up the contract for one thousand dollars payment for leasing the farm and D.C. gave Roy the money to pay it. The truck that was housed at Pinkie's Farm Store was seen bringing beer in to the barn to be stashed while Roy brought most of the whiskey in himself. Pinkie was at the farm only once. He was welcomed by Roy's wife, because Roy was out making his usual run.[10]

CHAPTER FORTY-ONE

*"Pinkie masterminded a stunning,
incredibly profitable scheme to incorporate
a tiny precinct totally surrounded by Abilene,
the so-called Buckle on the Bible Belt."*[1]

Pinkie was raised close to Fort Worth, Texas. As a young boy he worked as a bellboy at a hotel where "he was exposed to the sins of the flesh, and their first cousins, whiskey and gambling."[2] Quitting school at sixteeen, after learning that people in a dry county would pay a high price for alcohol, he learned the bootlegging business from Clem Connally, a chum whose father was a bootlegger.[3]

Another mentor was a salty old woman, Oma Coleman, who boasted that she "taught the little SOB everything he knew."[4] Pinkie was a man who learned to get what he wanted and it didn't matter what price other people had to pay for it.

Pinkie continued his bootlegging business without even a pause after our accident. Roy Maxey was charged with and convicted in July of 1951 of negligent homicide of the second degree for the death of my mother, Pearle Edwards.[5]

While Mr. Maxey was appealing the decision, which he appealed all the way to the Texas Court of Criminal Appeals, my almost sixty-year-old grandpa had many new hats to wear. Having quit his job working in a chemical plant outside Brownfield, he reacquainted himself with farming life by taking over my dad's farm to make a home for my sister and me.

Granny's health problems, the financial stress of reentry into farming, enduring the court procedings over the car accident, being a replacement father to two small and needy children, applying to the court for guardianship of my sister and me, as well as handling the financial situation with insurance companies and hospitals gave my Grandpa more than enough to do. How could it have been anything less than the most stressful time in his life?

While Grandpa was dealing with what life had dropped in his lap, Pinkie was rolling in the money. Pinkie controlled, "through a system of demand notes," ten liquor stores which grossed in their legal operation $8,788,711 in 1951 and 1952.[6] That was a whole lot of money! And it doesn't say anything about the money he made through his illegal operations of bootlegging. It's hard to imagine the amount of money he pocketed from that.

And, yet, when Roy Maxey asked him for the money to take a bus to Galveston to have his leg amputated, Pinkie refused to give him bus fare.[7] Pinkie had promised, "regardless of what happens, you will be taken care of."[8]

I don't remember Christmas of 1951, but it must have been difficult for my family, especially my grandparents. The first Christmas without my parents and the first Christmas in years my Granny, in poor health or not, had to do Santa Claus for two small children.

The day after Christmas in 1951, a civil lawsuit was filed in court by our attorneys against S.F. Wells Jr., Roy Maxey, and Tom Roden for death of parents of minors for the sum of $160,000+.[9]

Mr. Wells was named in the suit, because the Lincoln Mr. Maxey was driving was registered in Mr. Wells' name. S.F. Wells, Jr. was no stranger to the law. He had been convicted once for possession, twice for transporting, and three times for selling alcohol in a dry area. He had been arrested and tried for hauling a truckload of beer through Lubbock to Amarillo, but was not convicted.[10]

When asked why he bought the car Mr. Maxey was driving, S.F. Wells, Jr. said, "My wife used it around here in town."[11] He said he had bought the new car in the last part of 1950 from the Truman Jones Auto Dealer.

When asked if he ever hauled whiskey in the vehicle he said no. Calloway Huffaker, our attorney, asked him what the overload springs were doing on the car and Mr. Wells admitted, "I imagine to haul whiskey with." In fact, he admitted to having the overload springs put on the car when it was fairly new.

Mr. Wells admitted he heard about the accident by reading about it in the paper the following morning, but he denied he came to Tahoka to check it out. He also denied the car was in his possession at the time of the accident. He said, "I let D.C. Turner have it right after the first of the year," and claimed he hadn't seen the car since.[12]

When asked about the transaction of selling the car to D.C. Turner, he said, "Well, I had known D.C. for a long time, and when I got the car, I was on a salary and I didn't make the deal whereby the car was needed, whereby I let him have it and he was going to pay me for the car."[13]

Although that might sound a little unbelievable, Mr. Wells had even more unbelievable things to say about the particulars of the sale of his car. When asked about payment he said, "We had set no price. I called D.C. Turner a couple of months after he had the car, and made a date to meet him, but something happened and we didn't get together."[14]

D.C. never paid Mr. Wells one penny for the car although Wells said he had given it to D.C. right after the first of the year. That meant D.C. had possession of the car for about five months without making a payment on it or even deciding on an amount that D.C. would pay for the car in the future. And six mornings out of seven, when they got out of bed, the car had at least two hundred more miles on it than it had the previous morning.

Mr. Wells bought the car for three thousand dollars and it was his first experience in borrowing money from a bank. Although he didn't pay anything down on the car, some time later he said he paid one thousand dollars in cash on his note at the First National Bank in Big Spring. Two years after the car was demolished in the accident, two thousand dollars was still owed on the car. Mr. Wells said he had recently received a notice from the bank saying the note was due. That 'recently' was over two years after the car had been completely demolished. Probably the most interesting part in the deposition was when Mr. Wells finally admitted that the bank required him to have a co-signer. It was none other than Pinkie Roden.[15]

CHAPTER FORTY-TWO

"Everybody wanted to be his (Pinkie's) friend. They damn sure didn't want to be his enemy."[1]

The depositions were taken two years after our accident. Uncle Robert said he felt Mr. Maxey testified, in part, because Pinkie did not pay his medical bills.[2] Several times in the deposition, Mr. Maxey said Pinkie promised to take care of everything, no matter what happened.[3]

I had to realize the powerful force of money. Having been raised in a home where money was not given much importance, I had a difficult time understanding it completely. In our home being a good, responsible, religious person was what was given importance. It's obvious Pinkie wouldn't understand our thinking, any more than I could understand his. If I understood his thinking, I suppose I would be just like him.

I couldn't help but feel compassion for the guy who was driving the bootlegging car. I could tell by his grammar in the deposition that he was uneducated. It was easy to be judgmental, but hard to know what life was like for Mr. Maxey. The most difficult part for me was understanding why the information in Mr. Maxey's deposition wasn't enough to charge and convict Pinkie.

I shared that information with Michael and Shirley and he said, "Elva, the real courtroom is not like it is on television. There are a lot of circumstances that create problems in a case." Michael was an attorney, so he should know, but it was hard for me to accept.

"But, Michael," I said, "we hear all the time about a small drug pusher giving state's evidence to put the bigger dope dealer in jail. I mean, bootlegging was against the law."

"I don't know what to tell you, Elva."

"You know the articles that were in the paper went on and on about the political clout Pinkie had in Austin as well as in the territory he bootlegged. The lawmen laughed about how clever Pinkie was." I couldn't help but feel emotional.

Shirley said, "That doesn't make any sense to me, Elva."

"I know. It doesn't to me either. In this deposition the man who was driving the car, Mr. Maxey, told all about meeting Pinkie and how the bootlegging business worked. The way Pinkie got around the law was by being further than arms' length away from the money or directing people. Talk about middle management! There was always a middle man paying the runners and directing their work so they could never say Pinkie gave them money or explicit directions. Everything was always done in cash."[4]

Michael said, "Well, if you are going to deal illegally, cash leaves less of a trail."

"Pinkie told Maxey no matter what happened, he would take care of it.[5] And, as I see it, Maxey got a dirty deal from his employer," I said as we crossed the street.

"What do you mean?" Shirley asked.

"Well, Pinkie said he would take care of him by paying all expenses, no matter what they were. Maxey's injuries were serious requiring multiple surgeries. He finally had an arm and leg amputated. He was in the hospital for most of three years.[6] Since this was such a high profile case and not just a ticket from the liquor control board, I'm sure Pinkie wanted to distance himself from it as much as possible. Besides, Mr. Maxey was no longer useful to Pinkie, so Mr. Maxey was, shall I say, expendable." I paused. "The reason Mr. Maxey did not serve the two years he was sentenced to for vehicular homicide in the death of my mother was because of his bad health."[7]

Shirley said, "I didn't know you had a choice. I thought if a court convicted you and you were sentenced to jail, I thought you had to go."

"I didn't know it either," I responded. "That is why it is hard for me to be at peace—knowing all of Pinkie's political clout and influence."

Shirley said, "It is hard to understand, but being married to Michael I've come to understand that what makes common sense, does not necessarily make legal sense."

"Pinkie always seemed to get what he wanted politically," I said. "But, did he ever consider the two little girls who no longer had parents?" I asked as my voice cracked.

Regaining my composure I said, "I think I've read everything about the trials stemming from our accident. I found the document saying Mr. Maxey didn't have to serve the two years in jail which the jury sentenced him. It said he was in constant and immediate need of medical attention.[8] I'd like to know why they went to all the trouble to try the case which was appealed all the way to the Supreme Court of Texas if he was too sick to serve the sentence? It said in the document that he was under technical arrest until the court determined he was physically able to serve his time and that he would at all times keep the court informed as to his whereabouts."[9]

"Do you think he did?" Shirley asked.

"I doubt that he did," I said, "but I guess it doesn't matter."

"What do you mean?" Michael asked.

I answered a bit reluctantly. "It appears as time went by, this case lost it's importance. I mean, it couldn't be on the front burner for forty years. The document said any time the court wanted, Mr. Maxey had to get a physical examination to determine if he was well enough to serve his time. I wonder if they ever, even once, had him submit to a physical?"[10]

"What do you think?" asked Shirley.

"Well, if I were a betting person, I would say they did not," I answered.

"Why do you say that?" asked Michael.

"If they did wouldn't there be a document saying the court ordered the physical examination and here are the results? After all, the doctor would have to be paid and a report given to the court. Wouldn't all documents that went to the court be included in what I have?" I asked.

"Well, they probably should be," Michael replied.

"There weren't any in there," I said as my voice trailed off. "The man is dead now, but that kind of lack of follow-through keeps me from being settled about all of this, especially when they said Pinkie would send holiday gifts of ham, turkeys, liquor, and steaks to . . . officials in the counties or towns that weren't friendly toward him."[11]

"That is the most bizarre thing I've ever heard of," Shirley said.

"Yeah, and when I read that the judge in Tahoka signed off that Mr. Maxey didn't have to go to jail, and when I found no evidence that he ever took a physical exam, or informed the court of his whereabouts, I wondered what kinds of things happened that I didn't know about?" The three of us sat looking at each other for a moment.

After a pause, Michael said, "You can't substantiate anything."

I replied, "No, I can't. That's not the point. But don't you find it hard to believe this man Pinkie, a bootlegger, wrote the liquor laws in Texas?"[12]

"Who told you that?" Michael asked.

"Mike Cochran quoted one man as saying you didn't cross Pinkie on liquor laws. He said the legislature couldn't get a liquor bill passed while Pinkie was walking the halls."[13]

CHAPTER FORTY-THREE

*"Well, I'll tell you, sometimes
when Mr. Roden and Mr. Siegel and Mr. Leggett
are prowling the halls of the Capitol,
it's just mighty hard to move a liquor bill."*[1]

I was wondering how to further my investigation. Maybe I should listen to the ones who said just forget it? Get over it and get on with your life!! There wasn't anything I could do about it anyway. I'd even heard that it was dangerous to my mental and emotional health to be digging into the past. I wondered if that advice came from people who have known their parents in a way that was never possible for me. My granny always said "before you judge, walk a mile in their shoes."

One afternoon Shirley and I went for coffee in a quaint place in the neighborhood and we sat directly across the street from a business that had a blue neon sign that said "private investigator." We light-heartedly conversed about what we thought they might be investigating like husbands or wives who were having extracurricular activites. I had my own investigation going, but how could I find an emotional closure? Walking home, I decided to call Polly.

"Polly, I got all the court documents concerning our wreck and you know, after reading them, I am more upset about the articles in the newspaper than ever. What he said in the articles seems like a copy of what happened in my parents accident."

"What do you mean?" asked Polly.

"Well, in Pinkie's deposition he was asked if they had a warning system to avoid the liquor control board. He denied it. But in the articles Mike Cochran talked about it. I guess I shouldn't be surprised he wouldn't want to implicate himself but what bothers me is that much of what is in Cochran's articles corroborates what was asked, but denied in the court documents. He was so good at doing things illegally by buying loyalty and distancing himself from the illegal acts themselves. He was so good at it that the law could not tie him to the acts directly enough to convict him."

"Yeah, it sounds like he was pretty good at that," Polly said.

"Why anyone should be given glory for that, I can't understand. I wonder if my grandpa rolled over in his grave when those articles were published?" I couldn't keep the emotion out of my voice.

"We read your letter to the editor. Wilson took it to work and showed all of his coherts. He really got a bang out of it. We thought you really did a good job making the point that what Pinkie was good at shouldn't be saluted. But Elva, Wilson works in law enforcement and has for some years now, and he has asked around and no one feels you would have any kind of legal case."

"Oh, no, Polly, I know that. Really that was never my intention. It was forty years ago. I am doing this for me, for my heart, not for any kind of legal reason. I have to leave justice up to God." I was always surprised that people thought I was looking for a legal resolution—forty years after the fact! "When I read the deposition given by Maxey, the guy who was driving the bootleg car, I couldn't help but feel a lot of compassion for him. Here he was uneducated, had a family, didn't really mean any harm it didn't sound like, and look at what happened to him. Of course, he knew he was doing illegal work, but it just sounded like he had a certain kind of innocence in him. Times were tough back then. In the deposition, he said he had lost an arm and a leg. I have to wonder about what happened to his family? The man and woman in the car with him who were killed in the accident were his cousins and they had ten children. I wonder what happened to them? Uncle Robert said he thought some of them went to an orphanage. It makes me feel so grateful for my grandparents. I wonder how many lives were changed because of this one accident."

"Yes, a lot of people suffered over it. I have a niece named Elna. I am sure you remember her because she used to work at the cleaners in Tahoka when you were a little girl. She got married and they moved down to Odessa. She told me that she got to be real good friends with this woman who lived there in Odessa. They would do things together, and she was real fond of her. She said one day this woman came to her house and sat down in her kitchen and said 'I want you to sit down. I want to tell you something.' Elna said her friend seemed very serious so she sat down. She said 'I want to tell you this before someone else does. You know those friends of yours you've talked about several times who were killed in that accident between Tahoka and Brownfield?' Elna said 'yes'. She said, 'well, my father was driving that car.'"

"You're kidding, Polly!"

"Elna said her friend had really suffered over it too," Polly added.

"Yeah, I'll bet. Polly, when I look at how many lives were affected by this wreck, it is incredible. And that is why I am so upset about the articles praising Pinkie's accomplishments." I paused, and then said, "I would really love to talk to that lady who was Elna's friend. You know, the driver of the car had massive injuries, and I am sure it affected that family in a major way. Polly, could you get me your niece's number or ask her for her friend's number? I would love to talk to her. I guess maybe her address would be better, now that I think of it. I mean, she might not want to talk to me. A letter would probably be better," I said thinking out loud.

"I will call her and see if she can get it for me. If she can, I'll give it to you," Polly promised.[2]

CHAPTER FORTY-FOUR

*"A guy (Pinkie) who could socialize
with the governor or the state's top accountant
one night and shoot dice the next evening
with a legendary gambler."[1]*

One week later, Polly called.

"Well, we are doing just fine. I talked with my niece, Elna, and she gave me the address the phone book had for her friend we talked about. Do you still want it?"

"Oh yes, and thanks so much for doing this. I really appreciate it. I know it may not turn up any information for me, but heck, it is worth a try."

Polly gave me a name and an address. I was eager to write the woman a letter and yet I realized she might not be eager to communicate with me. I wanted to talk about our experience, and I was curious to see if she did. Would I have been willing to talk with her if she had contacted me in earlier years? I honestly didn't know. It was possible I would have refused. On the other hand, maybe that contact would have opened my heart and started me sooner on my journey of discovery.

Within a few days I had a letter written to Glenda.

> *4/16/93*
> *Dear Glenda,*
> *My name is Elva Jo Edwards. I got your name from Edna Mays. She said she had known you in years past.*
> *I don't know if you know who I am, so I will take a minute to explain. I had your phone number and considered calling you, but under the circumstances I felt perhaps it would be better to write.*
> *I am actually from Tahoka, Texas. I am 43 years old. When I was 19 months old I was in a car accident with my parents, Pearle and Calvin Edwards, who were killed. The accident was on the Tahoka-Brownfield highway. My grandmother was also killed in that accident. I understand your father was the driver of the other car. And, I understand this accident had serious ramifications for your family as well as mine.*

My mother was an only child. Her mother was also killed in the accident. Her father had died a few years earlier. So basically, that was the end of that side of the family.

My father's parents lived in Brownfield. They moved to Tahoka and took over my father's farming operation and raised my sister and me. They were good, loving people. Their youngest daughter graduated from high school the same week my parents were killed. I'm sure it was difficult to go back to diapers, but they really dedicated their lives to raising us. My grandfather often said, "I just want to live long enough to get you girls raised." Both of my grandparents had health challenges during my childhood, but their desire to raise us helped them make it through.

My grandfather died in September 1969. It was the first day of my sophomore year in college. He did, indeed, live just long enough to get us raised.

My grandmother is ninety-seven years old and in the nursing home in Tahoka. She has really lost her mind in this last year. I just went to visit her over Easter. I've been scared she would die since I was ten years old. She is really something else.

My father had one brother and two sisters. They all had children and we were raised very close. We do feel we have a close extended family.

My family has had its dysfunction around the death of my parents. Basically 'things' were never talked about. I never really felt it would be OK to ask too many questions or appear to have too much feeling around the situation. It was sort of like—don't talk about it and nobody's feelings will be hurt. In this day and age, people would take children to counselors and learn to deal with the grief, but that wasn't really done in the early 1950's.

In October 1991, I went to Tahoka over Halloween to visit my Granny and family. My cousin pulled me aside and told me there was a series of articles that were in the Lubbock Avalanche-Journal about Pinkie. She had written a letter to the editor, but it was never published. I ended up writing a letter to the editor and eventually spoke with the publisher a couple of times. This made me realize I didn't really know what happened with the accident of my parents. So I started investigat-

ing. I found there were three trials regarding my parents and the accident. I was shocked!!! I never knew that!!! I really felt a bit betrayed by my family, but came to realize they really never dealt appropriately with the pain involved with the tragedy. The way they handled it was by repressing it, not remembering, etc. It feels a bit ridiculous that I'm past forty years of age and am discovering something this BIG in my life.

I had written a judge and he gave me the court case numbers and eventually I got copies of the depositions etc. If I understand correctly, your father lived—actually was the only adult who survived the accident. When I was young, I had this idea that the person who was driving the other car hated my parents, hated me, was mean, etc..... You know how the mind can work. However, in reading the deposition of the man I think was your father, I found myself having a lot of compassion for a person who found himself in a tight spot—jobless and having a family to feed. The money Pinkie offered looked good. And, who would ever have imagined such a tragedy. In the deposition, he explained all about his connections with Pinkie etc. I found it fascinating reading.

Through all of this, I have entered the process of healing from the pain of not having parents and not being able to express my pain as a child. The purpose of the investigation is really for my own healing.

One of the aspects about the accident is that basically twelve children were left orphaned from that accident. I am wondering what happened to each of them? My sister and I are the only two I know about. (I am a chiropractor in Denver and my sister is an executive secretary in San Diego. Her daughter, my niece is expecting a baby soon. She also lives in San Diego. My sister had the one child. I have none.) I am hoping you can help me. I think they are your cousins. I'd like to know:

1) Name
2) Age at time of accident
3) Current address and phone number if they don't mind
4) Anything else you want to tell me

There were many ripples from the accident. One of them is your family. What happened to you guys? I understand your father didn't live that many more years. When did he die? He lived through the accident but I understand he had a lot of problems resulting from the accident. What about your mom? Your siblings? You? How do you feel you have come to terms with our mutual history?

I am hoping to hear from you. I hope that you are at a place in your life where we can connect on some level. If not, I do understand and perhaps in the future things will change.

If you have any questions, feel free to ask.
Sincerely,

Elva Jo Edwards[2]

CHAPTER FORTY-FIVE

*"Associates say Pinkie played a leading role
in shaping package store legislation, including
hours of operation, and a less visible but pivotal role
in a Texas mixed drink law that could mean
more business for him and fellow store owners."[1]*

The more days that went by without a response from Glenda, the more my hopes of a response dimmed. Although I had promised myself I would be satisfied with whatever happened, I couldn't help but feel sadness creeping in. But, I finally got what I wanted.

> *"May 4, 1993*
> *Dear Elva Jo,*
> *I wanted to let you know your letter finally reached me. It went to my ex-husband. We divorced in 1983 after twenty-nine years of marriage and I remarried in 1986.*
> *Needless to say your letter was quite a surprise. Even though it brought back some painful memories, I was glad to hear from you. I, too, had wondered in the past what happened to the other lives of those involved. I am sorry to say I won't be much help on the other orphaned children. These children were like third cousins and not well known to me and I don't know what happened to them. Even though all of my father's immediate family is gone, I may have an avenue of contact which I will explore later.*
> *This is just a short note to let you know I have received your letter. I am leaving May 5th for Germany for two weeks, so your letter arrived at a very busy time for me. I will write more and give you some update on our lives when I return. ...*
> *Just briefly: My mother is still living. I have one brother who has one son..... I have two children. ...*
> *As I said, this has to be short at this time. I am sure we have a lot in common to talk about and I will look forward to that.*
> *Sincerely,*
> *Glenda"[2]*

I was full of appreciation for her willingness to correspond with me about such a painful situation for us both. Much of my life had been filled with people without the capacity or desire to talk to me at length and in depth about something that brought such raw pain to the surface. The pain was not just mine, but theirs, too. I couldn't say I was comfortable with the pain, but in order to heal my broken heart, I was consciously developing the capacity to tolerate the pain instead of pushing it away as I had always done before.

Glenda's letter felt very healing. Corresponding with others who were involved made me feel less like I was alone in my pain. I called the only person who would understand and appreciate the significance of this letter—my sister, Calva.

CHAPTER FORTY-SIX

*"Pinkie wrote an awful lot
of liquor law in Texas."*[1]

It was only about a month later when Glenda made good her promise of writing when she returned from her trip. I was please to find another letter in the mail.

> *"June 10, 1993*
> *Dear Elva,*
>
> *I have meant to write ever since I returned from vacation, but have just procrastinated. I had a very nice time on my trip, but came back very tired and suffered from jet lag for the first time.*
>
> *I have contacted a distant relative inquiring about the other orphaned children. She gave me the name of another who she thinks might have some information, but I have not been able to reach her. I will keep trying. If I can just contact one, I will be able to find out about the others.*
>
> *In your letter you said you had copies of depositions, etc. of the court cases which I would love to have copies of and would be glad to pay for if you don't mind sharing them. I was as surprised as you to know there were three trials. I only knew of one, which I did not attend and that was my parents suing Pinkie. Like you said it wasn't discussed a lot around us either; however, I wasn't around much. It was a pretty busy time for me. I went to work part-time to get through high school and to help out as well. My Dad was in the hospital the most of three years. Of course Mother had to go to work and never having worked before was unable to get a job that paid much. I carried the full load of solid subjects and worked half-day during school and full time summers. That was before the days of DE and DO in school, so unfortunately I didn't earn credits for my job. When I got out of high school, I went to work full time and was unable to go to college. All this was unfortunate, but*

> *I feel fortunate compared to you, because I still had my parents. I read an article that was sent to me from the Lubbock paper in 1991 that I believe was from you. It was very touching and I definitely see why you speak so highly of your grandmother.*
>
> *I will keep trying to locate the other children. I look forward to hearing from you.*
>
>
>
> *Sincerely,*
> *Glenda"*[2]
>
>

I was deeply touched by her letter and telephoned Glenda to speak with her personally. She answered the phone, and I heard a voice that sounded kind and sweet, and I liked her from the moment we began speaking. We shared the difficulties we and our families experienced after the accident and the dysfunction that developed around it. I felt close to her as if we had known each other many years. I felt compassion for her life after the accident. People behaved toward her in such a way as to blame her for her father's problems. As a teenager, a deduction was taken from her paycheck to pay for her father's medical care that was incurred by the county. When she married she told her employer she was no longer responsible for her father's medical bills and the deduction ceased. From our conversation, I understood Mr. Maxey was basically addicted to pain medication the rest of his life. I felt if I met Glenda, I would like her, and we could be friends.

I told Glenda I had the depositions and would send her a copy of them. Most of the court action and the law suits were news to her. I noticed in her letter her father did sue Pinkie. I found it interesting, because in his deposition he said he had no intention of doing so.

CHAPTER FORTY-SEVEN

"Another of Pinkie's Austin contacts was Montford, a widely respected Democrat from Lubbock."[1]

The Rocky Mountain area was beautiful and where I felt at home. My family wanted me to return to West Texas, but the thought of enduring the sand storms I've lived through in West Texas kept me in Denver. The people in West Texas were wonderful, but the scenery was spectacular in Colorado. I appreciated the beauty of West Texas more than ever, but my nervous system couldn't tolerate sand storms.

Just as in Texas, July was a hot month in Denver. I came home for lunch and found another letter from Glenda. It read:

> *"July 5, 1993*
> *Dear Elva,*
>   *Thanks so much for sending the depositions to me. I haven't had time to read them as yet. I am sorry I have not acknowledged them sooner, but I have been busy as usual, but a little more so as my Mother has been pretty ill. After we talked and Mother was feeling better, I talked to her about the trial we discussed. She advised me that it never came to court, that Pinkie gave my Dad $1500.00 to settle the case. I guess that looked like a lot to him at that time, because he was even without bus fare to get to the Galveston hospital where they amputated his leg. Mother said he asked Pinkie to buy him a bus ticket and he refused.*
>   *I have sent a request to the Postmaster of Crane Tx. for a forwarding address to one of the other surviving children. I had received his address from the distant relative I mentioned when we talked. I found out he had moved when I tried to contact him. I hope to receive that any day now. I have tried two others, but to no avail. If I can ever locate one of them, I should be able to find all of them.*
>   *I hope you had a nice Fourth holiday.*
>   *Sincerely,*
>   *Glenda"*[2]

I found it so interesting to see how Pinkie used people! Fifteen hundred dollars was a drop in the bucket for the injuries Mr. Maxey received in the accident and meaningless pocket change to Pinkie. Bootlegging made Pinkie wealthy, but it didn't do much to kindle his compassion. Mr. Maxey was expendable to Pinkie, but for Glenda and her brother, he was more than a commodity; he was their father.

I was sensitive to the emotional needs of children in large part because I didn't have my parents. Not having children myself, my niece has been very important in my life, and in April 1993, she blessed me with a great-niece, Kalia, whom I simply adore. Although I was not her parent, I experienced a well of love and desire to assure her well-being from the moment I laid eyes on her. This child has helped me understand more fully how my mom and dad were cheated out of the joy of loving and raising their children.

I was reminded of the other children that were left orphaned in the accident and again wondered about their lives when I opened my mail and found another letter from Glenda.

> "August 16, 1993
> Dear Elva,
> Yes, I have had contact with one of the Riley children (Billy Riley, who is now 64 years old). I had traced them as far as Crane, Texas, but by the time I got that address, they had moved. I went through the Post Office there and got a change of address and with that I got his phone number through information and called. I spoke with his wife. She and Billy married in January before the accident in May. She gave me a brief run down on the children: There were ten children, in age order, Orville, Billy, Jack, Doris, Donna Ruth, Dorothy Nell, Dora Marie, Della Mae, David, and John. After the accident the last six children went to Bo's Orphanage in Quinlin, Texas, where they all remained until they finished school. Jack died in a car accident in California in 1968 and Doris died of lung cancer in 1988. The others are still living. I didn't get where Oville lived, but Donna Ruth is in Northern California, Dorothy Nell and Dora Marie are in Reno, Della Mae is in Bonham, David is in Roundsboro (near Tyler), and John is in

Dallas. She said she had a clipping of the accident that she would send me. I told her if she would that I would make copies and return it. I gave them my address and phone number and I have had no contact. I don't know if they are just busy like everyone else or after thinking it over, opted not to make further contact. I did tell her that I was seeking this information not only for myself, but for you. I mentioned Pinkie and she didn't even know who I was talking about.
Sincerely,
Glenda"[3]

My heart was touched by her persistence in finding these people with whom I shared history.

CHAPTER FORTY-EIGHT

*"Montford delights in recounting
his first meeting with Pinkie."*[1]

Would Billy Riley communicate with me? I could understand that Billy might not be in an emotional place to want to speak with me. He may be like many people and want to leave the past in the past. What had been most difficult for me to tolerate was that with all my efforts that reporter, Mike Cochran, never responded to any of my communication. I wanted an answer to my question: did you not think there were a lot of innocent people left crippled in the wake of Pinkie's power and influence? With all of my wanting, again I was left unsatisfied.

But with Billy I felt differently. I had so much compassion for him and his siblings. I was aware of the built-in defense mechanisms we have that don't allow us to be open to something new, especially if it might be painful. I wrote him a letter knowing I couldn't be attached to the results. On a hot day in August of 1993, I sat at my computer and wrote the following letter.

> Dear Billy,
> I'd like to introduce myself. My name is Elva Jo Edwards. I live in Denver, CO. I was in the accident that killed your parents May 21, 1951. On that date, at least 14 children's lives were changed forever with you and I being included.
> My parents were Calvin and Pearle Edwards and my Grandmother was Mrs. Rogers. They were all killed. I was the smallest of the two children in the accident. I was nineteen-months old. I am now forty-three.
> Life was difficult for all of us I'm sure. In some ways I wonder if my sister and I were the most fortunate in that we had grandparents that loved us a great deal. Only others who have lost a parent as a child can know the hole that is in your heart. I understand you weren't a child, but I am sure it affected you deeply.
> There are a lot of twists about that accident that I've only learned about in the last couple of years. My investigating was prompted by a series of articles in the Lubbock-Avalanche Journal about Pinkie Roden. Through my investigation I was able to make contact with Glenda who seems like a very nice lady.

I am writing you for several reasons. After investigating this, I have a deep desire to attempt to understand what everyone else in the situation experienced. It feels to me we are connected in a deep way even though we do not know each other. I would like to hear and understand everyone else's perspective on how this accident has affected their lives. I would like to know from you and your siblings, if you are willing to share this with me, your age at the time of the accident, where you lived and how that situation worked out for you, and how you feel the experience has made an impact on your life.

I know this dredges up old memories and old pain. Some of my family are not eager or willing to talk about this as it is too painful. However, it was a big event in all of our lives and my intention is to actually go through the process of grief so I can get to the other side of it and live my life without that influence. In other words, instead of pushing away from it, I want to embrace it and process it so I won't be bound by it anymore.

I too realize I can hardly expect you or your siblings to be in the same space I am about our mutual past. What I do know is that we all survived the most major of childhood traumas and in that there seems to be a bond.

I would have called you, but felt it would be more appropriate to write and give you a chance to consider the things I've said.

I am willing to share my information with you if you are interested.

I will wait to hear from you and your siblings.
To your good health,
Elva Edwards[2]

I mailed the letter and said a prayer that God's will be done, because I didn't know what would be best for all concerned.

CHAPTER FORTY-NINE

*"The tots lost a mother, and a grandmother
in what was almost the twinkling of an eye,
and their father died a few short hours later."[1]*

December 10, 1994

Time passed as I worked through more and more of my history with my spiritual teacher.

One Saturday I had returned from a class with a friend. She dropped me off in front of my house, and as I was clawing my way through my purse looking for my keys, I walked to the front door of my house. I glanced up at my front door and noticed a note taped to the door from Shirley. It said, "Elva, come over as soon as you get in. I want to talk to you."

I opened the door and walked toward my telephone to call Shirley. I picked up the telephone and noticed the indication that I had a message waiting. I dialed the number to retrieve the messages and found I had three messages: two messages from my cousin, Donna, in Tahoka and one from Calva, my sister, in San Diego. Before I called them, I would call Shirley to tell her I needed to return calls and do a few things before I could come over. I had been in a meeting all day and was supposed to go back the next day, so I was tired. I dialed her number and she answered.

"Hi, Shirley. What's up?" She had never left me a note before, so I was intrigued at her method to reach me, but needed to take care of a little business first.

"I want you to come over here."

"I have some things to do first," I replied.

"I want you to come over here first." Shirley was unusually persistent. I was tired and with time zone changes for each person involved, I felt it would be best to make my calls first.

"Why? I have to call Calva and my cousin and..."

"I want you to come over here first," she continued to persist.

Suddenly, I sensed something was wrong. "What is wrong Shirley?"

There was hesitation. I felt the rush of adrenaline through my body. I repeated, "Shirley, tell me what is wrong."

"Elva, your grandmother died today." Many, many times I had expected this moment, but I didn't expect it today.

Shirley continued, "Calva called me, and I told her you were at your class. I didn't have the phone number there. Elva, why don't you come on over here and have dinner with us? You can call Calva and your cousin from here. I've been checking the airlines for you, and I have all the information written down."

As the tears fell, I told Shirley, "I'll be over in a minute."

Suddenly I couldn't remember my plans for the evening. Gathering my coat and purse, I drove the few blocks to Shirley's where Michael met me at the door with a hug. Shirley was not far behind. Their compassion allowed me to feel their love and my sorrow at the same time. I'd called Granny "my little sweetie," as the last year or so, she only weighed about seventy-six pounds, less than one-half of her normal weight of days gone by.

At this time my life was in chaos. It wasn't a good time in my life for this to happen, but when would be? I decided to drive to Tahoka as I felt too stressed to worry with flying. Shirley felt that I was too stressed to drive. I really wanted the time alone that driving would offer me, and if I left early in the morning, I would arrive about dark since it was an eleven hour drive.

On the day I drove to Texas, I woke up ready to get an early start and was on the road by ten minutes after six. The trip was full of vacillations between crying because Granny's physical form was gone to feelings of calmness and peace that Granny was finally free. I was sad because she would not be available for me, but she hadn't really been available to me for years. If I got upset when driving, I sensed my body as deeply as possible and I calmed down. I noticed this phenomenon all the way to Tahoka.

When I pulled off of U.S. 87 in Tahoka, I stopped at the one red light in Tahoka, and then continued to Donna's house. I pulled into the driveway. Suddenly, I had a rush of intense emotion and felt I couldn't get out of the car. It felt like it would really be true, really be final if I got out of the car, even though I knew it was already final. My mind played interesting games. Dan, Donna's husband, noticed I was parked in the driveway. He approached the car, opened the door, found me crying, gave me a hug, and told me he was sorry. He and Davy, his son, carried my luggage into the house and I unpacked.

I showered, dressed, and immediately went to the funeral home. Walking into the room where Granny's body was lying in a casket, I felt calmer. She looked like she had looked twenty years before when we had so many good times. She still had many wrinkles, which reminded me of the day she had told the local mortician that when she died, she didn't want her to remove all of her wrinkles. I guess she felt she earned her wrinkles. Granny was never embarrassed about her age. Perhaps she dealt with getting older before I became a part of her life.

I looked at her body and saw that the torment was gone. Her pain, agony, and suffering had vanished. She was free—free at last. There was peace and serenity in feeling her presence, but as people walked in and said some words of sympathy or gave me a hug, I began to feel emotional as if their words or actions took me away from the contact I had with Granny. Sensing my body as deeply as I could, I became calm and felt the contact with Granny's essence once again. The calm felt like the hand of God on my shoulder. It was the first time I had experienced sadness and loss so purely. It wasn't about taking care of someone else because they were not strong enough to handle mourning on their own. It wasn't about being the strong one everyone could lean on, or about being the weak one who needed a strong shoulder. It wasn't about any ideas my mind was usually full of. The time for me was about saying good-bye to my granny's physical expression and non-physical spirit, a very personal and intimate good-bye, just between the two of us.

That evening, we met as a family at Donna's house and shared our love for Granny. People in a small town know how to be of service to a family in sorrow by providing food and kind words. Granny had been a long time member of the community as well as a member of the First Baptist Church, and although she outlived most of her peers, she was not forgotten. Many of the people of Tahoka respected Granny in a special way for her devotion to her family, especially for raising an extra family because back then, it was rare. Many of the townspeople had seen her at death's door numerous times, only to bounce back and participate in life as if nothing had ever happened. All in all, she was an amazing woman.

My family gathered to make decisions about the kind of funeral service we wanted for Granny. I was a little surprised to find I didn't have any preferences other than I wanted us to sing the song that she had always told me was her favorite song. Byron Norwood, the vocalist, stopped by to assist us in selecting music for the service. Donna had a song in mind and, while standing in her living room, he sang it for us. We agreed it was a perfect song for Granny and it seemed fitting for Byron to sing at her service as he was, at that time, living in the house she raised us in on the farm. The "coincidence" didn't get lost on me. Surely he had been able to feel her presence in the house.

Granny's funeral allowed me the opportunity to see people I hadn't seen for years. She'd been the oldest living member of our extended family for about eight years. Several of her nieces were present whom I had not seen for some time. Beautiful flowers surrounded her casket and pink carnations, which were her favorite, topped the casket. The funeral itself was a wonderful service which would have met with Granny's approval. Byron's wonderful tenor voice sang about how Granny was ready for the struggle of life to end, and how she had been waiting for heaven's call.

I'd been concerned that the smaller children wouldn't have fond memories of Granny, because most of the time, she wasn't that pleasant for them to be around. Drew, her eighteen-year-old great-grandson, read an essay written the previous year by his little sister, D'Lynn, who was eleven years old, and proved my fears to be groundless.

MY SPECIAL GRANNY

I have a special great-grandmother. Her name is Nellie Edwards. She is ninety-seven years old and lives at the Tahoka Care Center. Every time we go to the care center she is usually asleep. Sometimes she is singing and is happy as a lark. Nellie Josephine Boyd was born November 20, 1895. Nellie was the youngest of nine children. Her mom died when she was six-years-old and her dad died when she was nine-years-old. She lived with different relatives in Poncha City, Oklahoma, Boyd and Crawford, Texas. In Crawford she met and married, Carroll Edwards, my great-grandfather on December 14, 1913. In the fall of 1922 they moved by train to Lynn County. They lived in a small community near Tahoka called Three Lakes. My great-grandfather was a farmer. They came to Lynn County to be closer to the rest of the Edwards family. Mr. Edwards, my great-great grandfather owned some land which he divided among eleven children.

Granny tells the story how everyone had wagons except Mr. Edwards, Granny's father-in-law. He had a car. That was very unusual in those days. Life in Three Lakes was difficult for them. In 1930, Granny said a tornado was so bad it picked up their house and moved it about 100 feet while the entire family was inside the house. Luckily, no one was hurt. In 1939 the Edwards family moved to Brownfield. In 1951 tragedy struck the Edwards family when their son Calvin and his wife Pearle were killed in a car accident. My great-grandparents returned to Tahoka to live and care for their young granddaughters who were three-years-old and eighteen-months-old. Our family has always been important to Granny probably because growing up she never had a real family. Granny has had many sicknesses in her lifetime. She has been in the hospital many times. She is a really strong and brave woman. On September 1, 1969, Carroll Edwards died. Granny always depended on him for everything. She didn't even have her driver's license. Her family wanted her to get her license, but she was afraid she was too young. She was only seventy-five. She passed her driver's test and drove for several years. My great-grandmother is a good granny because she gives good hugs. When she hugs me she feels all snugly and warm.

Sometimes my mema, my mother, and I walk Granny to the dining room. There they have coffee and visit with her. I play the piano for her. I can tell she enjoys the music because she taps her foot and sings along with me while I play. Granny has always enjoyed music. She played the piano in church when she was young. I enjoy spending time with her.

When my cousins come and visit her, I have to share Granny with them. Sometimes we bring her to my house where we can all visit with her. One day Granny was spending the day with us. She and I sat on the porch swing together. We sang together, talked, and played with my dog. This was a very special time for me and my granny. Granny is special to me because she is my great-grandmother. She plays with me, she laughs with me, and she has a big smile when we have our picture taken together. Granny's birthday is November 20. Mine is November 21. We always have our birthday party together. Granny will always be a special person to me. Even though her health is not good now, I can remember all the good times and fun times we had together.[2]

I was touched by D'Lynn's expression of love and compassion for Granny and was glad she had a sense of her life. Brother Jerry Becknal, the pastor of the First Baptist Church, had not known Granny as a functional woman since he had pastored her church for only a few years, and yet from his words at her funeral, I could tell he had a sense of Granny. I didn't feel any pastor she had known could have captured her essence any better than he did. His service was truly a tribute to her life.

During the funeral service I kept hearing the sweet cooing sounds of a baby. I looked around my shoulder and saw my cousin, Bobby Martin, holding his child who was less than a year old. Granny's life was dedicated to children which made it seem so appropriate for a child to attend Granny's memorial service. It reminded me of when I was in elementary school. Granny taught the three-year-old children in Sunday School. Even when she could take a break from children for a few hours, she chose to be with children. The presence of Bobby's child blessed our farewell to Granny.

People filed out of the church service a pew at a time, stopping to view the body before exiting the church. The seating arrangement left me the last person to bid farewell to Granny's body. Kena, my niece, filed out of the pew before me. As she left the pew, Kena walked to the front of the church and pulled a red rose from a bouquet and carried it with her to the casket and laid the flower on Granny's chest. The pallbearers, who were Granny's grandsons and great-grandsons, lined the walls of the foyer waiting for their task of carrying out the casket. I stopped before Granny's body, kissed my fingertips, and put them to her lips. It took all of my strength to leave, to walk out of the church knowing there would be no turning back. I walked into a group of people waiting to offer their kind words of love for Granny and compassion for me.

We went to the cemetery and bid her body farewell. When my parents died, my grandpa had bought a cemetery plot for four in case my sister or I, or both, did not live to adulthood. When Grandpa died we decided most likely I would marry and have my own family, so we decided to bury my grandparents with my parents. I felt it was the right decision as they were all my parents. They shared children, why not a cemetery plot?

The cemetery service was a prayer. After the prayer, we mingled with family and friends. I had to wonder, where were the Associated Press writers now? I suppose she was not the material for a series of articles for an Associated Press writer who was easily impressed by money, power, and greed. She was not politically savvy or motivated by money. However, she was excellent at rocking a child to sleep, or making tea cakes for her grandchildren. I remember her holding me and rocking me when I was tall enough my feet would hit the floor.

Upon leaving the cemetery we went to the hospital where Aunt Wilma was hospitalized with pneumonia. She was distressed that she could not attend the funeral, and it was unfortunate as even though she was a daughter-in-law, she took care of Granny and loved her as if she were her own mother. She came to Granny's aid countless times. It seemed unfair.

Aunt Wilma and Aunt Freda were the major players in taking care of Granny when she was in the nursing home. They checked on her daily, took her to the doctor, fed her, and washed her clothing. Aunt Wilma was a hairdresser and cut Granny's hair and occasionally gave her a permanent. One day after Granny had become a bit difficult to deal with, Aunt Wilma was giving her a permanent in the nursing home hair salon. Granny was yelling at the top of her lungs "you're killing me," all through the rinsing. It was heard all the way down the hall. That was probably the last permanent Granny ever received.

As the afternoon came to a close, and the sun began to descend toward the horizon, I returned to the cemetery alone. The gravesite had freshly turned dirt which was topped by bouquets of flowers. I sat on the large granite headstone that said EDWARDS and looked at the gravesites of the four people who were my parents.

I walked around and smelled the flowers. My fingers passed over a leaf from each flower arrangement. Granny loved beautiful flowers. I picked a red rose out of one of the flower arrangements and walked around with it at my nose. What a fragrance! What a life!

CHAPTER FIFTY

*"An outlaw cited for upholding the tradition
of American justice and an erstwhile bootlegger
publicly honored for his accomplishments
under the free enterprise system."*[1]

I returned to Denver and back into my hectic life. It had all started about a year before Granny died when I had a bad car accident in the mountains west of Denver. Car accidents and I were no strangers. My car was totaled. I choose to buy a new SUV, although I had no idea how popular they were. One Saturday morning I walked out my front door to go to a class and my truck was gone. I was so shocked I went to the people next door and asked if they had seen my truck. It finally sank in that my truck had been stolen! When the police arrived, they assured me the neighborhood was good and that this theft was a fluke. My truck was recovered, but was never the same.

That was the beginning of ten acts of crime against me in just over a year's time. My office was broken into two times and money was stolen. I was naive to leave the money there, but I always had before I moved locations. My learning always seemed to come in traumatic ways.

Within a short time, my truck was stolen a second time. Each time it was found, it had damage to it. It appeared it had been taken for a joy ride. The wheels had been removed and the truck abandoned.

One night I had just gone to bed when I heard glass breaking. I thought my neighbors in my duplex must have broken something. But, the breakage continued and I couldn't determine exactly where the noise was coming from. I walked into the bathroom and in the dark I could see the glass window was broken and a pipe was sticking through the window and moving. I ran to my neighbors who shared my duplex and beat on their door. They let me in and I called the police. They never found the perpetrator. Even though I wasn't hurt, it was terrifying to be afraid for your life.

I decided I would have my garage door replaced and keep my truck in the garage. I had to enter my garage from the alley and had felt that my safety was more important than the truck's. But after having the truck stolen twice, I knew something needed to change. I made an appointment with a garage door business to install a new door and repair the doorframe. Only one day before they were to begin the work, my truck was stolen for the third time. I was beside myself. The police said, "You're being stalked." No kidding.

In the meantime, I went to the grocery store one day and was approached by a real professional. As she pulled my attention away from my cart, her cohort stole my purse. Before it dawned on me what was happening, she ran out the door of the grocery store. I had over three hundred dollars in my purse, but it was empty when a man called that evening. He said he retrieved my purse out of the trash can, and if I wanted, I could come and get it. He said there was no money, but my credit cards and driver's license were there. I was afraid to go to this man's apartment to get my purse. What if it was a set-up? I assumed he didn't steal it as I saw the woman, but I was still shaking inside. I called the police and asked if an on-duty policeman would stop and pick up my purse and they obliged. I was relieved to have my credit cards back, although I had already called and cancelled them.

My truck was once again in the shop after being abandoned after another joy ride. My garage door was replaced and only some repairs on the framing were left to be completed. I left work and drove my rental car home. I wanted to see my new garage door so I drove down the alley. It was dark as I approached my garage door, but it looked like someone had thrown mud on the new white door. I got out of the car to inspect the door and found someone had actually smashed into my new garage door. I had thought the shadows from the dents were mud. I couldn't believe it! That was the last straw!! I couldn't take it anymore. Within a week, I sold my duplex.

One day I was at my office and sat down to pay bills. I opened my telephone bill and it was over five hundred dollars. I looked at the details and noticed they had charged someone else's number to my bill. I called the telephone company with the complaint.

The telephone employee looked up my records and asked me to repeat the number on my bill. "That is your telephone credit card number," he said.

"I don't have a credit card for the telephone."

"Yes, you do," he replied.

"I do?" I asked. "When did I get it?"

"August 1989," he replied.

And suddenly, it all fell into place. That was the date I opened my chiropractic office. When my purse was stolen, they took the one credit card that I didn't even remember I had and used it repeatedly. I was dumbfounded.

A couple of days after my purse had been stolen, a police officer came by my office and had photos of six women. "Was one of these people the one who stole your purse?"

"Yes, that woman right there," I answered.

He said the district attorney's office would be in touch, and they were. They asked me to come to court on a certain date, and of course, they couldn't tell me exactly the time the case would be heard or how long it would take. In an effort to support justice, I cancelled my whole work day to go to court. That morning before leaving for court, I received a telephone call.

"Dr. Edwards, we won't need you to come to court today."

"Why not?" I asked.

"There was a paperwork mix up and the prison didn't send the women for this case."

How inefficient, I thought. But, I knew the system wasn't perfect and so I agreed to go another day which requried another day of closing my office.

Early that morning I received another call. The date would be put off again. This time I was not so nice and suggested they get their act together. I had been told that the two women had recently gotten out of jail when they robbed me. No wonder our justice system had so many problems. I was beginning to see just how inept it was.

So, once more I agreed to take off a day of work to go to court to identify these women. They had stolen not only my purse, but the purses of about thirteen other women in a short period of time. The day before mine was stolen, in the same grocery store they stole a ninety-five-year-old woman's purse. In fact, on the news, they reported that they were stealing the purses of "elderly" women. My friends and I laughed, because I was only forty-five years old!

The day arrived to go to court, and once again, I received a call that there was another mix-up. That was too much and pushed me over the line. I yelled at them and told them to not call me again. I wanted to help put criminals behind bars, but I had reached my limit. No wonder justice was so hard to come by.

I had never considered living in the suburbs before that night, but I vowed to move. It required many trips south, west, and east to finally decide I wanted to live west of the city, mostly because it offered easy access to the city. I found a house I wanted in one of the suburbs of Denver called Lakewood. I moved to the foothills, and eventually, I moved my practice within a mile of my home as I soon learned that I didn't like being a commuter. And, for awhile, life was calm.

CHAPTER FIFTY-ONE

*"He (Pinkie) was an outlaw,
'but he was a good outlaw,' said his widow.
'An outlaw with heart.'"*[1]

As the years passed and I processed more and more of my traumatic history, I felt less and less reactive, almost as if my body was less and less rigid with my "story" about not having parents. Ever so slowly it felt like understanding my history helped squeeze, drop by drop, the trauma out of my body. I was indebted to my spiritual teacher for my increased understanding of my childhood and its lasting effects on me. In some ways, understanding how trauma was patterned in my life at such an early age allowed me to deal better with trauma each time it found me. I learned that the traumas I endured didn't make a statement about me.

As life lived through me, a pattern was being played out. I learned how important the first three to six years in a child's life are, because they become the blueprint of their life in the future. My blueprint was filled with traumatic experiences, and at the same time I was not those experiences. I was learning who and what I was regardless of my circumstances.

My circle of chiropractic friends got together once a month to give and receive from each other the gifts of the Neuro-Emotional Technique, a technique designed to take the emotional charge of a traumatic incident out of the body. The Neuro-Emotional Technique, my teacher and my chiropractic buddies had been my life savers in my adulthood, just as my grandparents had been in my childhood. My God, what would I have done without them?

Every time I was in yet another traumatic incident, the many body sensations, that were imprinted early in my life and in subsequent traumas, were re-stimulated. That meant I would have more body reactivity than the situation warranted, because part of what was stimulated was bodily held tension that got locked in my body in the original traumatic experience. The reaction would not only be emotional, but physical as well. Sometimes I felt like I had just touched an electric fence or was plugged into a light socket. My hair would stand up on my neck and back. I would feel a tightness inside my body that I could not let go. Sometimes I felt like I was on a downhill run-away train which was headed for impending doom. My chiropractic friends were very generous in helping me. They understood my traumatic history, and had compassion as my body would lead them back to the incident of our accident that created the original imprint of overwhelming emotions; emotions so strong that no child could handle them. That is why they were stored in my body in the first place. It wasn't enough to do this work once. With the kind of traumatic history I'd had, there was much work to be done.

After studying trauma, I understood the "game" my sister and I played everyday. Therapists called it re-enactment, where a child plays out what happened to her over and over. No child is too young to be traumatized. When a child is pre-verbal, or under three, their experience is not in their verbal memory, so they can't tell you what happened to them. Their memories are in their bodies, and they behave in such a way as to show you what happened to them. Sometimes the play is grim and obsessive, but it is still unable to relieve the anxiety of the child. The child is stuck.

Once I was at a retreat with Dr. Scott Walker, the founder of the Neuro-Emotional Technique™. Another doctor and his wife, Dave and Rhonda, and I had planned to meet at the seminar and catch up on each others' lives. I arrived at the airport in Kalispell when Dr. Deb Walker walked up to me and said, "I guess you heard about our friend Dave."

"What are you talking about?" I asked.

"Unfortunately, he was in a bad motorcycle accident two days ago and they aren't sure he is going to make it."

"Oh, my goodness. I didn't know."

"His son was with him, and he is in the hospital, but not as serious as Dave. They said Dave is clinging to life with a thread."

All I wanted to do was to go home. I needed to escape the intense feelings that were surfacing and I thought going home would bring relief. I didn't feel I could stay and participate in the retreat in a meaningful way because I was too upset about Dave's condition. I knew Dave's life was in God's hands, but I couldn't help being overwhelmed by the assumed needs of his wife and three children. All the left-over trauma from the overwhelming events of my earlier life sprang forth from the past to the present. I was basically experiencing post-traumatic stress syndrome again. There really wasn't any way for me to leave the meeting unless I rented a car and drove back to Denver, so I stayed, but isolated myself that evening.

At the first meeting of the retreat, in front of over a hundred chiropractors, Dr. Walker worked on me, leading time and time again to my emotional upset about Dave being related to the imprint from the original catastrophic event in my life, our car accident and the loss of my parents. Dr. Walker found that the grief that I was experiencing, related back to age one when my parents died. The accident of my friend stimulated old emotions hidden and trapped in my body. They were resurfacing because they were restimulated by Dave's accident. Sadness, grief, anguish, lack of control over events and paralyzed will, as well as other emotions were competently traced back to my original accident and the feelings I had at one-year-of-age. At times like that, it felt in my body as if I were on a run-away train going downhill with the speed continuing to accelerate, and a crash imminent. It was difficult to describe the feelings in my body at a time like that. I can simply say they were overwhelmingly devastating which might be an appropriate way to describe my reaction to my parent's death. After tracing my reactions to their original source, Dr. Walker made the appropriate corrections on my body.

Dr. Walker worked on me for about an hour that morning, and within thirty minutes after the treatment, I was participating in the retreat in a meaningful way while I also held my friend in my heart. His work was able to eliminate some of the bodily-held memory from my earlier accident. Thank God and Scott. The way I saw it, God was working through Scott to help me.

Becoming a chiropractor had helped me understand the mind-body connections, and being my grandfather's granddaughter, I understood how the lack of satisfaction, or justice, likely led him to have a major heart attack after having to settle a case I'm sure he felt he should have won. He probably felt he had to push away his intense feelings of anger, hurt and sadness, but the result was a major heart attack. Typically, being in touch with our feelings will not hurt us physically, but the repression of those feelings can cause us physical symptoms. Those hidden emotions or "glitches" can run our life. I often thought the feelings would be so intense I would "go nuts." I was re-experiencing the overwhelming feelings that my body experienced as a child. I experienced it internally the way I did as a child, but the external reality had changed. I was an adult who in many ways could help herself. Mentally healthy people tend to have internal controls that allow only a little to come forth at a time, allowing us to process hurtful emotions without becoming non-functional. That is the reason one treatment is not usually enough. And it is why time is important in the healing process: it takes time to process all of the pain and hurt, because we can only handle a little bit at a time.

Once in a conversation with Granny I suggested someone's physical problem had an emotional element. She behaved as if I were attacking the other person and said, "When you were in the hospital with bronchitis, was that caused from emotions?"

I responded, "Yes, Granny, I think it partially was. If you remember I left my ex-husband and landed in the hospital a few weeks later with bronchitis. Energetically, the lungs have to do with grief, and I was deep in the throes of grief over the split in my marriage. I wasn't aware of it at the time, because that was before I was a chiropractor, but it makes sense to me now that the emotional burden I was carrying affected my health."

After my divorce, I felt overwhelmed with my feelings of hurt, sadness, fear, and grief. All the feelings that come with a marriage that didn't work out. I dealt with the feelings the best way I knew how. Most of the emotions revolved around ideas I had of me being unlovable, alone, foolish, a failure, and deficient in what makes a man love a woman. Afraid of the intensity of my emotions, I buried the pain in my body. If I had felt the emotions deeply, I might have cried in front of Granny more than I deemed appropriate. I felt I needed to protect her from my pain, because I felt it would hurt her to see how devastated I was. I was afraid I would be hit by a powerful wave of emotion that would leave me out of control. That situation had the overlay of the previous traumatic events in my life, the death of my parents, which in fact did overwhelm me. But at the time, I couldn't see it.

As an adult I had a great deal more capacity to deal with the end of my marriage than I had as a child to deal with the demise of my parents. But the feelings of hopelessness and the sensation of too much stimulation came from the past and landed on the more current situation. I was unable to see which feelings were from the past and which feelings were from the dissolution of the marriage. I didn't look at my past, because I still had not seen that my past had anything to do with my present. I didn't seek professional help, because I didn't realize I needed it. Since I needed to function and desperately needed for Granny not to be upset, I felt it necessary to avoid that place of pain as much as possible. My attempt to push the pain away only distorted the energy in my body and I got sick. Of course, none of this was conscious or within my control.

What I did not do was give Granny the credit she deserved. Look what she had been through in her life! For me to be so grandiose as to think she couldn't handle my feelings about my marriage dissolving was underestimating her ability. But as a child, I was shown in unspoken messages not to show my pain about my parents. Instead, I felt I needed to protect others from my pain. Unfortunately, the pain from the loss of my parents was always right behind any current situation I was in, just waiting to break forth, which always gave me the feeling that whatever suffering I was experiencing was too much for other people to bear.

Thank God for the people and techniques I found to help me. While I was understanding my history more and more and experiencing the Neuro-Emotional Technique™, traumatic events continued to occur.

GRANNY AND GRANDPA

Carroll and Nellie Edwards, Elva's grandparents, are on their way to church. Although Grandpa was more comfortable in farming clothes, he always wore a suit and tie to church. The family went to the First Baptist Church in Tahoka every Sunday. Grandpa was a deacon of the church and Granny taught the children in Sunday School.

THE EDWARDS FAMILY

This is a special family photo made for the church directory when Elva Jo was in the eighth grade. Carroll, Nellie, Elva Jo, and Calva An Edwards.

A Texas Tragedy

FARM LIFE

Carroll Edwards

Grandpa loved to go to the ballpark and watch the children play little league baseball. This photo was taken in 1962. His visible trademarks: the hat, the cigarette in the right hand, sitting with his hand on his knee and with his knees wide apart, and his smile.

This is a photo of the farmhouse in which Carroll and Nellie Edwards raised Elva Jo and Calva An. It was the same farmhouse Calvin and Pearle lived in with Granny Rogers when they died. However, the house looks different because they built onto it in the early 1960's as Calva An and Elva Jo entered their teenage years.

CALVIN'S SISTER
ELVA'S AUNT

Albert and Mona Rae DeBusk and their daughter Mary Nell

Mona Rae was Calvin's older sister. They lived in Hobbs, New Mexico. Albert DeBusk died in 1970 and Mona Rae DeBusk died two months after her mother, in 1995. When Elva was a child, they visited in Tahoka for a weekend once a month. Elva Jo and Calva An would go to Hobbs and spend a week in the summer where they were shown a wonderful time.

CALVIN'S BROTHER
ELVA'S UNCLE

Robert and Wilma Edwards

Robert is eight years younger than Calvin. Robert married Wilma Gresham and they lived in Denver City until Robert moved to Tahoka to help his dad by farming the land Elva Jo and Calva An inherited from their Great-Granddad Pierce. Wilma worked as a hair dresser. When Elva Jo and Calva An were girls, Aunt Wilma always cut their hair and gave them permanents.

CALVIN'S SISTER
ELVA'S AUNT

Wayne and Freda Jeffcoat

Freda had three children from a previous marriage. She married Wayne when Elva Jo was a senior in high school. Elva Jo and Calva An saw Freda almost daily when they were children because Granny kept her children while she worked.

FIRST COUSINS

Front Row: Robert Gage, Donna Edwards, Rayfard Gage
Back Row: Milton Edwards, Elva Jo Edwards, Mary Nell DeBusk, Calva An Edwards

During our childhood we spent many hours together: in the cotton seed bin, in the cotton trailers, watching the pigs, playing football, swimming, watching comedies, riding our tricycles, and having the occasional argument.

A Texas Tragedy

FIRST COUSINS
FORTY YEARS LATER

All of Granny's grandchildren on the day of her funeral in December 1994.

*Pictured in front are Donna Stone, Jamie Rivera, Mary Nell Ford
And Standing are Calva Ledbetter, Milton Edwards,
Elva Edwards, Robert Gage and Rayfard Gage.*

LEAVING HOME

This photo was taken of Elva in 1970 while she was a student at Texas Tech University in Lubbock. She graduated with a B.S. in 1972.

Granny and Elva spent a few minutes together on the day of her wedding in 1972.

GRANNY AND HER GREAT-GRANDCHILDREN

*Granny and nine of thirteen great-grandchildren.
It was during this time Granny told Elva, "I'm enjoying my life as much as ever."*

Granny made her famous teacakes for three generations of children who always loved to eat the dough. Great granddaughter, Kena, sits on the kitchen counter, as Granny shapes a batch of teacakes. Kena is Calva's only child. She was born one week before Grandpa died in 1969.

Granny and great-granddaughter D'Lynn celebrated their birthdays together, Nov. 20 and 21.

A Texas Tragedy

FURTHER EDUCATION

Graduation Day —
Elva and Geary Benson, her study partner in chiropractic school.

Elva with Drew, Davy and D'Lynn Stone on Drew's wedding day, June 27, 1998. At Granny's funeral, Drew read the sweet essay that D'Lynn wrote about her Great-Granny.

Milton and Mary Ann Edwards married in 1984. Milton and Elva are first cousins. Mary Ann was new to the family when the series of articles were published about Pinkie Roden in 1991. It was Mary Ann who first approached Elva asking if she had seen the articles. That conversation was the impetus for Elva's investigation and ultimately this book.

GRANNY TURNS 90!

With all of the concern over Granny's health when Calvin and Pearle died, everyone was surprised at Granny's long life. Even with all of the hardships life had for Granny, she enjoyed her life. For Granny, her life was her family.

A Texas Tragedy

FRIENDS

Calva and Elva, along with Mike and Shirley Nosler, celebrate Elva's 40th birthday. Shirley and Elva have been best friends since 1975.

GRANNY WITH HER CHILDREN

Granny with five of the six children she raised, Calva Ledbetter, Robert Edwards, Elva Edwards, Freda Jeffcoat, and Mona Rae DeBusk.

An Edwards' cousins reunion the mid-90s.

CHAPTER FIFTY-TWO

"Bizarre?
Not Down in West Texas, it ain't."[1]

October 1998

On October 21, 1998, I realized the following day would be my mother's birthday. As a child, we never celebrated my mother or father's birthday. In fact, I'm embarrassed to admit that I didn't even know when my mother's birthday was until I spent some time at the cemetery when Granny died. I noticed my mother's headstone indicated her birthday was October 22. Even though Granny's funeral was four years prior, this was only the second time I had realized the significance of the day as it approached. In fact, as I fell asleep on the twenty-first, my last thought was, "tomorrow will be my mother's birthday." Even with that, I was a little surprised when I woke up the next morning with my first thought being, "today is my mother's birthday."

My heart swirled with a sweetness for my mother simply because it was her birthday. As I meditated, showered, and dressed for work, I sensed my love for her. It wasn't often I could think of her without sadness arising, but this time the feeling of sweetness was a form of love I was holding in my heart for her.

With that sense of sweetness at its height, I walked out my front door and picked up my morning newspaper, *The Denver Post*. After returning to the house, I opened the paper and pulled the first section back exposing the next section where the headline read, "Bizarre? Down in Texas, it Ain't."[2] Being a native of Texas, I was curious and started reading the article. Within a few seconds, I read a line that was very familiar to me. "It is a place where folks considered bootlegging not a crime but a public service."[3] I could sense the hair on my neck standing straight out. The overwhelming body sensations I'd become familiar with began having their way with me again. As I flipped the paper to page thirty-one where the article was continued, my body began to feel internally like a train running out of control. All I could do was watch what was happening as I was unable to stop what had been put into motion. It was less scary to me than previous times because I understood more of what was happening. But no amount of understanding could have made it easy for me.

Half-way through the article I read, "Then there was 'The Wizard of the West,' the late Tom 'Pinkie' Roden...During his earlier days, investigators quietly bought his souped-up used cars for a better chance to catch his drivers. 'He drove us crazy,' the late Coke Stevenson Jr., once the state liquor board administrator and an improbable admirer, had said. 'But I couldn't help but like him.'"[4]

Recognizing that the information had come from the articles written in 1991, I turned back to the first page to see that the author was none other than Mike Cochran. I was furious. I wanted to kill him. I was literally beside myself. How dare he so blatantly ignore the pain and suffering Pinkie caused me and my family. In 1991, when he wrote the series of articles about Pinkie, I had called him many times asking him to call me. He never did. I sent him a letter. No response. I mailed him copies of all the depositions I had retrieved from the Lynn County court house, and again no response. After this second assault, I made a vow to never give up. I would call him every day for the rest of my life until he responded, or I was arrested for stalking. I decided to become this man's worst nightmare. I was irate because he had totally ignored the letter I sent him, had never responded, and had the gall to write another story about how "cute and clever" Pinkie was even after I had brought my parents' deaths to his attention. That evening I wrote a letter to *The Denver Post* expressing my indignation about the article and requested a reply, but never received one.

I called the Associated Press in New York where they gave me the number for Mike Cochran at the *Fort Worth Star Telegram*. I left him a 'not-too-kind' message! Every day thereafter I left him at least one message, all of them angry. As my body calmed down over the next few days, my messages were less angry. It took five days for my body to approach its normal feeling again. On Monday morning, the fifth day, I decided to ask to speak to an editor at the *Fort Worth Star Telegram*.

The operator connected me and a man answered. I asked, "Could I speak with the editor who supervises Mike Cochran?"

"Well, he doesn't really work here," the editor informed me.

I said, "He has an office there doesn't he?"

"No, not really," he advised me. "He just comes by once in awhile and picks up his mail."

"Where is his office?" I asked.

The editor gave me a number for the Associated Press in Dallas.

Immediately I dialed the number. The woman who answered sounded young and frankly, unreliable. She asked me to spell Edwards. In my mind's eye, on the other end of the telephone line was a young woman polishing her nails, unconcerned with my request.

However, my assessment of the young woman was definitely wrong. Within thirty minutes, the telephone rang. Finally, after seven years, Mike Cochran called explaining to me that the woman who received my call had paged him and told him to call me because I was upset with him.

"I have a question for you," I asked attempting to control my anger. "I wonder if you are as enthralled with the criminal element as it sounds like in your article in *The Denver Post* on Thursday, or are you just making a buck?"

He rushed back a defensive response with, "I didn't make a dime on that article."

Trying to best him I said, "Well, you have a job don't you?"

He continued defending himself with, "It is just the truth. Pinkie was a character. I mean, when you have the head of the liquor control board saying we chased him for years and couldn't ever catch him, but couldn't help but like him, that is a character."

I said in a slow, commanding voice, "No, what that is is a bunch of Texas, good-ol'-boy, BULLSHIT! That is what that is. He was a criminal."

For a moment, there was silence. Then Mr. Cochran said, "Well, I didn't mean to be insensitive."

"But you were insensitive," I responded, not about to let him get by with that kind of apology. "Do you know who I am?"

"It had something to do with a tragic accident. When we talked before,—"

I interrupted him in mid-sentence, "What do you mean? I've never talked with you before."

"Didn't we talk a few years ago," he asked.

"No, we didn't. In fact, that has been a source of great pain for me. I called you numerous times after the series of articles you wrote in 1991 about Pinkie. I wrote you a letter. I even sent you all the depositions, and I never heard one word from you."

"I thought I talked with you a few years ago," he stated. I could sense him doing a mind search trying to locate how he knew I had something to do with a tragic accident.

"Perhaps you talked with the editor of the *Lubbock Avalanche-Journal* because he is the man I talked with in 1991, and I was pretty upset with you." I realized upset didn't even begin to describe what I'd gone through in 1991. "By the way, how many articles have you written about Pinkie?"

"I've just written the series in 1991 and this article that was printed Thursday in *The Denver Post*," Mike said.

"It is pretty incredible really." My throat tightened and my voice revealed my pain. "Both of those articles were published on my mother's birthday, seven years apart."

"You know, I really didn't mean to cause you any pain," Mike said with seeming genuineness.

"Yes, I understand that you probably didn't know about our accident when you wrote the articles in 1991, but you did this time. It isn't so much that you wrote about Pinkie, but the tone of the articles makes it seem like his behavior is funny, really hysterical. I believe your article said that Pinkie was such a great bootlegger he taught his runners to go the back roads to evade the liquor control boys." I paused with the sadness arising once again. "That is what happened when my parents were killed. What I want to know is, where are the articles about the pain Pinkie caused?" As I finished my sentence, my voice cracked, the sadness of my experience overflowing. "You know, six children found themselves living in an orphanage because of this accident."

We continued our conversation. I informed Mr. Cochran of the long search and investigation of the last seven years. "I'll send you the information I have about my parent's accident if you will read it."

He agreed to read the information, so I got his address. We both seemed to soften as we felt each other's humanity.

Although I had years of anger for him, I knew I wanted to speak with him again in the future. I couldn't help but like him, even though I didn't want to. He had tolerated my having my say about his articles and his particular slant toward Pinkie's illegal activities, and that meant a great deal to me. He even said he would consider writing an article from my perspective. What more could I ask for?

We ended our conversation with an agreement that we would speak again in the near future. In a certain way, I felt friendly toward him.

After hanging up the telephone, I sensed my body had calmed down. When in that place of traumatic overload, I have a feeling of bigness which allows me to say exactly what I want to say without any fear of reprisal. I wouldn't be so bold without that kind of energy. When my body calmed down, the sadness resurfaced. The sadness from the years of suffering sprang forth again. I wondered, would I ever stumble on to the accident and not have an emotional reaction? Just when I thought I had processed my history, I became painfully aware that there was more. It may never end.

CHAPTER FIFTY-THREE

*"Thanks to the good Christians of Abilene,
I will die a wealthy man."*[1]

Several weeks later I spoke with Mike Cochran again. I was anxious to hear if he had read the information I sent him, because I planned to dog him until he did. "Hi, Mike, this is Elva Edwards."

"Oh, hi Elva. I'm glad you called. I've been in and out of town and have intended to call you," Mike responded with a perkiness in his voice.

"I figured you had been out of town. I was wondering if you have had the opportunity to read the information I sent you?"

"Yes, as a matter of fact I did. It was interesting information, and now I have a better idea why you were so upset with the articles I wrote about Pinkie."

I smiled. He had read the information! "Yeah, I know what you mean. It is more complicated than just saying I'm angry about it," I said.

"I was glad to see that you got to the point of seeing that the accident wasn't really Pinkie's fault. It was really Maxey's fault, because he was driving the car."

I would not let this slide. "No, Mike, I disagree. If right now, in Pinkie's legal liquor operation in Lubbock, a driver of one of his trucks had an accident and someone was killed, legally the responsibility would fall on the employer. The liability would be Pinkie's, not the driver's. That's the law."

"Oh, I see what you mean," Mike said.

I didn't exactly want to belabor the point, but that was THE POINT, and if he didn't get that point, all my conversation with him was for naught. "First of all he was involved in an illegal business. But if it were his legal business, he would still be responsible. If anything it is worse because he was running an *illegal* business, and he didn't take responsibility for his employee. Pinkie was just a master at distancing himself from the law by putting in middle men like D.C. Turner. Pinkie told Maxey all of his orders and all of his pay would come from D.C. Turner. The reason for that was so no one could say that money went from Pinkie's hands into his runner's hands. My grandpa was right. Pinkie probably did think he was awful smart."

"You were right about the way the liquor control men acted toward Pinkie," Mike said. "I wonder if they laughed about the way Pinkie manipulated them, because they were embarrassed about not being able to catch him."

"Well, one man said in your original article that he could have caught him at any time. But, I suppose the man liked living." My tongue could be awfully sharp at times.

Mike chuckled. "You know, I talked to the sheriff of Odessa, and he told me that he could have arrested Pinkie many times, but if he had, he would have been run out of town."

"Yeah, Mike," I answered, "See what I mean. Money is power, and as we both know, Pinkie had a lot of money."

"He did have that."

Changing the subject, I said, "Mike, I want to meet you in person. I can come to Texas to see you, but I can't come before Christmas. I can come in January or February. Would that work out for you?"[2]

We both had to check our schedules and after numerous conversations we decided on a date and time that Mike and I would meet— in Tahoka.

CHAPTER FIFTY-FOUR

"It would be difficult to fault Tom "Pinkie" Roden's choice of political cronies, since one, Bob Bullock, is arguably the most powerful person now (1991) in state government. And another, State Sen. John Montford, is headed that way."[1]

February 1999

As I found my seat aboard the airplane, it struck me that my meeting with Mike Cochran was a culmination of eight years of investigation and work. After all these years, I was experiencing a satisfaction that had evaded me most of my life. With the satisfaction was a joyful lightness. Could it be happiness? I wondered.

It was easy to forget just how flat the land could be, until my airplane landed in Lubbock. After leaving Colorado, I was in awe for a few minutes at the difference in landscape. My family met me at the airport and the party began. It was always fun to see and visit them. Being with my aunts, uncles, and cousins always let me see what I had missed by not having parents as well as a family of my own. Yes, I got to go to lunch or go shopping with my Granny when I was young, and I loved it. But my cousins got to do the same thing with Granny then, and with their moms, now.

The next day I was standing in the doorway of my cousin's house in Tahoka as I watched Mr. Cochran park his car and approach the house. I opened the door and our eyes finally met, after all these years. We shook hands and the appropriate introductions were made.

With time limited, we soon found ourselves at the graveyard where my parents were buried. I pointed out the granite headstone that said "EDWARDS." Mike noticed my grandmother had lived twenty-five years longer than my grandfather. I noticed Granny's one life would have equaled three of my father's lifetimes. He died at thirty-three, and she at ninety-nine.

Within an hour we were at the intersection where my mother's life had ended and my life was changed forever. The area around the intersection had changed a great deal. The little country store and the gin were gone. Even though I had driven through the intersection numerous times before, I was struck by how ordinary it was and how extraordinary was the indelible imprint it left on my life.

I had brought several notebooks full of court documents to allow Mr. Cochran to verify that I, indeed, knew what I was talking about when it came to Pinkie Roden. We sat down for lunch and I said, "Mike, what stressed me the most about the articles you wrote was your implication that the people who were supposed to enforce the law thought it was funny that Pinkie was such a rascal," I offered. "You romanticized many of Pinkie's misdeeds."

"Well," Mike said, "it's certainly unusual for the people who have chased you and never caught you, to like you. That is what made Pinkie such a character."

We ordered lunch and continued discussing many aspects of the accident, the people involved, bootlegging, attorneys, court proceedings, and growing up without parents.

I explained to Mike the circumstances of the civil case that was spawned from our accident.

"Mike, this is the lawsuit that was filed with the court about seven months after our accident. The original petition was against S.F. Wells, Jr. because he was the owner of the car that Roy Maxey was driving. The lawsuit states Mr. Maxey was working within the scope of his employment, bootlegging forty-six quarts of whiskey and twenty-six cases of beer, was driving at an excessive rate of speed, was driving without his lights on, did not heed a stop sign, failed to yield right of way, operated the vehicle while under the influence of intoxicating beverages, and drove into oncoming traffic."[2]

"That's a lot of charges," Mike said.

I continued reading from the papers, "The suit claims the resulting injuries and deaths were caused by the negligence and carelessness of the driver and suggests Mr. Maxey was working for S.F. Wells, Jr. while transporting his load of whiskey, beer, and wine which was a criminal offense. The suit said he was driving at excessive speed and without lights to avoid being detected while bootlegging."[3]

"So they thought it was S.F. Wells' load of whiskey and beer?" Mike asked.

"The prosecution was presenting the case that way since it was Wells' car. They knew it was Pinkie's load of liquor. The truth was obvious to the attorneys, but you know how the law is. Normally, if you employed someone, they might drive your car. But Pinkie had his employees' drive someone else's car. That is one of the ways he protected himself legally," I said.

Continuing, I said, "In the lawsuit, it states bootlegging itself constituted negligence and not having lights on the front or the rear of the car was a violation of the law, as well as running a stop sign."[4]

"We know that is true," Mike commented.

"Pinkie and Wells bought that car together, but it was registered to Wells. Pinkie signed the note for Wells. And, the bank didn't ask for the money owed on it for two years after the car was wrecked. I find it unbelieveable! Wouldn't you like that kind of relationship with a bank?" We laughed. "So in plain talk, Mike you and I know that the car, although it was registered in Wells' name, was owned by Pinkie."

"Yeah, it looks that way," Mike agreed.

Iced tea was placed before us and the waitress informed us our food would be out soon. We had bread and butter to snack on in the meantime.

I said, "Mike, the part of this lawsuit that sent me straight through the roof was the money. You can see on this document that the suit requested damages for

1. our wrecked car which was a financial loss of $1750;
2. the mental pain and anguish my father suffered for the seven hours he survived for $5000;
3. my father's hospital bills, as well as my sister's and mine were about $325;
4. $1000 for the cemetery headstone for my parents;
5. $4,500 for the funeral expenses for my mother, father, and grandmother;
6. since my father was thirty-three-years-old and had a life expectancy of thirty-three more years and was making an average of $10,000 per year, his counsel and guidance was priced at $100,000;
7. since my mother was thirty years old and had a life expectancy of thirty-four more years, her guidance, care, and support was priced at $50,000.[5]

It is outrageous that they consider my father's life worth twice as much as my mother's. And Mike, I want you to guess how much my physical and mental suffering was considered to be worth?"

"How much?" Mike asked.

"Five hundred dollars.[6] Just think about that Mike. Five hundred dollars!!"

I had to excuse myself and go to the ladies room. I felt our society's view of children's pain was heartless.

People did not seem to think the pain felt by children was as severe as the pain of adults, but before reading the court documents I had thought those were unconscious beliefs and ideas of adults. It seemed like society wasn't aware of our bias because we hadn't consciously explored our feelings, beliefs, and actions as a society. But to actually see in print that my father's seven hours of mental and physical pain was felt to be worth $5000, while my suffering from physical injuries that kept me in the hospital a week and my mental anguish of needing and wanting my parents for the rest of my life was valued at $500 enraged me.

I was certain my father was in physical pain. He had numerous fractures. And I was certain he was in mental anguish, because he knew my mother had died and we had been injured. Just because my mother died quickly didn't mean she wasn't in pain. Perhaps, the pain of my mother and father ended with their death and perhaps it didn't. Mine on the other hand continued indefinitely.

Society has not changed much in the way we view children or the way we view women. A very small child was killed in the Denver area by the parent and at trial a verdict of guilty was rendered and punishment was a number of years in jail. An article in the paper quoted the prosecutor as saying that she did not understand the verdict of the jury, as on any given day an adult murdering an adult would receive a life sentence. The child was helpless to fight back and yet there was a lesser sentence handed down. It simply reflected that we, as a society, did not think the life of a child was as important as the life of an adult. If we want to see what we believe, we only need to look at how we behave.

I returned to the lunch table and our food arrived. Mike and I chit-chatted about the restaurant and the people having lunch. I met the attorney, an acquaintance of Mike's, who had advised the *Lubbock-Avalanche Journal* not to print my original letter. Mike and I chuckled at the coincidence of meeting him there. Our conversation veered again toward Pinkie.

"Mike, perhaps in the eyes of the law, Pinkie was not directly linked with our accident because he did not give Mr. Maxey a W-2 form, but in my eyes, he was responsible. I've never heard of any illegal drug trafficker giving their runners W-2 forms for taxes, and yet our jails are full of people who have been convicted of drug dealing. Anyone who wants to can see that Pinkie directed the illegal work and provided a car for the illegal work. I don't feel Mr. Maxey was absolved of responsibility, but Mr. Maxey's life was completely compromised after the accident while Pinkie kept right on doing what Pinkie did best—breaking the law while laughing in the lawman's face. Let's not forget his throwing his power and money around to get what he wanted politically. The death of my parents was not even cause for him to skip a beat in his illegal business. The winks and blinks and chuckles his antics received from the lawmen cheapened the lives of my parents and my loss, especially when I read those depositions and the settlement."

"What exactly did the settlement agreement say?" Mike asked after taking a drink of his iced tea.

"An agreement was made for a $12,000 settlement. I saw the work the attorneys did because I read the many petitions they filed in court, and the depositions. They traveled for depositions and investigation. They supported and advised my grandpa, and for that the lawyers got $6000 of the settlement. They probably earned it. In a certain sense it didn't matter that my suffering was only considered worth $500, because we didn't get even a penny," I said dabbing my mouth with my napkin.[7]

"What do you mean you didn't get a penny?"

"When you add up the money we lost from the accident, not counting my parents, but just the actual material loss like our hospital bills, the funeral bills, the money for the car, the headstone for my parents, and so forth, we ended up over $1500 in the hole. And, in 1951, $1500 was a lot of money, unless of course you were the kingpin of the bootlegging business."

"Yeah, it was a lot of money. It is still a lot of money," Mike said.

I continued, "No wonder after that agreement my grandpa had a major heart attack. After that heart attack, Grandpa always told me the doctor said he could drop dead any moment. I could have gone about eighteen years without hearing that."

We sat silently for a moment when I decided to give Mike my idea about Pinkie's psychological make-up. "You know Mike, I think there is the distinct possibility that Pinkie had a flaming personality disorder." I began digging in my purse and pulled out a sheet of paper and positioned it in a way Mike and I could both see it. "Prisons and jails are full of criminals who have personality disorders. If you portrayed Pinkie correctly in your articles, you gave a good description of a person with a sociopathic personality disorder. I brought the list of characteristics that are listed in the diagnosis book for a sociopath:

> 1. 'fails to conform to social norms with respect to lawful behavior . . . destroying property, harassing others, stealing, pursuing an illegal occupation
> 2. repeatedly fails to honor financial obligations . . .
> 3. has no regard for the truth. as indicated by repeated lying, use of aliases, or "conning" others for personal profit or pleasure
> 4. is reckless regarding his own or others' personal safety . . .
> 5. lacks remorse (feels justified in having hurt, mistreated, or stolen from another)'[8]

What do you think Mike?"

"Well, you may have something there. It isn't too normal for the sheriffs and politicians to have so many good things to say about a person who has broken the law as much as Pinkie did," Mike confessed as he thanked the waitress for bringing our food.

"Pinkie fits the description. Sociopaths like to be dangerous, riding that fine line of being caught, and certainly we could say that about Pinkie," I concluded.

Of course, Pinkie was dead and in a certain way it did not matter if he did or did not have a personality disorder. But, I found it interesting, because sociopaths have a way of endearing themselves to others even when they do so many bad things. Otherwise, why were people, especially the enforcers of the law, so taken by this man?

Mike and I spent the day together and began a friendship that continues. Mike had the opportunity to read the depositions of Mr. Maxey, Mr. Wells, and Pinkie. After reading Pinkie's deposition, Mike looked up at me and said,

"After reading this, what I want to know is why wasn't Pinkie tried for perjury?"[9]

I smiled.

CHAPTER FIFTY-FIVE

*"As Ector County's top cop at the time,
Slim Gabriel, now retired, explained:
'I wasn't a very good sheriff, but I was a wise one.
If I'd arrested Pinkie, the oil show people
and the Chamber of Commerce
would have run me out of town.'"*[1]

Mike Cochran and I bid each other farewell with Mike offering to write an article from my perspective for the Associated Press about my journey and the pain Pinkie caused others. And for this, my appreciation for him soared.

After we went our separate ways, I could feel my longing for my grandpa. I once told a friend that I could have used a father's guiding hand for about ten more years. She said, "You think that Elva, but kids don't want to listen to their parents at that age and you wouldn't have listened to your grandpa either." She was probably right, but it was easy to idealize how it could have been with my grandpa, just as it was easy to idealize how it could have been with my parents.

Once I told a friend I wished I had parents. She responded with, "You can have mine." I had to giggle, but I needed to be reminded of how few parents and adult children have worked out their issues. It was easy and fun to idealize all the wonderful things about having parents, but I never seemed to think of the limitations or difficulties we would have had.

I had the sweetest elderly man and wife as patients. In our conversation, I told her about my parents being killed when I was one-and-one-half-years old, and some of what I had gone through. The lady stood rigidly at the front counter in my office, looked me in the eye and said, "My mother died when I was four years old and I have suffered from that all of my life." She understood. Without her saying anything more, I felt soothed and comforted to have someone validate and understand my experience. She didn't have to ask how I felt about it, or if I was looking for a legal remedy. Nor did she ask why I was curious about my parents and the trials surrounding their deaths. She understood, because she, too, suffered.

I remember the day I realized that the feeling of deficiency I've had throughout my life had nothing to do with my actually being deficient, but instead with ideas that not having parents created in my mind. My ideas were something to the effect that I wasn't as good as other kids, because I didn't have parents. Or that I wasn't loveable enough to have parents. Basically my mind said there was some kind of inherent flaw in me that kept me from having parents. Those ideas were there to help my childlike mind try to understand why my life was different, why I didn't have parents. My mind dwelt on those things long enough that my heart believed them. In fact, there was a solid conviction that it was so. And one day my eyes opened, and I could see that there was no inherent deficiency or flaw. I realized it had all occurred between my own ears. The flaw was in my thinking. When I realized that, I was filled with compassion for myself and all the suffering I'd experienced in my life over not having parents.

CHAPTER FIFTY-SIX

"Pinkie's clout with the Liquor Control Board was almost mystical."[1]

April 1999

Mike Cochran wrote a feature article for the Associated Press about my experiences in investigating the accident that imprinted my life at such an early age. The article was written from my perspective and was his answer to my original question of "where are the articles that show the pain Pinkie caused?" The article was picked up by many newspapers throughout the state of Texas. A few days after the article was published, I received a telephone call.

"I'm calling for Elva Edwards," the gruff Texan voice said on the other end of the telephone line.

"This is Elva Edwards," I said as I sat vigilant, wondering who was calling with this deep, unfamiliar, male voice.

"I read the article in the Midland newspaper this weekend about the accident you were in back in 1951, and I was there," he said. My mind was awhirl. *He was there?*

Who could this be? I knew the article had been published around Texas over the weekend. But I'd had no idea anyone was still alive who was at the scene in 1951.

"Now who is this?" I asked trying to find an appropriate way to proceed with the conversation.

"I'm Leonard Coffman. My dad was Kevil Coffman," he explained.

"Really," I commented recognizing the enormity of what he was saying. "It was your dad who carried me to the hospital that night," I stated.

"Yes," he said. "I was there. I was out the door right behind him that night. I was only ten years old."

"You were there," I said in amazement as my thoughts went back to that night of which I had no conscious memory. It had never occurred to me that Kevil Coffman had a child. Nothing was ever mentioned about that in any of the newspapers or court documents. I was focused for the next few hours while Leonard and I pieced together what we each knew about that fateful night of May 21, 1951.

Toward the end of our conversation he said with a wavering voice, "It really shook up my Dad." He admitted it had affected his own life a great deal too.

"When you were old enough to get your driver's license, did the accident influence the way you drove?" I asked.

He responded with each word emphasized, "Yes, it did then, and for the rest of my life."

The orphans may have been affected the most, but Leonard said the accident left a permanent impression on everyone in his family. In our last moments on the telephone, I shared with him how much I appreciated Mike Cochran and his articles, because if they had not been printed, we would never have connected. Our telephone conversation lasted until it drew to a natural conclusion when I asked him to meet with me the next time I visited Texas.[2]

Hanging up the telephone, I let what he had said percolate in my mind. Leonard said his parents never talked to him about that night when he witnessed more than any ten year old should have. It was evident that my trauma became his trauma, too. Going back in my mind to the accident invariably left me with feelings of sadness.

CHAPTER FIFTY-SEVEN

"...the little girls are far from the scene now, that is if they will ever be far from it..."[1]

February 2000

The howling winds of Texas called me once again. D'Lynn, my cousin who had written the touching essay about my Granny that had been read at her funeral, was playing basketball as a high school sophomore and wanted me to come watch her play. It was time for a trip to Texas to see my family and I also wanted an opportunity to meet Leonard Coffman.

Several weeks before my trip, I wrote Leonard a letter and told him the dates I would be in Tahoka and asked if he would be able to meet me. He called and we agreed on a time and place in Tahoka to meet. We met in a convenience store. As I walked in, our eyes met. We were the only older people in the store. I looked at him and said, "Are you Leonard?"

He answered, "Yes."

Leonard drove his wife, Brenda, and me to the accident site where he pointed out where each car had landed that night in 1951. He delineated all the physical changes in the West Point area since he was a ten-year-old boy. We spent several hours together discussing the event that had been important in shaping both of our lives.

"The article Mike wrote about you sure brought up a lot of emotion for Leonard," Brenda said. The couple told me what they had been going through for the last year. Reading the articles stirred him emotionally just as Mr. Cochran's original articles about Pinkie had stirred me. Emotions that had been subconscious for all these years surged through to his present awareness, making it necessary for him to deal with his past. For both of us, our meeting was, in part, one way to heal from our shared past.

I told them about a situation in Denver which had stirred me emotionally, again bringing feelings from the past to a current situation. "A six-year-old girl was killed in Denver several years ago as she darted in front of a young man who stated that he never saw her. He was driving and the sun was in his eyes when the little girl ran right out in front of him. The driver was distraught and went to the hospital to check on the little girl. He and his parents attended the little girl's funeral. He was truly sorry with all of his heart. And, you know, I feel it's because his sorrow was so real and he was so open and honest, the parents of the little girl said on television, 'We understand, and we forgive you.' Now, there was nothing but sadness in the situation, but no one was irresponsible. The little girl was simply being a little girl. The driver wasn't on drugs or alcohol or speeding or in any way affected because of his own misdeeds or carelessness. It was an unfortunate morning where the sun was just on the horizon creating difficulties for drivers. That driver hit her, but if she'd run in front of me, it would have been me that hit her."

We all nodded our heads in a knowing way, understanding that accidents can and do happen without any irresponsibility.

After a long pause I continued, "Several years ago there was a man in Denver who was driving drunk and hit a woman and her two little girls. He killed the mother and one of the little girls. Her husband was a professional bike rider and was in Europe at the time. I remember reading the article in the paper when the driver went to court. He said he was sorry. I wanted to yell at him 'It's too damn late to be sorry,' especially for that little girl who needed her mother. He should have thought about that before he got behind the wheel drunk."

I noticed my body was getting triggered, or as my grandpa would say, "all riled up." I was aware of how little tolerance I had for irresponsibility. At this point I had learned I could calm my body down by being very present to what feelings were in my body. My focused attention often diffused the stress reaction. It was a practice I learned through meditation.

Brenda, Leonard and I had returned to my cousin's house where we drank glasses of iced tea while sitting around the dining room table. Our conversation turned away from the accident itself to Pinkie and bootlegging and Mike Cochran. Brenda said, " It doesn't do you any good to hate Pinkie. That will only hurt you, not him."

I agreed, "No, it doesn't. But it was important for me to go through all of the feelings I had that had been stored all these years. The more I understand it, the less reactive I am about him. This may sound strange to you, but in a way, I have compassion for Pinkie. I don't think he could help himself. If you look at all of the characteristics of a sociopathic, or an anti-social personality disorder, he fits it to a tee, or at least from the information in Mike Cochran's articles."

"Really," Brenda said with curiosity. "What makes you think so?"

"If you think about it, how would you feel if you were responsible for an accident like the one I was in?" I asked.

"Oh, my gosh, I don't know if I could live with myself having killed five people," Leonard said.

"Normal people would say something like that. It would be a life changing event. They would feel a heaviness for having been responsible for taking another's life, let alone taking five people's lives and leaving twelve children orphaned! Normal people would have to go to counseling and do a lot of work on themselves to be able to step back into life in a meaningful way. But, from all I could tell, it didn't even cause a pause for Pinkie."

"Well, yeah," Brenda said, "It seems like a normal person would feel guilty."

"And that is one reason why I think Pinkie was a sociopath. Most people would be in agony over it, but a sociopath would not because they don't have a conscience. Our accident didn't seem to bother Pinkie that much. And, that brings me to how I have found some compassion for him. A person is not a sociopath for no reason. It is often a parenting problem. There may be some tendency toward it inherently, but usually there was little attunement to the child by the parents. Or there was some huge kind of disruption for him in his early life where he didn't get what he needed to develop in a normal way.

"From what I understand, sociopaths feel such a huge emptiness inside because they don't have the normal ego structure. They attempt to fill that emptiness with all kinds of things. He tried to fill it with money and power, and in 1951, over eight million dollars in his legal operation wasn't enough to fill him. He needed more, so he also bootlegged. He made much money and held nothing sacred—nothing got in his way. Even if his driver's health was ruined and twelve children were orphaned, it didn't matter. Nothing and no one was more important than Pinkie getting what Pinkie wanted no matter who or what he had to manipulate or destroy. He was so grandiose as to have liquor control agents transferred if they caused him a problem."

"How could a liquor agent have done his job and not have caused Pinkie a problem?" Leonard asked.

"It is a mystery, isn't it? But in the articles Mike Cochran wrote that Pinkie's wife admitted he did.[2] Our accident didn't seem to cause him to reflect upon himself and his life. So in a way I have to feel sorry for him that his development was so lacking that he was left with this kind of personality disorder. Of course, I'm not a psychiatrist, but he did, according to the information I read, fit the diagnosis.

When I see people who have a difficult time taking responsibility for their life, I realize how much my grandparents gave me. I know how to be a responsible person. So when I track it like that, having a personality disorder wasn't his fault in a certain way." I paused. "That doesn't mean he didn't have any responsibility for the accident, but just that he didn't have the capacity to have normal feelings and behavior. And that, in and of itself, is sad for anyone, even Pinkie."

"Yeah, I guess your right," commented Brenda.

"As I have understood more and more about my history and Pinkie, I see it is not for me to judge. I have to leave justice to God. My job has been to heal, in a real way, not in the superficial way of saying 'oh, I'm fine.' For me, investigating the people and the events related to the accident was a big piece in the healing process. At some point in my understanding there was a kind of liberation in just knowing the truth, and in the center of that liberation was a transformation. The transformation was in how I saw myself, especially in relationship to the rest of the world."

"How did you see yourself differently?" asked Brenda.

"All these years, in the back of my mind and in the bottom of my heart, I felt it was my fault I didn't have parents. There was something about me that was bad and caused me not to have parents. I remember once thinking that maybe I had caused the accident by crying or something." I had to chuckle at such an absurdity. "But seriously, others inherently had what I didn't and that meant something was wrong with me. Going through the sadness of my loss has been almost like a cleansing. None of the facts have changed, but the way I relate to them has changed considerably. The change is internal, my inner experience. I'm sure it doesn't look any different to the external world."

Brenda says, "It sounds like it has been good for you."

"It has been because now I understand my life a lot better. At nineteen-months-of-age a child is attempting to find an optimal distance from the mother. The child wants some independence, but in two minutes they want mommy back and being without her creates anxiety. So the conflict is between being independent and having the closeness and love of the mother. Obviously, I didn't get the closeness with my mother which, I think, has manifested in my feeling very alone in this world. I know it looks like, to the outside world, that I am independent. And, I am. But I am also alone."

"Well, it must have been hard to work through a loss as great as yours," Brenda said.

"I'm healing from hurts that even I was unaware were present, but nonetheless ran my life. I'm not saying I'm through. I guess we don't finish until we die. But I do thank God for the understandings I have. I've shed many tears, but I remember the day when I woke up and looked myself in the mirror and said out loud, 'I do not need parents.' I was somewhat surprised. I'd been going through my life feeling this emptiness, this hole in my heart, and suddenly I realized I didn't need the same thing I needed as a child, like a mom. It sounded silly, but it was a revelation to me. Yes, it would be nice to have a mom to share my life with and it would also be nice to have a million dollars, but I don't need either to feel as if I am a whole human being, a complete person. I realized when I felt like I needed my mom, it was because inside I felt like a little girl, since a little girl does need a mom."

We continued our conversation about our families and Leonard told me his granddaughter was writing an essay about her great-grandpa, the hero who saved a little girl's life. It was sweet.

Before we parted I said, "Leonard, one of your friends called me one week after I spoke with you the first time. Do you remember Bill Pendleton?"

"Oh, yeah. We were friends when we were kids. His grandparents ran the grocery store at West Point," he said.

"Do you remember the day you two were looking at the accident site together after the wreck," I asked.

"Yeah, we talked about the accident and walked over to the site to see how much glass was left in the ditch until it was all gone."

"Do you remember that he found a penny he thought had been in our car?" I asked.

"Yeah," he chuckled, "but we didn't know if it really came out of one of those cars or if it was there before."

"Bill kept that penny all these years! I thought that was amazing! He called after reading the article Mike Cochran wrote about me. He said he wanted to send the penny to me and about two weeks later it arrived in the mail. He said he didn't really know if it was from our car, but as a little boy he wanted to think it was. And he said the accident really left a huge impression on him."

"No bigger than the impression it left on you, I'm sure," said Brenda.

"Oh, the impression was quite deep because I was so young. Some people think the younger you are, the less it affects you. That is absurd. The younger you are, the less ability you have to help yourself, ask for help or even understand what is happening to you."

"It makes sense it would make you feel insecure," Brenda said.

"Yeah, and that's why it has bothered me when people have told me I was too small to notice or care that my parents suddenly disappeared. I beg to differ with them, and I think current child psychologists would, too. It creates such a hole in your heart when your parent dies early. I had a deep feeling of not being wanted. It felt like I had no value because I thought, 'if my parents don't want me, who would?' People would tell me how lucky I was. I didn't get it, because I thought kids who had parents were lucky. My friends who had parents were never told they were lucky. It was very confusing, even though my grandparents were the greatest. They really were."

"It sounds like they were, but it doesn't mean you didn't suffer from not having your parents," Brenda said.

"Yes, I must say it makes me feel almost as if I have a new life, with a lighter heart. You know, Pinkie's wife said he died a lonely man and with a broken heart.[3] Pinkie said you could count your real friends on one hand and have fingers left over.[4] For a sociopath that would be true because they don't have a clue about real friendship. Money bought him political favors, but it didn't buy him real friends."

"No," Leonard said, "it never does."

"So who was the unlucky one? Maybe Pinkie was the unlucky one. My granny had a difficult life, but she died with her family devoted to her even after a lifetime of illness and fifteen years of being dependent on us for her care. She was never forsaken by friends or family. She was loved, even though her body and her mind were worn out years before her passing. My life hasn't been perfect by any means, but I have been blessed with family and a multitude of wonderful friends. My love for my grandparents was so huge, and still is. Even though I didn't have my parents, I did have a lot of love. I now have the kind of understanding of my life that has given me some peace. In death, Pinkie only had his wife."

There was a moment of silence.

"Is there anything left unresolved for you?" asked Leonard.

"I have no doubt that unconsciously there is because it keeps arising, but with less intensity than before. Consciously, the main thing I keep asking myself about is, where are the Riley orphans and how has this complex set of circumstances played out in their lives?

It does still bother me that the politicians, like John Montford, who is the chancellor of Texas Tech right now, where I graduated, were Pinkie's Austin 'contacts.' I still don't understand the lawmen laughing about how funny it was that Pinkie got by them. But in a way, that too is a sign of Pinkie being a sociopath. In counseling, they say there is no help for the sociopath, because he is so manipulative he gets the counselor wrapped around the sociopath's little finger. That is sort of what Pinkie did with the politicians and lawmen—manipulated them into getting what he wanted."

"Yeah, it sounds like he did that all right," Leonard said.

"It meant a lot to me that Mike Cochran wrote that article. He didn't have to respond to me, or listen to my side of the story. He certainly didn't have to write an article from my point of view about Pinkie Roden, but Mike is a man of conscience—unlike Pinkie. You know, when Mike was interviewing me, right before we were going our separate ways, I said, 'I just want you to know I appreciate this.' And you know what he said?"

"What?" the Coffman's asked in unison.

"Mike Cochran said, 'Let me make my amends.'"

THE NEXT GENERATION

Elva looks forward to the future with her great-niece and great-nephew, Kalia and Cody Galvan. They are the children of Kena and Raymond Galvan. They are Calva's grandchildren.

APPENDIX

Dr. Elva Edwards
13318 West Exposition Drive
Lakewood, CO 80228

email address is elva@ecentral.com

Dr. Elva Edwards is in private chiropractic practice in Lakewood, Colorado. She is available for seminars, lectures, and consultations and provides a mail order service for patients. For seminars and lectures contact Bookings Publicity at 303-986-8738.

To review the articles Mike Cochran wrote about Elva's jouney, go to www.lubbockonline.com and go to the April 11, 1999 edition. The title of the story was "Murder She Wrote."

APPENDIX

CAST OF CHARACTERS

Elva Jo Edwards .... orphaned by accident
Calva An Edwards .... orphaned by accident
Calvin Edwards .... father of Elva and Calva, died in accident
Pearle Edwards .... mother of Elva and Calva, died in accident
Elva Rogers .... grandmother of Elva and Calva, died in accident
Tom "Pinkie" Roden .... bootlegging kingpen of West Texas
Roy Maxey .... driver of bootlegging car
Samuel Riley .... passenger in bootlegging car, died in accident
Mrs. Samuel Riley .... passenger in bootlegging car, died in accident
Carroll Edwards .... father of Calvin Edwards
Nellie Edwards .... mother of Calvin Edwards
Robert Edwards .... brother of Calvin Edwards
Wilma Edwards .... wife of Robert Edwards
Freda Jeffcoat .... sister of Calvin Edwards
Mona Rae DeBusk .... sister of Calvin Edwards
Milton Edwards .... son of Robert Edwards
Mary Ann Edwards .... wife of Milton Edwards
Donna Stone .... daughter of Robert Edwards
Dan Stone .... husband of Donna Stone
Drew Stone .... son of Dan and Donna Stone
Davy Stone .... son of Dan and Donna Stone
D'Lynn Stone .... daughter of Dan and Donna Stone
Melvin Burks .... high school counselor
Mitchell Williams .... county attorney for Lynn County in 1951
Truett Smith .... the Edwards' attorney in 1951
Calloway Huffaker .... the Edwards' attorney in 1951
Wilson Edwards .... best friend and cousin of Calvin Edwards
Polly Edwards .... best friend of Calvin and Pearle Edwards
Glenda Mathers .... daughter of Roy Maxey
W.T. and Esta Mae Kidwell .... friends of Calvin and Pearle Edwards
Ruby Harvick .... nurse at Tahoka hospital
Lawrence Harvick .... Ruby Harvick's husband
Kevil Coffman .... gin manager and first on scene of accident
Marie Coffman .... wife of Kevil Coffman
Leonard Coffman .... son of Kevil and Marie Coffman
Brenda Coffman .... wife of Leonard Coffman
Billy Pendleton .... boyhood friend of Leonard Coffman
Jeno Jones .... ambulance attendant
Benny Moore .... man who informed Carroll Edwards of the wreck

ENDNOTES

CHAPTER ONE
1 Cochran, Mike. "Pinkie's liquor empire was hard-earned, well-respected," Lubbock Avalanche-Journal, (TX) 21 October 1991, sec. A, p. 8.
2 Cochran, Mike. "Pinkie's' life filled with success, odd mix of acquaintances," Lubbock Avalanche-Journal, (TX) 20 October 1991, sec. A, p. 5.
3 In re Elva Jo Edwards and Calva An Edwards vs. S. F. Wells, Jr. Et. Al., No. 1989 (District Court of Lynn Co., Tx. 1953).
4 Cochran, Mike. "Pinkie's' life filled with success, odd mix of acquaintances," Lubbock Avalanche-Journal, (TX) 20 October 1991, sec. A, p. 5.
5 Ibid.
6 Ibid.
7 Ibid.
8 Cochran, Mike. "Pinkie's liquor empire was hard-earned, well-respected," Lubbock Avalanche-Journal, (TX) 21 October 1991, sec. A, p. 8.
9 In re Elva Jo Edwards & Calva An Edwards vs. S. F. Wells, Jr. Et. Al., No. 1989, (District Court of Lynn Co., Tx. 1953).
10 Cochran, Mike. "Pinkie's liquor empire was hard-earned, well-respected," Lubbock Avalanche-Journal, (TX) 21 October 1991, sec. A, p. 8.
11 Ibid.
12 In re Elva Jo Edwards & Calva An Edwards vs. S. F. Wells, Jr. Et. Al., No. 1989, (District Court of Lynn Co., Tx. 1953).
13 Ibid.
14 Ibid.

CHAPTER TWO
1 Cochran, Mike. "Pinkie's liquor empire was hard-earned, well-respected," Lubbock Avalanche-Journal, (TX) 21 October 1991, sec. A, p. 8.
2 Edwards, Robert. Personal interview. 1991.

CHAPTER THREE
1 Cochran, Mike. "Pinkie's' life filled with success, odd mix of acquaintances," Lubbock Avalanche-Journal, (TX) 20 October 1991, sec. A, p. 5.
2 Coffman, Leonard. Personal interview. April 1999.
3 In re The State of Texas vs. Roy Maxey, No. 2,862, (County Court of Lynn Co., Texas, 1952).
4 Coffman, Leonard. Personal interview. April 1999.

CHAPTER FOUR
1 Cochran, Mike. "Pinkie's liquor empire was hard-earned, well-respected," Lubbock Avalanche-Journal, (TX) 21 October 1991, sec. A, p. 8.
2 Kidwell, Este Mae. Personal interview. 1991.
3 Edwards, Polly. Personal interview. 1992.

CHAPTER FIVE
1 Cochran, Mike. "Pinkie's liquor empire was hard-earned, well-respected," Lubbock Avalanche-Journal, (TX) 21 October 1991, sec. A, p. 8.
2 In re The State of Texas vs. Roy Maxey, No. 2,962, (County Court of Lynn Co., Texas, 1952.)
3 Hall, Jerry. "Crash Tragedy For Youngsters," Lubbock Avalanche-Journal, 23 May, 1951, sec. 2.
4 Mathers, Glenda. Personal interview. 1993.
5 Edwards, Robert. Personal interview. 1996.
6 Ibid.
7 Unknown. "Five Killed In Two-Car Crash Near West Point," The Lynn County News, (TX) 25 May 1951, p. 1.
8 Edwards, Polly. Personal interview. 1993.
9 Edwards, Robert. Personal interview. 1996.

CHAPTER SIX
1 Hall, Jerry. "Crash Tragedy For Youngsters," Lubbock Avalanche-Journal, 23 May, 1951, sec. 2.
2 Edwards, Polly and Wilson Edwards. Personal interview. 1991.

CHAPTER SEVEN
1 Hall, Jerry, and Hank McKee. "Four Die, Four Hurt in Crash," Lubbock Avalanche-Journal, 22 May, 1951, sec. 1.
2 Edwards, Polly and Wilson Edwards. Personal interview. 1991.
3 Ledbetter, Calva. Interview with Ruby Harvick. 1991.
4 Edwards, Polly and Wilson Edwards. Personal interview. 1991.

CHAPTER EIGHT
1 Hall, Jerry. "Crash Tragedy For Youngsters," Lubbock Avalanche-Journal, 23 May, 1951, sec. 2.
2 Edwards, Robert. Personal interview. 1996.
3 This is one of the two scenes in this book where I do not have documentation. I took the liberty of using information from Pinkie Roden's deposition and Mike Cochran's newspaper articles together to create this scene.
4 Coffman, Leonard. Personal interview. 1999.

CHAPTER NINE
1 Cochran, Mike. "Pinkie's liquor empire was hard-earned, well-respected," Lubbock Avalanche-Journal, (TX) 21 October 1991, sec. A, p. 8.
2 In re Elva Jo Edwards and Calva An Edwards vs. S. F. Wells, Jr. Et. Al., No. 1989, (District Court of Lynn Co. Tx., 1953).
3 This is the second scene for which I did not have documentation. I combined information from the depositions available and the newspaper articles. These are the ONLY two scenes in this book for which I do not have documentation.

CHAPTER TEN
1 Cochran, Mike. "Pinkie's' life filled with success, odd mix of acquaintances," Lubbock Avalanche-Journal, (TX) 20 October 1991, sec. A, p. 5.
2 Pool, Harvey. Personal interview. 1998.
3 Edwards, Polly and Wilson Edwards. Personal interview. 1991.

CHAPTER ELEVEN
1 Unknown. "Five Killed in Two-Car Crash Near West Point," The Lynn County News, (TX) 25 May, 1951.
2 Ledbetter, Calva. Personal interview. 1991.
3 Edwards, Nellie. Personal interview. 1982.
4 Edwards, Polly and Wilson Edwards. Personal interview. 1991.

CHAPTER TWELVE
1 Cochran, Mike. "Pinkie's' life filled with success, odd mix of acquaintances," Lubbock Avalanche-Journal, (TX) 20 October 1991, sec. A, p. 5.
2 Coffman, Leonard. Personal interview. April 1999.
3 Edwards, Polly. Personal interview. 1995.
4 Edwards, Carroll. Personal interview. 1968.

CHAPTER THIRTEEN
1 Hall, Jerry. "Crash Tragedy For Youngsters," Lubbock Avalanche-Journal, 23 May, 1951, sec. 2.
2 Edwards, Carroll. Personal interview. 1968.

CHAPTER FOURTEEN
1 Hall, Jerry. "Crash Tragedy For Youngsters," Lubbock Avalanche- Journal, 23 May, 1951, sec. 2.
2 Edwards, Nellie. Personal interview. 1969.

CHAPTER FIFTEEN
1 Hall, Jerry. "Crash Tragedy For Youngsters," Lubbock Avalanche- Journal, 23 May, 1951, sec. 2.

CHAPTER SIXTEEN
1 Hall, Jerry. "Crash Tragedy For Youngsters," Lubbock Avalanche- Journal, 23 May, 1951, sec. 2.

CHAPTER SEVENTEEN
1 Cochran, Mike. "Political sidekicks delighted in 'Pinkie's' law making antics" Lubbock Avalanche-Journal, (TX) 22 October 1991, sec. A, p. 8.

CHAPTER EIGHTEEN
1 Cochran, Mike. "Pinkie's' life filled with success, odd mix of acquaintances," Lubbock Avalanche-Journal, (TX) 20 October 1991, sec. A, p. 5.

CHAPTER NINETEEN
1 Cochran, Mike. "Pinkie's' life filled with success, odd mix of acquaintances," Lubbock Avalanche-Journal, (TX) 20 October 1991, sec. A, p. 5.

CHAPTER TWENTY
1 Cochran, Mike. "Pinkie's' life filled with success, odd mix of acquaintances," Lubbock Avalanche-Journal, (TX) 20 October 1991, sec. A, p. 5.

CHAPTER TWENTY-ONE
1 Cochran, Mike. "Pinkie's' life filled with success, odd mix of acquaintances," Lubbock Avalanche-Journal, (TX) 20 October 1991, sec. A, p. 5.

CHAPTER TWENTY-TWO
1 Cochran, Mike. "Pinkie's' life filled with success, odd mix of acquaintances," Lubbock Avalanche-Journal, (TX) 20 October 1991, sec. A, p. 5.

CHAPTER TWENTY-THREE
1 Cochran, Mike. "Pinkie's' life filled with success, odd mix of acquaintances," Lubbock Avalanche-Journal, (TX) 20 October 1991, sec. A, p. 5.

CHAPTER TWENTY-FOUR
1 Hall, Jerry. "Crash Tragedy For Youngsters," Lubbock Avalanche- Journal, 23 May, 1951, sec. 2.
2 Cochran, Mike. "Political sidekicks delighted in 'Pinkie's' law making antics" Lubbock Avalanche-Journal, (TX) 22 October 1991, sec. A, p. 8.
3 Cochran, Mike. "Pinkie's' life filled with success, odd mix of acquaintances," Lubbock Avalanche-Journal, (TX) 20 October 1991, sec. A, p. 5.
4 Cochran, Mike. "Friends say Pinkie lived, died a well-liked, yet lonely man," Lubbock Avalanche-Journal, (TX) 24 October 1991, sec. A, p. 7.
5 Ibid.
6 Cochran, Mike. "Political sidekicks delighted in 'Pinkie's' law making antics" Lubbock Avalanche-Journal, (TX) 22 October 1991, sec. A, p. 8.
7 Cochran, Mike. "Pinkie's liquor empire was hard-earned, well-respected," Lubbock Avalanche-Journal, (TX) 21 October 1991, sec. A, p. 8.
8 Cochran, Mike. "Pinkie's' life filled with success, odd mix of acquaintances," Lubbock Avalanche-Journal, (TX) 20 October 1991, sec. A, p. 5.

CHAPTER TWENTY-FIVE
1 Cochran, Mike. "Pinkie's' life filled with success, odd mix of acquaintances," Lubbock Avalanche-Journal, (TX) 20 October 1991, sec. A, p. 5.
2 Edwards, Mary Ann. Letter. 22 Oct. 1991.

CHAPTER TWENTY-SIX
1 Cochran, Mike. "Pinkie's' life filled with success, odd mix of acquaintances," Lubbock Avalanche-Journal, (TX) 20 October 1991, sec. A, p. 5.
2 Hunt, Jon. Personal interview. 1991.

CHAPTER TWENTY-SEVEN
1 Cochran, Mike. "Pinkie's' life filled with success, odd mix of acquaintances," Lubbock Avalanche-Jour-

nal, (TX) 20 October 1991, sec. A, p. 5.
2 Unknown. "Five Killed in Two-Car Crash Near West Point," The Lynn County News, (TX) 25 May 1951, p. 1.
3 Ibid.
4 Ibid.
5 Ibid.
6 Hall, Jerry. "Crash Tragedy For Youngsters," Lubbock Avalanche-Journal, 23 May, 1951, sec. 2.

CHAPTER TWENTY-EIGHT
1 Cochran, Mike. "Pinkie's liquor empire was hard-earned, well-respected," Lubbock Avalanche-Journal, (TX) 21 October 1991, sec. A, p. 8.
2 Cochran, Mike. "Pinkie's' life filled with success, odd mix of acquaintances," Lubbock Avalanche-Journal, (TX) 20 October 1991, sec. A, p. 5.
3 Ibid.

CHAPTER TWENTY-NINE
1 Cochran, Mike. "Pinkie's' liquor empire was hard-earned, well-respected," Lubbock Avalanche-Journal, (TX) 21 October 1991, sec. A, p. 8.
2 Ibid.
3 Ibid.
4 Ibid.
5 Cochran, Mike. "Pinkie's' life filled with success, odd mix of acquaintances," Lubbock Avalanche-Journal, (TX) 20 October 1991, sec. A, p. 5.
6 Cochran, Mike. "Political sidekicks delighted in 'Pinkie's' law making antics" Lubbock Avalanche-Journal, (TX) 22 October 1991, sec. A, p. 8.

CHAPTER THIRTY
1 Cochran, Mike. "Pinkie's' life filled with success, odd mix of acquaintances," Lubbock Avalanche-Journal, (TX) 20 October 1991, sec. A, p. 5.
2 Cochran, Mike. "Political sidekicks delighted in 'Pinkie's' law making antics" Lubbock Avalanche-Journal, (TX) 22 October 1991, sec. A, p. 8.

CHAPTER THIRTY-ONE
1 Cochran, Mike. "Pinkie's' life filled with success, odd mix of acquaintances," Lubbock Avalanche-Journal, (TX) 20 October 1991, sec. A, p. 5.
2 Ibid.
3 Cochran, Mike. "Pinkie's' liquor empire was hard-earned, well-respected," Lubbock Avalanche-Journal, (TX) 21 October 1991, sec. A, p. 8.
4 Ibid.
5 Cochran, Mike. "Friends say Pinkie lived, died a well-liked, yet lonely man," Lubbock Avalanche-Journal, (TX) 24 October 1991, sec. A, p. 7.
6 Hall, Jerry. "Crash Tragedy For Youngsters," Lubbock Avalanche-Journal, 23 May, 1951, sec. 2.
7 Cochran, Mike. "Pinkie's' liquor empire was hard-earned, well-respected," Lubbock Avalanche-Journal, (TX) 21 October 1991, sec. A, p. 8.
8 Cochran, Mike. "Pinkie's' life filled with success, odd mix of acquaintances," Lubbock Avalanche-Journal, (TX) 20 October 1991, sec. A, p. 5.

CHAPTER THIRTY-TWO
1 Cochran, Mike. "Friends say Pinkie lived, died a well-liked, yet lonely man," Lubbock Avalanche-Journal, (TX) 24 October 1991, sec. A, p. 7.
2 Hall, Jerry. Personal interview. 1992.

CHAPTER THIRTY-THREE
1 Cochran, Mike. "Pinkie's' life filled with success, odd mix of acquaintances," Lubbock Avalanche-Journal, (TX) 20 October 1991, sec. A, p. 5.
2 Cochran, Mike. "Political sidekicks delighted in 'Pinkie's' law making antics," Lubbock Avalanche-Journal, (TX) 22 October 1991, sec. A, p. 8.
3 Edwards, Polly. Personal interview. 1992.

CHAPTER THIRTY-FOUR
1 Cochran, Mike. "Political sidekicks delighted in 'Pinkie's' law making antics," Lubbock Avalanche-Journal, (TX) 22 October 1991, sec. A, p. 8.
2 Edwards, Elva. Letter. Lubbock Avalanche-Journal. 1991.

CHAPTER THIRTY-FIVE
1 Cochran, Mike. "Family, friends remember 'Pinkie' as big-hearted, magical guy," Lubbock Avalanche-Journal, (TX) 23 October 1991, sec. A, p. 7.
2 Edwards, Elva. Letter to Judge Truett Smith. 1991.

CHAPTER THIRTY-SIX
1 Cochran, Mike. "Pinkie's' liquor empire was hard-earned, well-respected," Lubbock Avalanche-Journal, (TX) 21 October 1991, sec. A, p. 8.
2 Smith, Judge Truett. Letter to the author. 1991.

CHAPTER THIRTY-SEVEN
1 Cochran, Mike. "Pinkie's' liquor empire was hard-earned, well-respected," Lubbock Avalanche-Journal, (TX) 21 October 1991, sec. A, p. 8.
2 Williams, Mitchell. Letter to the author. 1991.
3 Cochran, Mike. "Pinkie's' liquor empire was hard-earned, well-respected," Lubbock Avalanche-Journal, (TX) 21 October 1991, sec. A, p. 8.

CHAPTER THIRTY-EIGHT
1 Cochran, Mike. "Friends say Pinkie lived, died a well-liked, yet lonely man," Lubbock Avalanche-Journal, (TX) 24 October 1991, sec. A, p. 7.
2 Williams, Mitchell. Personal interview. 1991.
3 Burks, Melvin. Personal interview. 1991.

CHAPTER THIRTY-NINE
1 Cochran, Mike. "Friends say Pinkie lived, died a well-liked, yet lonely man," Lubbock Avalanche-Journal, (TX) 24 October 1991, sec. A, p. 7.
2 Edwards, Robert et.all. Personal interview. 1991.
3 DeBusk, Mona. Personal interview. 1968.

4 "The Elephant In the Room" by Terry Kettering. Reprinted by permission of Bereavement Publishing, Colorado Springs, CO. 1-888-604-HOPE

CHAPTER FORTY

1 Cochran, Mike. "Friends say Pinkie lived, died a well-liked, yet lonely man," Lubbock Avalanche-Journal, (TX) 24 October 1991, sec. A, p. 7.
2 In re Elva Jo Edwards and Calva An Edwards vs S.F. Wells, Jr., ET. AL., No. 1989, (District Court of Lynn Co, Tx, 1953).
3 Ibid, p. 39.
4 Ibid, p. 39.
5 Ibid, p. 9-11.
6 Ibid, p. 40.
7 Ibid, p. 9.
8 Ibid, p.47-48.
9 Ibid, p. 67.
10 Ibid, p. 13-18.

CHAPTER FORTY-ONE

1 Cochran, Mike. "Political sidekicks delighted in 'Pinkie's' law making antics" Lubbock Avalanche-Journal, (TX) 22 October 1991, sec. A, p. 8.
2 Cochran, Mike. "Pinkie's' life filled with success, odd mix of acquaintances," Lubbock Avalanche-Journal, (TX) 20 October 1991, sec. A, p. 5.
3 Ibid.
4 Ibid.
5 In re The State of Texas vs. Roy Maxey, No. 2,962, (County Court of Lynn Co., Texas, 1952.)
6 Cochran, Mike. "Pinkie's' liquor empire was hard-earned, well-respected," Lubbock Avalanche-Journal, (TX) 21 October 1991, sec. A, p. 8.
7 Mathers, Glenda. Letter to the author. 1993.
8 In re Elva Jo Edwards & Calva An Edwards vs. S. F. Wells, Jr. Et. Al., No. 1989, (District Court of Lynn Co., Tx. 1953).
9 Ibid.
10 Ibid.
11 Ibid, p. 29-30.
12 Ibid, p. 33-34.
13 Ibid, p. 32-33.
14 Ibid, p. 33.
15 Ibid, p. 33-48.

CHAPTER FORTY-TWO

1 Cochran, Mike. "Friends say Pinkie lived, died a well-liked, yet lonely man," Lubbock Avalanche-Journal, (TX) 24 October 1991, sec. A, p. 7.
2 Edwards, Robert. Personal interview. 1993.
3 In re Elva Jo Edwards and Calva An Edwards vs S.F. Wells, Jr., ET. AL., No. 1989, (District Court of Lynn Co., Tx. 1953).
4 Ibid, p. 3-71.
5 Ibid, p. 13.
6 Mathers, Glenda. Personal interview. 1993.
7 In re The State of Texas vs. Roy Maxey, No. 2,862, (County Court of Lynn Co., Tx., 1953.)

8 Ibid.
9 Ibid.
10 Ibid.
11 Cochran, Mike. "Pinkie's' liquor empire was hard-earned, well-respected," Lubbock Avalanche-Journal, (TX) 21 October 1991, sec. A, p. 8.
12 Cochran, Mike. "Political sidekicks delighted in 'Pinkie's' law making antics" Lubbock Avalanche-Journal, (TX) 22 October 1991, sec. A, p. 8.
13 Ibid.

CHAPTER FORTY-THREE

1 Cochran, Mike. "Political sidekicks delighted in 'Pinkie's' law making antics" Lubbock Avalanche-Journal, (TX) 22 October 1991, sec. A, p. 8.
2 Edwards, Polly. Personal interview. 1993.

CHAPTER FORTY-FOUR

1 Cochran, Mike. "Pinkie's' life filled with success, odd mix of acquaintances," Lubbock Avalanche-Journal, (TX) 20 October 1991, sec. A, p. 5.
2 Edwards, Elva. Letter. 1993.

CHAPTER FORTY-FIVE

1 Cochran, Mike. "Political sidekicks delighted in 'Pinkie's' law making antics" The Lubbock Avalanche-Journal, (TX) 22 October 1991, sec. A, p. 8.
2 Mathers, Glenda. Letter to the author. 1993.

CHAPTER FORTY-SIX

1 Cochran, Mike. "Political sidekicks delighted in 'Pinkie's' law making antics" Lubbock Avalanche-Journal, (TX) 22 October 1991, sec. A, p. 8.
2 Mathers, Glenda. Letter to the author. 1993.

CHAPTER FORTY-SEVEN

1 Cochran, Mike. "Political sidekicks delighted in 'Pinkie's' law making antics" Lubbock Avalanche-Journal, (TX) 22 October 1991, sec. A, p. 8.
2 Mathers, Glenda. Letter to the author. July 1993.
3 Mathers, Glenda. Letter to the author. August 1993.

CHAPTER FORTY-EIGHT

1 Cochran, Mike. "Political sidekicks delighted in 'Pinkie's' law making antics" Lubbock Avalanche-Journal, (TX) 22 October 1991, sec. A, p. 8.
2 Edwards, Elva. Letter. 1993.

CHAPTER FORTY-NINE

1 Cochran, Mike. "Friends say Pinkie lived, died a well-liked, yet lonely man," Lubbock Avalanche-Journal, (TX) 24 October 1991, sec. A, p. 7.
2 Stone, D'Lynn. Essay. 1992.

CHAPTER FIFTY

1 Cochran, Mike. "Friends say Pinkie lived, died a well-liked, yet lonely man," Lubbock Avalanche-Journal, (TX) 24 October 1991, sec. A, p. 7.

CHAPTER FIFTY-ONE
1 Cochran, Mike. "Friends say Pinkie lived, died a well-liked, yet lonely man," <u>Lubbock Avalanche-Journal</u>, (TX) 24 October 1991, sec. A, p. 7.

CHAPTER FIFTY-TWO
1 Cochran, Mike. "Bizarre? Not down in West Texas, it ain't," <u>The Denver Post</u>, (CO) 22 October 1998, sec. A, p. 25.
2 Ibid.
3 Ibid.
4 Ibid, page 31A.

CHAPER FIFTY-THREE
1 Cochran, Mike. "Political sidekicks delighted in 'Pinkie's' law making antics" <u>Lubbock Avalanche-Journal</u>, (TX) 22 October 1991, sec. A, p. 8.
2 Cochran, Mike. Personal interview. 1998.

CHAPTER FIFTY-FOUR
1 Cochran, Mike. "Political sidekicks delighted in 'Pinkie's' law making antics" <u>Lubbock Avalanche-Journal</u>, (TX) 22 October 1991, sec. A, p. 8.
2 In re <u>Elva Jo Edwards and Calva An Edwards vs. S. F. Wells, Jr. Et. Al.</u>, No. 1989, (District Court of Lynn Co. Tx., 1953).
3 Ibid.
4 Ibid.
5 Ibid.
6 Ibid.
7 Ibid.
8 American Psychiatric Association: Diagnostic and Statistical Manual of Mental Disorders, Third Edition, Revised. Washington DC, American Psychiatric Association, 1987. *Reprinted with permission.*
9 Cochran, Mike. Personal interview. 1998.

CHAPTER FIFTY-FIVE
1 Cochran, Mike. "Family, friends remember 'Pinkie' as big-hearted, magical guy" <u>Lubbock Avalanche-Journal</u>, (TX) 23 October 1991, sec. A, p. 7.

CHAPTER FIFTY-SIX
1 Cochran, Mike. "Pinkie's' liquor empire was hard-earned, well-respected," <u>Lubbock Avalanche-Journal</u>, (TX) 21 October 1991, sec. A, p. 8.
2 Coffman, Leonard. Personal interview. 1998.

CHAPTER FIFTY-SEVEN
1 Hall, Jerry. "Crash Tragedy For Youngsters," <u>Lubbock Avalanche-Journal</u>, 23 May, 1951, sec. 2.
2 Coffman, Leonard and Brenda. Personal interview. 2000.
3 Cochran, Mike. "Friends say Pinkie lived, died a well-liked, yet lonely man," <u>Lubbock Avalanche-Journal</u>, (TX) 24 October 1991, sec. A, p. 7.
4 Ibid.